Bullets i

"These life stories of academics from around the globe tell a vivid, inspiring and sometimes poetic history of modern Iraq."

—miriam cooke, Braxton Craven Professor of Arab Cultures, Duke University

"Searing! The American assault aimed to 'end' the Iraqi state and shatter the culture that sustained it. Yako retrieves the stories of some sixty displaced Iraqi academics. Distillations of their experiences read as if written on shards of glass that penetrate the skin and wound the heart."

—Raymond W. Baker, Board Director, International Council for Middle East Studies, Washington, DC

"Luis Yako's thinking is as compelling as his writing. *Bullets in Envelopes* persuasively shifts the politics of argumentation. He uses anthropology to convey the existential turbulence of academics in exile after the US invasion, instead of using academics to advance the discipline."

—Walter D. Mignolo, author of *The Politics of Decolonial Investigations*

Bullets in Envelopes

Iraqi Academics in Exile

Louis Yako

First published 2021 by Pluto Press
345 Archway Road, London N6 5AA

www.plutobooks.com

British Library Cataloguing in Publication Data
A catalogue record for this book is available from the British Library

ISBN   978 0 7453 4197 2   Hardback
ISBN   978 0 7453 4198 9   Paperback
ISBN   978 1 7868 0744 1   PDF eBook
ISBN   978 1 7868 0746 5   Kindle eBook
ISBN   978 1 7868 0745 8   EPUB eBook

This book is printed on paper suitable for recycling and made from fully managed
and sustained forest sources. Logging, pulping and manufacturing processes are
expected to conform to the environmental standards of the country of origin.

Typeset by Stanford DTP Services, Northampton, England

Simultaneously printed in the United Kingdom and United States of America

To all those who were burned by the fires of war, but insist on living to tell their stories ... To all those who didn't survive to bear witness to what happened...

To my first Iraqi educators who taught me how to breathe when they taught me my first alphabet...

To all those who loved Iraq sincerely then and now...

To the many poets and writers who taught me: how to let my heart and mind beat in harmony with every word I put on paper ... that one can be a sniper carrying a pen ... that the cooperation between humans and injustice is like a cooperation between a wound and a dagger ... and if injustice is to end, the wound must stop cooperating with the dagger...

To a future that is yet to be born ... one in which everyone gets their fair share of bread and love...

Contents

Preface

In what I call "the genealogy of loss," this book traces the losses of Iraq and its people through the eyes of academics, one of the country's most educated demographics, to show the extent to which wars, sanctions, and the 2003 invasion have damaged Iraqi society. The invasion had an enormous impact on education and educators. It not only destroyed many achievements Iraqis had built for decades but also erased and forced out some of the country's brightest minds that had helped train Iraqis and shape the skills essential for running and preserving the entire society. Academics are the engineers of the society in the sense that they train almost everyone else to contribute to it, whether doctors, engineers, professors, workers, lawyers, and many other professions. The destruction and restructuring of Iraqi academia and the killing and/or forcing out of many of its academics can only be seen as a political tactic aimed at restructuring and disabling Iraqi society.

While most Iraqi people I know from different walks of life are politically savvy because their lives have been determined by politics, I wanted to research a population that is as close to politics and the centers of power as possible, yet also one that can critically examine and interrogate power from multiple perspectives. Academics are uniquely positioned to do so. They can look critically at their lives in Iraq before the invasion, while equally critically articulate and analyze the consequences of Iraq's invasion and the current regimes of power. As a cultural anthropologist deeply committed to the Middle East and Iraq, I wanted to select a population that is near and dear to my heart. Looking back at my own life in Iraq, from primary school all the way to graduating from Baghdad University, few groups have influenced and shaped my vision as much as Iraqi educators have. Many of the educators who taught me were deeply committed to Iraqi society—to creating knowledgeable students and citizens who see themselves as equal to rather than superior or inferior to anyone else in the world. And because most of these educators simultaneously influenced and were affected by wars and politics, I knew that their voices could add nuance to the story I was trying to tell.

Furthermore, having closely studied much of Western scholarship on Iraq and the Middle East, I saw that the stories of the region and its people are seldom told through the lenses of its most educated populations. If we consider that the former Ba'ath regime made education available for free to every Iraqi citizen from kindergarten all the way to the PhD level, then it follows that Iraq's most educated people are as diverse in gender, class, and politics as the society itself. Iraqi education was a basic human right available to all—not the privilege of a chosen few—and the diversity of voices in Iraqi academia reflects that reality, not that of a privileged group only. There are many important works that paint a picture of the region from the viewpoint of its refugees, gender issues, dissidents, and other important populations, but few are the works that examine the region through the eyes of its academics, who, since the beginnings of the pan-Arabist project, have been key actors in building their societies.

Telling Iraq's story through the eyes of its academics challenges the stereotypical images of war-torn countries as destroyed places with people in tents and in need of humanitarian aid in the form of basic foods and blankets: children with worn out clothes, and countless other such images whether propagated through certain types of scholarship, humanitarian organizations raising funds, or mainstream media. I am not suggesting that these stories are not important. I am instead suggesting that such narratives only tell us how things are at present, not *how they became that way*. I wanted to choose a group that could trace the genealogy of events. Thus, it is my hope that the testimonies in this book will not just be projected as sad stories from "that part of the world," but rather considered as expert and experienced voices that can make cultural, political, and epistemic contributions to how we understand the region's challenges.

STARTING FROM THE END:
RETURNING TO IRAQ AFTER A DECADE IN EXILE

Once upon a time, I was born and raised in a place I used to know only as "home." Once upon a lonely night in 2005, I had to leave Iraq to save my life after receiving a death threat for working as a Linguist/Interpreter with the occupying forces. I wanted to leave with my dignity intact, so I chose to leave as a scholar to pursue higher education rather than live in refugee camps. My love and passion for learning helped me do that, but little did I know that the more education I received in Western institutions, the more I would realize how subjugated and indoctrinated one can become when trying to learn under the grip of age-old colonial and imperial institutions. Nevertheless, as a scholar, I was determined to gain and use every critical tool possible, including tools and ammunition from the imperial universities, to understand what was done to Iraq, to my beloved home that was lost forever.

After one decade in exile, I returned to Iraq to take stock, to have a better understanding of what happened, how it happened, and why it happened. I returned this time as a trained cultural anthropologist from Duke University, Durham, North Carolina, to conduct fieldwork on a population that has had a lasting impact on my life—Iraq's academics. In them, I saw some of the most well-positioned people to testify not only to the destruction of Iraq's once solid education system but also to the intentional destruction, erasure, and dismantling of Iraq's culture, society, and memory. This book tells that painful story through one of Iraq's most well-educated populations—its post-2003 exiled academics.

After two previous summers of field research in the UK and Jordan, 2013 and 2014 respectively, I decided to spend one academic year in Iraq because I knew that the internally displaced academics trapped inside—those not "successful" or "fortunate" enough to escape through the bottleneck—had so much to say about what had happened. After all, I am a child of wars, sanctions, and political upheavals. I know what it means to be trapped inside and what it means to squeeze through the bottleneck, without ever truly recovering from the wounds inflicted upon us. I opened my eyes to this world in the 1980s, to the then ongoing Iran–Iraq War. I witnessed much violence and destruction. I saw countless dead bodies during the First Gulf War. The 13 years of UN sanctions robbed me of some of the most beautiful childhood and teenage years. The 2003 US invasion of Iraq barely allowed me to finish my undergraduate studies at Baghdad University, before forcing me to leave Iraq in 2005 to escape death and violence. By the end of my first week back in Iraq in 2015, my personal observations and experiences started to paint a picture about the story this book was going to draw. What I experienced between the first moments of being at the airport in Sweden on my way to Iraq in September 2015 and the end of the first week in Iraq confirmed the intertwinement of the personal, the political, and the anthropological.

In that first week back after one decade in exile, I learned that the only way I could tell this story as sincerely as possible was to keep alive every bit of it that is personal—personal not just for me but also for each of my interlocutors. I learned that the biggest epistemological scam produced in history is the notion that one can be fully "objective." Like the proverbial writing on the wall, I saw that the word "objectivity" had been the most vicious disguise to hide subjectivity. Indeed, it can also be the perfect guise to hide the malice and prejudice of those who claim to have it. At that defining moment in my scholarship, I understood Johann Wolfgang Goethe's words, "I can promise to be sincere, but not to be impartial" (Goethe 2014: 91). I understood that scholarship, or indeed any type of writing and thinking, is powerful when it is sincere without hiding behind the vain guise of "objectivity." I understood that to be human automatically disqualifies us from being "objective," but it does not disqualify us from being sincere.

After ten years in exile, I was in Stockholm in September 2015 packing my bag to go back to Iraq. I could not believe it was going to happen in less than 24 hours. I was anxious that entire day; I could not sleep or do anything. I went out roaming the streets. I greeted a stranger and had a short conversation. He turned out to be an Armenian in his twenties, thirsty for warm human connection after many lonely, long, and cold Scandinavian winters. He was delighted to meet an Assyrian from Iraq. He invited me for a meal at a nearby Middle Eastern restaurant followed by a walk. It was an ideal way to spend those few hours before heading to the airport. I spoke little. He spent most of the time talking about how much he hated Turkey and the Turks; how racist the Swedes are toward immigrants, no matter how much they like to sugarcoat this fact and claim otherwise.

Toward the end of the evening, the Armenian stranger, who was no longer a stranger, asked what I thought about "home" and "exile" because he had been struggling for years with those notions in Sweden. I told him that life had taught me that it is possible that things, ideas, concepts, and feelings can mean the opposite of what might seem apparent. It was possible for people to be the opposite of what they claimed. It was possible for "home" to signify "exile" and vice versa. Laughter may be tears in disguise. Revolutions could be about oppressive powers pulling the carpet from under the feet of other oppressors. Climbing to the top might not really mean "going up," it could in fact be a harsh form of falling; reaching the pinnacle of fame, surrounded by camera flashes has led to the demise of countless souls on this planet. In brief, it was possible that everything we are told and taught is the opposite of what we think, or that it might be outright false. I told him that I go through life remembering my mom's earliest advice that "succeeding in an unjust world is the first sign of failure because it means we're cooperating with injustice." I told him that I carry like a talisman around my neck André Gide's words: "Fish die belly upward and rise to the surface. It's their way of falling." My Armenian acquaintance took an interest in these reflections and asked that we stay in touch. He walked with me to the door of the apartment building, we said goodbye like two old friends, and he vanished in the crowd as though the whole encounter had been nothing but a dream. I thought that my year of fieldwork—wrestling with home, exile, and displacement as some of the most political and politicized concepts of our time—had already started in Stockholm.

The day was September 11, 2015. The place was Arlanda Airport in Stockholm. The time was an early hour in the morning. I was waiting in line to check in my luggage on a flight headed to Erbil, the capital city of Iraq's northern Kurdistan region. After an entire decade, I was going back to see how the many people, places, and things I left behind had continued their lives (and gone to their deaths) in my absence. I reminded myself that just as I was changing in exile, so were all the people and things I had left in Iraq. I reminded myself that it was going to be an encounter between two changed and constantly changing worlds. I had to be prepared for the fact that some (or many) images of what Iraq used to be in my head may no longer exist.

The check-in line was long. I started watching the faces of the people waiting, their look, their clothes, their luggage. The guy behind me had his headphones on blasting a traditional Turkman folk song from Kirkuk. I could hear the song oozing out of his headphones. It was a song that many of our Turkmen neighbors and friends in Kirkuk used to play at weddings. My ears immediately recognized the words: "Beyaz gül kırmızı gül güller arasından gelir ..." ("White rose, red rose, she comes through roses ...". I hadn't particularly liked the song as a child but, in that moment, I did because it was much more than a song. Time had transformed it into fossilized moments and faces of distant people, places, and moments that I may never see again, except in my daydreams. In front of me in the line, there were two Kurdish families. They seemed to have just met at the airport. They were speaking in two different Kurdish dialects (Kurmanji and Sorani). These two groups usually do not like each other, particularly since the intra-Kurdish struggle in the 1990s, which continues by other means to this day. But I thought to myself, in exile, people have no choice. They simply learn how absurd their differences at home are compared to what they endure in foreign lands. They learn how to love the remotest things, scents, and traces that remind them of a lost home and a lost life. The husbands were talking about how convenient it was to have a direct flight from Stockholm to Erbil, although they complained about its early-morning hour. The wives were discussing the "right" age for children to start articulating their first words. Further down the line, I saw a few guys joking and laughing loudly in a Baghdadi Arabic dialect. They were making sarcastic remarks without taking notice of anyone around them. I already felt like I was in a small version of the Iraq I knew and missed so much, though I realized this might not be the case when I arrived. Perhaps, the Iraq I had known was now more accessible in exile than at home.

Most passengers in the check-in line were Iraqis. Many were Kurds. Some were Arabs. I spotted a few Christian families. I heard two ladies speaking neo-Aramaic with a golden cross hanging around the neck of one. I overheard one talking about how a relative, a refugee in Lebanon, had just been accepted to immigrate to Australia. These conversations were hardly strange to my ears. Before I left Iraq, many people were either talking about leaving or celebrating that some of their friends or relatives had managed to leave, hoping they would be next. Most people want to leave, even without knowing whether they would ever arrive somewhere. After living in the West for one decade and witnessing the gradual rise of hate, racism, and prejudice against anyone and anything from the Middle East, I felt uncertain at that moment about which was the safer option: to stay in war-torn countries or to escape to increasingly hateful and systemically racist Western ones. This question would only get harder to answer in the coming decades.

Ironically—or maybe not—all the passengers had foreign passports in their hands, myself included. I spotted Swedish, Danish, German, and other EU passports. This, too, did not come as a surprise. Because of the wars and devastation of the last few decades, the only way an Iraqi could be treated with dignity, whether in Iraq or elsewhere, was to hold a foreign—meaning Western—passport. A "good" or a "fortunate" Iraqi is almost by definition one who holds a Western passport. An Iraqi passport is paralyzing. It is "suspect" at every airport, checkpoint, or point of entry. As an Iraqi, one is unwelcome almost everywhere. One is questioned almost to death before being allowed entry to any country, and one is always welcome to exit with no questions asked. Every authority and official thinks they have the right to interrogate an Iraqi without a second thought. Iraqis know well that holding that useless document called an "Iraqi passport" is a curse at this point in history. But, of course, this is hardly the only such case. Most passport holders who come from nations whose people count as, using Frantz Fanon's words, "the wretched of the earth," experience different forms of discrimination and exclusion. Some experiences are harsher than others. It is all about power, or lack thereof. Your passport has power. It is not just a document that helps you pass; it can become a symbol of humiliation that prevents you from passing. Many Iraqis I know joke about the words on the inside cover of Iraqi passports: "All competent authorities are requested to accord the bearer of this passport protection to allow him/her all possible assistance in case of need." Every place an Iraqi goes to, they experience the opposite of this statement. These words are just one more example of how things can have the exact opposite meaning of their appearance as with "home" and "exile," "peace" and "war," "honesty" and "dishonesty," and countless other words in different languages. I had become irritated about my first language, my second language, my third language, and all the languages I speak. Words increasingly do not mean what they are supposed to mean in all these languages. Languages are increasingly becoming tools for disguising ideas and reality rather than disclosing them. It suddenly crossed my mind that perhaps one day I will be forced to put every single word I write inside quotation marks. Nothing means what it is supposed to mean. I dreamt of a world in which everyone means what they say and say what they mean.

When my turn came, the cordial, blond female Swedish airline employee checking passports and handing boarding passes looked at my American passport and said, "I see that you were born in Iraq. Do you have an Iraqi passport?" I answered that it had expired. She went on, "You know people over there are not crazy about American passports. Let me see your Iraqi passport, even if it's expired." She took a quick look, checked in my bag, and directed me to the appropriate gate.

I arrived in Erbil shortly after 10.30am. I greeted the friendly Kurd female officer at the passport control in Kurdish, she stamped my passport, and there I was, officially in Iraq. As I walked over to the baggage claim area in the modest but clean airport, I remembered that no one from my blood family or relatives was coming to meet me. My immediate family members had all left Iraq over the last ten years because of the war. My remaining relatives, on both parents' sides, do not live in the city and I had not let them know that I was coming. I wanted to land in the airport *for real* before I could tell anyone with certainty that I was in Iraq.

The only person who was waiting for me at the airport was my American brother-in-law! I wondered what the Swede who checked my passport at Arlanda would have thought about that. My American brother-in-law came to Iraq after 2003, fell in love with the country, and decided that he would rather live in Erbil than in the USA. He says he feels "freer" in Iraq, and he is not alone. Many expats I know love so-called Third World countries. Many do not mind settling and getting married there, while the locals in those countries are escaping in all directions. The reason is simple: expats are treated better than local citizens in such countries, and even better than in their own so-called industrialized countries in the "developed" world. Despite my gratitude that he had come to pick me up, I still found this ironic and painful. An American is the only one at the airport to pick me up in my own country. It felt as though that complex line between "home" and "exile" was being challenged from the moment I landed in Iraq. I decided, however, that it was not helpful to dwell on this thought. I didn't want anything to spoil my first intimate moments of embracing Iraq's skies, lands, trees, roses, buildings, streets, faces, scents, and everyone and everything that had been living and growing in my imagination during the past decade.

I spent the first couple of days in Erbil, mostly with my brother-in-law and some of his foreign expat friends who gave me some tips about life there. They shared things they knew better than me because they had been there and I had not. I soon learned about the new malls, the best hotels, the residential buildings where many expats and rich locals live in places with names like the "English village" or the "Italian village." I thought about how in every "Third World" country that gets "liberated" from its dictators, the first things that go up are luxury hotels and residential areas for Western expats and gated communities from which to administer the newly formed governments in places like Baghdad's Green Zone. The expats in Erbil also told me about things as simple as where to get a local phone sim card, the best haircut, and the cost of basic foods.

I felt alienated on my first night. The feeling was identical to how I felt on my first night in the United States in 2006. In the evening, I went out into the well-known Christian district of Ankawa on the outskirts of Erbil to buy a sim card. It was a hot September evening. As I greeted the salesperson at the random shop I entered, he paused, stared at me, and asked: "Are you Louis?" "Yes, I am. Wait, don't tell me who you are. I think I also recognize your face, but I have to add ten years to it." I recognized him. He was one of our old neighbors in Kirkuk. They had to move to Erbil as security deteriorated after 2003. That was a comforting first connection. It made me feel I am less of a stranger. I am still remembered, I thought. I still exist. But that was not enough. I wanted more closeness than an old neighbor to feel at home again. I immediately activated my sim card and called my aunt in Duhok, two and half hours north of Erbil. She could sense how sad my tone was on the phone and said, "I will be waiting for you tomorrow. Come here. Come start your fieldwork here and by the time you finish with Duhok, your sister will be back from the USA in Erbil and then you could head back there." I went to the bus and taxi station in Erbil the next day to get a taxi and headed to Duhok, a beautiful town sandwiched between two mountains, where I spent the early years of my childhood.

At around 1.30pm, in the shared taxi heading to Duhok, the passengers were all friendly Kurds. I greeted the driver and the passengers in Kurdish and then started looking out the window to check out the scenery. I heard the two guys next to me saying: "thank God there are no Arab passengers in the taxi. Arab passengers always cause delays at the checkpoints." As the taxi moved, I started checking out all the new buildings and streets. It was clear that whereas some people had become better off, others were worse off or had simply stagnated. Infrastructure reveals so much about a place and its culture, politics, and people. The disparities between the poor and the rich neighborhoods in Erbil, in a sense, show that "time" was not ticking at the same pace for everyone. Time was not moving favorably for everyone. Even time is like power in that it moves some people forward, some backward, and some to the sides and the margins. Time also buries some people under the ground. I noticed many unfinished construction and apartment buildings. It looked as though there had been an investment boom that had been abruptly halted by an unexpected economic crisis that made other parts of the city look like dilapidated ghost towns. As we were exiting Erbil, at every traffic light we stopped at, there were poor Syrian or Yazidi women and children begging drivers to buy gum, tissues, and other simple items. Some of these women, ranging from 11 to 30 in age, were so beautiful that it would not be surprising if they were forced to sell other things to get their meals for the day.

Over time, I discovered that many of the women living in tents and dilap-idated buildings had been selling their bodies to make a living. Talking with taxi drivers in Ankawa, I found out that many beauty salons had been turned into places where customers (men) parked their cars and waited to pick up internally displaced women doing sex work. Some people told me that some high-ranking officials obtained sex in return of favors such as renewing the residency cards of displaced women from places like then ISIS-occupied Mosul, and other war-torn parts of Iraq and Syria. These women choose to be in this Christian district away from conservative Kurdish neighborhoods where such practices would not be tolerated. One taxi driver literally said: "Christians are cool, open-minded people. They do not make any judgments. We can come here to drink alcohol and fuck women then go back to our closeted neighborhoods." It seems like the Christian district is turned into a place where an encounter between mainly Muslim sex workers and their Muslim customers takes place in an environment seen as "open-minded."

The driver taking us to Duhok was talking to the front seat passenger about how bad the economy was, saying that public sector employees weren't being paid, and so on. I understood that the Kurdistan region was being crippled by a bad economy. Consequently, public sector employees, who make up most of the employed, were only getting their salaries once every few months due to deep divisions and disagreements over oil revenues between Kurdistan and Baghdad. Baghdad had been withholding Kurdis-tan's 17 percent share of oil revenues because the Kurds have been drilling, extracting, and selling oil through illegal contracts with foreign companies without Baghdad's permission. Iraqi officials in Baghdad, the passengers explained, told the Kurds that if they want to get their share, they must share what they are selling from their region with the central government. The refusal of the Kurdish officials to abide by this, and the fact that much of Kurdistan's oil exploration had been less successful than originally antici-pated, caused a serious economic problem in the region. This was the main topic the passengers discussed during most of the trip.

As the taxi continued on its way, I kept looking out of the window to check out the many villages and small towns we passed through, as we left Erbil behind. Not much had changed in these villages and little towns, except one could see more "fancy" houses at least by village standards. Some individuals had clearly been making plenty of money to renovate or build all these new houses. They looked expensive but also indicated recently acquired financial wherewithal. Many places that had been beautiful verdant agricultural lands on the way had been turned into depressing, half-finished cement buildings. There was a clear disparity between how extravagant many individual houses looked versus the poor state of public services like sewage and roads that were mostly unchanged from the Ba'ath era. During its 35 years in power, the Ba'ath regime had made serious efforts to modernize Iraq's infrastructure in cities and villages. The road from Erbil to Duhok was the same: the only thing that had changed since the Saddam Hussein years was that it has become even narrower, dangerous, and the potholes had only worsened over the years. I saw a clear pattern of how most wealth was being used for individual rather than communal interests. These images reminded me of the anthropological literature we studied on "development." Here, development looked so much like destruction and impoverishment.

My thoughts were interrupted when we stopped at a checkpoint—there were so many of them—and the officer asked everyone to present their IDs. I presented the only valid ID I had on me, my American passport. As soon as he looked at it, he asked me to get out of the car. He said to the officer next to him in Kurdish, "We need to check this to make sure it's an authentic passport." The checkpoint looked like a kiosk, with barely a wooden cover on top to protect against Iraq's unforgiving summer sun. I wondered how they were going to check the passport's authenticity when they did not seem to have any equipment or machines in place. I decided to just talk to them. I spoke in Kurdish and told the officer that I was from the region and had just returned after ten years in the United States, which is why I did not have a valid local ID. My IDs had expired. As soon as I spoke in Kurdish and he heard my name, his tone changed 180 degrees, "Welcome home, my dear brother!" I got back into the taxi and it drove away.

I told the driver the same brief story about why I had no valid local IDs, so this helped for the rest of the trip. He did the talking on my behalf at the other checkpoints and everything went smoothly. I realized that the first task before I could even begin my ethnographic work was to renew my local IDs. I could only imagine how a non-Kurd would feel and be treated when going through all these checkpoints where one could pass just by simply speaking Kurdish or be stranded if they did not speak the language, even if their IDs were valid. In many ways, the language, the sect, and the ethnicity are the IDs in post-US occupation Iraq—the "new Iraq." In fact, at many checkpoints, I observed that they would not even ask for an ID. The first thing they would do is profile the person based on their face and language. If it became clear that they did not speak Kurdish, they would be stranded and interrogated. I noticed over time that some displaced Arabs had learned what one might call "basic checkpoint Kurdish." But even that was no guarantee for being allowed to "pass." The officers could recognize faces. Arabs or Arab-looking people were to be interrogated. Further, sometimes they would prolong the conversation and by the second or third question, the Arab's "checkpoint Kurdish" would fail, causing serious difficulties for them.

My impressions from the first day, and even before reaching Duhok, was that the region functioned on an ethno-nationalist system where language acted as a metonym for power (and disempowerment) and residency cards were a prerequisite for the existence of non-Kurds, especially Arabs. What all these elements have in common is their incredible resemblance to the pan-Arabist project. In fact, Kurdish ethno-nationalism seemed like an amplified and more intense version of pan-Arabism, which seemed to be over and done with. But it was not over: it had simply been passed on from Arabs to Kurds to implement this new project called "the new Iraq" or "the new Middle East" imposed and facilitated by the American invasion. There was such a deep anti-Arab sentiment that it was a blessing not to be an Arab then and there. Little did I know that these first observations and encounters from the early days were going to be central for understanding the lives of the exiled and internally displaced academics and, in turn, to understanding what had happened to Iraq and how things *became that way*.

Acknowledgments

Looking back at the journey of writing this book that started as a doctorate dissertation, I feel like a fortunate bee that was blessed with vast fields of colorful wildflowers. I am deeply grateful for the many beautiful souls and minds, who nurtured, pollinated, and cross-pollinated my thinking. I am indebted to those who mentored and supported me in conceiving, thinking, researching, and writing this work. I am primarily grateful for the 63 Iraqi academics in the UK, Jordan, and Iraq. Although I cannot name them to protect their privacy, this research would not have been possible without each one of them. I hope that I was able to sincerely capture their voices and stories. I ask them to forgive me for any potential human failures and limits. To my best friend on the path of life, Todd Heath, for the great love and encouragement, for being with me every step of the way. To my brother and best friend, Yako, for all the conversations and the wisdom. For making me laugh even at the most difficult moments. To my parents and my sisters Linda, Lina, Lana, Lorin, and Lowana.

I am grateful for my PhD committee members for their love, intellectual support, and tireless work during all the phases of writing. Their diverse and rich knowledge about different parts of the world has enormously enriched my thinking. I am grateful for my advisor, Charles Piot, for embracing me and believing in my work. I thank him for his wisdom and for allowing me all the intellectual freedom I needed to breathe, think, and write creatively; and for all the encouraging and constructive feedback on each chapter. On top of Charlie's academic support, I am grateful for his responsiveness and guidance on all the administrative and logistical matters that were extremely important for going through this process. Charlie always responded to my questions and needs within less than 24 hours, despite the fact that he chaired our department during most of my time as a PhD candidate. His academic and work ethic are humbling. I could not have asked for a better advisor.

I am grateful for the unlimited and heart-warming support from Professor Miriam Cooke. I will never forget the many hours of conversations and mentorship. I thank her from the bottom of my heart for reading everything I wrote, whether it was academic or creative work. I thank her for believing in me. Miriam's scholarship and mentorship have been extremely important in informing and shaping my thinking in this project. Her commitment and genuine love for the Middle East and the Arabic language and literature are rare. I would not have been able to complete this journey without her boundless energy and care.

Professor Diane Nelson's passion, intellectual and political courage, and her beautiful mind are inspiring. I thank her for understanding my life and intellectual interests with deep compassion: for understanding my words and silences alike; and for everything I learned in her class, Anthropology of the State, which significantly informed and inspired my work. Diane's comments and ideas over the last five years were instrumental in this work. I will never forget all the conversations in her office where she allowed me to express and to listen to my inner voice, as I was searching for what really matters in my work.

Professor James Lorand Matory inspired me from the first day in his class, Theories in Cultural Anthropology, during my first year at Duke University. I will never forget the many occasions when I simply showed up in his office and had some of the most inspiring and intellectually stimulating conversations about my work and other topics of mutual interest. I am speechless every time I think about Professor Matory's accessibility and attentiveness during this journey. His passion for anthropology and the richness of the different human cultures and societies always fills me with life and energy.

I will never forget my first conversation with Professor Walter Mignolo at the end of the first class of his course, Decolonial Aesthetics. Walter and I talked for two hours that evening. Every word he said during that conversation connected deeply with my life experience and journey. When Walter speaks about the "colonial wounds," I feel as if the two of us grew up under the same roof. I cherish the many beautiful conversations Walter and I had during my time at Duke. Knowing how busy Walter is, every minute we spent together meant the world to me. I thank him for always believing in my work, for treating me as an equal, for reading and supporting my public writing, and for teaching me how to decolonize everything under the sun.

I am grateful for the Duke Graduate School for the financial support without which research for this work would not have been possible. I am also thankful for the summer research travel awards from the Asian and

Middle Eastern Studies Department and the Duke program in Gender, Sexuality, and Feminist Studies in summer 2013.

I am indebted to many faculty members for the insights and the learning experience I gained in their classes at Duke University and the University of North Carolina at Chapel Hill (UNC), which immensely informed my work and thinking: Rey Chow's class on Foucault Legacies; Frances Hasso and Nadia Yaqub's course on Critical Genealogies in Middle East Studies; Laurie McIntosh's class on Research Methods; and Anne Allison's inspiring course on Critical Ethnographies. I remember with great fondness the many intellectual and poetic conversations with Professor Irene Silverblatt. I thank Professor Bruce B. Lawrence for the encouragement and the wonderful conversations along the way. I am indebted to Professor Abdul Sattar Jawad from the Middle Eastern Studies Department at Duke University for connecting me with interlocutors in Jordan. I thank Duke's librarian for Middle East and Islamic Studies, Christof Galli, for making available many resources that helped my research.

I am forever grateful for many family members and friends in different parts of the world. I thank Professor Nadje al-Ali for supporting my project, her invaluable insights in the early stages of this work, and for connecting me with interlocutors in London during my summer research in 2013. Al-Ali's sincere work and passion for Iraq have greatly informed and inspired my work. In Jordan, I am indebted to Dr. Lucine Taminian. My research there would not have been possible without Lucine's immense logistical support. In Iraq, I am grateful for my family and friends whose help was instrumental in conducing this research in 2015–2016. For my dear friend and interlocutor, Salman Turki, for his immense contribution and inspiration in this work. For Vivian Tallo from Duhok University and Kawther Akreyi from Erbil, for connecting me with many interlocutors. From Ireland, for my dear friend, Gerard Deering, for engaging with my work, calling me almost at the end of every day to check on the writing, for listening to me read drafts of this work, and for really believing in the importance of this project beyond academia. From Russia, I am indebted to my dearest friend, Elena Demchenko, for always being there for me, for the academic and personal advice on everything, and for her beautiful friendship. From Belgium, I am grateful for my friends, Dirk and Hilde Adriaensens. From Pennsylvania, I am humbled by the endless love from the most amazing friends, Addison and Mary Louise Bross; Ilhan and Francesca Citak; and my dearest friend,

Jennifer Hasty. I thank them for always opening their homes and hearts for me. I am deeply thankful for the meticulous editing and helpful comments of Maia Tabet during the early stages of editing the manuscript. Last but certainly not least, I am deeply thankful for the meticulous, caring, vigorous, and truly admirable work the Pluto Press staff have bestowed upon me during the process of publishing this book. I am especially grateful for Neda Tehrani and Thérèse Wassily Saba's extremely helpful feedback, comments, and edits to my manuscript. I am also grateful for all the readers who will read and engage with this work.

Introduction
The Story of This Story

This book is a reflection through the eyes of those who survived, continue to endure the consequences, and insist on living to honor everything that was destroyed and lost in Iraq over the last few decades. Through what I call a "genealogy of loss," I trace the relationship between academia and power in contemporary Iraq, as experienced by Iraq's currently exiled and displaced academics, a group uniquely well-positioned to bear witness to the ways in which academia is entangled in vicious and violent political systems, wars, and occupation. As I learned from many interlocutors, academia cannot be understood separately from politics. This work shows that academics, while vital for society, are also some of the most susceptible groups to political violence. I call the trajectory of their lives a "genealogy of loss," because by tracing their stories in Iraq's contemporary history, it becomes clear that the losses they have incurred have had drastic effects on the entire society.

Iraqi academics moved from a centralized, secular state into occupied death zones marked by foreign occupation and sectarian violence, which in turn pushed many of those who had fallen out of grace with the post-occupation political regimes into exile to face yet other sophisticated, degrading, and inhumane forms of power and methods of governance just to stay alive. This book examines these stages with ethnographic data captured through the voices of those who were there before 2003, who were there after the occupation, and who are now in exile insisting on living to tell the story. It is a work ultimately about people trapped between a past still alive in their memories, a present that is unbearable, and a future that is not born yet.

QUESTIONS AND CONTRIBUTIONS

The two central questions driving this work can be summarized as follows: what does the trajectory of the lives of academics from contemporary Iraq (including the Ba'ath era, the occupation, exile, and displacement) teach us about the complex relationship between academics, as key engineers of

1

society, and the states under which they live or find themselves forced into living? And, how should we understand the post-occupation assassinations, liquidation, forced internal displacements, and external exiles of these academics as part of dismantling the Iraqi state (or any state), its institutions, and society? In other words, what do the stories of these academics reveal about new forms of governance, and consequently, about the reconfiguration of key terms in this work: state, academics, and exile?

After I examine these academics' lives during the Ba'ath era, I look at their lives during the post-2003 occupation, focusing on the death threats they received. Most threats were sent in the form of bullets inside envelopes, along with threatening notes to leave or be killed. Many academics were assassinated, liquidated, silenced, displaced, and exiled. Many were forced to put their lives and skills "on sale," which turned them from respected and relatively stable actors in Iraqi higher education and society into what I call "lives under contract." My research shows that what happened to these academics in the post-2003 occupation of Iraq was not the result of circumstance or a unique case limited to the Iraqi context. The destiny of these academics, though intense and extreme, is part and parcel of a worldwide trend to reconfigure the role of academics and the terms of the contract between academics and the powers under which they live and think in the neoliberal age.

In capturing these testimonies, I take seriously what the decolonial thinker, Walter Mignolo, notes regarding scholars who have for too long assumed that the "knowing subject in the disciplines is transparent, disincorporated from the known and untouched by the geo-political configuration of the world in which people are racially ranked and regions are racially configured" (Mignolo 2009: 160). As such, one way to decolonize knowledge produced about other people is by bringing to the fore the "epistemic silences" of Western scholarship (Mignolo 2009: 162). The silenced voices of these Iraqi academics can change how we see Iraq and the Middle East to rethink some of the most challenging questions about the region and the world today. These stories also change the terms of the conversation, if there is a genuine desire to allow the subaltern to speak and to pay attention to what they have to say (Spivak 1988). Doing so can create, using anthropologist Lila Abu-Lughod's words, "new zones of theorizing" on the Middle East, a call that dates to 1989, but remains as timely and urgent today (Abu-Lughod 1989).

2

This work answers the call by diversifying the voices and testimonies that tell the story of what is happening in the region.

The book seeks to make three key contributions. First, it exposes the multifaceted and complex sides of the relationship between academics and different regimes of power. It expands our knowledge about the many complex faces of the state, the various methods of governance that emerge as a result of changing power relations, as well as how academics are entangled in these political and violent changes. Turning Iraq from a united, secular state ruled by a single-party, into divided sectarian, ethno-nationalist zones ruled by multiple sectarian and ultra-nationalist regimes and militias, has changed the definition, role, and place of academics and academia altogether. The "new academic" in post-occupation Iraq must fit with the new political realities on the ground. Therefore, unsurprisingly, anyone related to the old political order (or to any undesirable political order) was marginalized, killed, or displaced. This work shows that the three main cleansing methods used in post-invasion Iraq that best capture the reconfiguration of power included: assassinations and death threats, sectarian violence, and the application of "de-Ba'athification" policies. Consequently, those academics who either did not fit into this new political mold or who refused to play by the rules of the new game had no choice but to pay the price with death or exile.

Second, this work contributes to our understanding on how "exile" and "displacement" start at "home" through violent political changes. It suggests that we trace the problems—and the solutions—for refugees, exiled and displaced populations all the way back home rather than the current locations where these populations struggle or reside.

Third, academics are also citizens and, therefore, the political upheavals and violence they witnessed as a result of their positionality in post-invasion Iraq raise questions, as some scholars and analysts have previously suggested, about how sectarianism and ethno-nationalism are not simply chaotic consequences of the war, but perhaps the desired outcomes of it.[1] The new forms of governance that mushroomed in post-invasion Iraq have been determining who is worthy of living or who is left to die, or what the Cameroonian philosopher, Achille Mbembe, calls "necropolitics" (Mbembe 2003). Governance through sectarian militias (as in the case of Shi'a versus Sunnis) or ethno-nationalism (as in the case of Iraqi Kurdistan) determine who lives and who dies, who stays and under what conditions, and who leaves. In exile and internal displacement, the new conditions under which these academics live are anything but apolitical. They are determined by other forms of politics, citizenship, economics, identity, as well as new academic and social conditions that are primarily governed by the spread of Western neoliberal practices of higher education worldwide.

The second part of the book examines the conditions of Iraq's exiled academics to show that far from being unique to the Iraqi context, these conditions, though extreme and violent in many ways, are nevertheless part and parcel of the shifting realities of higher education worldwide, which are marked by corporatization, commercialization, precarity, and the suppression of resistance. Part II of the book shows that exiled Iraqi academics have been turned from actors who were formerly vital and relatively stable in their academic positions before the invasion, into lives under contract, as is the case in Jordan and Iraqi Kurdistan. This move into contingent academic existence, which also determines their residency status, raises serious questions about the role of academics in society in the neoliberal age.

Ultimately, these conditions combined create a culture of fear and instability for academics, who are constantly frightened about losing their contracts and residency status. They are constantly looking for short-term plans to survive. They are hardly able to think, write, and teach without any sense of safety or stability. Under such conditions, these actors with a pivotal role in any nation, become unable to fully contribute to society because they always live in what I call a "plan B mode of existence" to secure their next step in a cruel and precarious environment.

FIELDWORK AND RESEARCH

This work was born of extensive socializing as well as interviews (both structured and semi-structured), discussions, engagements, living experiences, social media interactions, and lengthy Skype conversations with a total of 63 exiled and internally displaced Iraqi academics in the UK, Jordan, and Iraqi Kurdistan respectively. Lengthy Skype interviews over multiple sessions were conducted with 7 of the 63 where a personal meeting was not possible. The fieldwork included two summer research trips: to London in 2013, and to Amman in 2014. Additionally, I conducted further fieldwork in Iraqi Kurdistan from September 2015 until April 2016. In each of these sites, I am deeply grateful for the generous help and support of many academics, intellectuals, family members, friends, and professors at Duke University,

Introduction

Baghdad University, Duhok University, Salahaddin University, University of London's School of Oriental and African Studies, and the Middle East University in Jordan. I am also grateful to the Council for At-Risk Academics (CARA) in London and Academics at Risk for connecting me with other Iraqi academics. I am also indebted to several individuals at the Iraqi Cultural Centre in London for connecting me with other academics and for allowing me to attend some of their events.

In 2013, I worked with 13 Iraqi academics (seven females, six males) from diverse academic backgrounds and disciplines residing in London and its surrounding areas. In summer 2014, I worked closely with 18 Iraqi academics (nine males, nine females) living and working in or near Amman. In 2015–2016, I was able, with the generous support of a fellowship from Duke University's Graduate School, to go back to Iraqi Kurdistan after ten years living in exile. There, I divided my time between the cities of Duhok and Erbil and worked closely with 16 academics (nine males, seven females) in Duhok and nine academics (six males, three females) in Erbil, the capital of Iraqi Kurdistan.

The academics concerned were not only from different disciplines, backgrounds, and cities around Iraq, but also from diverse religions, ethnicities, and political affiliations as follows: ten identified as Shi'i Muslims; 17 identified as Sunni Muslims; five identified as half Shi'i-half Sunni Muslims; seven identified as Kurds; four identified as Christians (both Assyrians and Chaldeans); two identified as Turkmen, the rest either refused to identify their religious/ethnic backgrounds, or identified as non-religious, communist, existentialist, or atheist. Since most of my interlocutors were either Sunni or Shi'i Arabs, my conversations with them were largely conducted in Arabic (a combination of Iraqi dialect and Modern Standard Arabic, depending on the topic discussed). A few academics, mainly Kurds who did not have a strong command of Arabic, spoke with me in Kurdish (Sorani dialect). Others, especially those teaching English language and literature, and linguistics, spoke in both Arabic and English, depending on the conversation. Interlocutors from the Iraqi Christian minority (Chaldeans and Assyrians) interacted with me in two different neo-Aramaic dialects. One individual used Turkmen and Arabic during our conversations.

Most of the academics concerned lived and worked in academic settings in Iraq during the Ba'ath era, roughly from the 1970s up to the 2003 occupation of Iraq, the most critical period for the purposes and scope of

5

this work. A smaller number—mainly those based in London—fled Iraq in the 1970s and 1980s due to their purported affiliation with the Iraqi Communist Party (ICP). Most of my interlocutors were displaced inside or exiled outside of Iraq: either during the 1990s because of the 13 years of suffocating UN sanctions; or following the 2003 occupation due to political, ethnic, sectarian, or religious tensions, threats, and assassination attempts; or during both of the above-mentioned periods. In fact, many interlocutors suffered from multiple exiles and displacements resulting from political upheaval.

The concerned academics' disciplines included: physics, engineering, literature and linguistics, political science and international relations, translation, education, agriculture, civil aviation, computer science, globalization and development, fine arts, pharmacology, management, economics, media and journalism, medicine, Arabic language and Islamic studies, archeology and anthropology, veterinary medicine and physiology, chemistry, mathematics, law, history, and teaching English as a second language (TESL).

The interlocutors were selected mostly through personal contacts, academic refugee organizations, or after knowing some interlocutors, they generously put me in touch with others either in their departments and universities or outside in other academic institutions. To protect their privacy and safety, particularly those in Jordan and Iraqi Kurdistan living under insecure and extremely precarious conditions, all the names used are pseudonyms. In Iraqi—and most Middle Eastern cultures—people are addressed with their first names. Even those with titles are usually addressed as "Dr./Prof. First Name" and the pseudonyms in the book follow that practice.

In the context of this work, I define an "Iraqi academic" as any Iraqi individual or an individual from an Iraqi origin currently living temporarily or permanently in exile outside of Iraq, or who is internally displaced within Iraq, who holds a postgraduate degree (a master's degree or higher) from Iraqi and/or foreign academic institutions, and who currently holds or has held in the past an academic position within Iraqi higher education institutions before the US invasion in 2003. Iraqi higher education, due to a shortage of PhD holders, has traditionally valued and hired holders of master's degrees, who could research, publish, and even advance on the academic track up to the rank of a full professor, without holding a PhD; many of these comprised a significant portion of the Iraqi academic workforce at both public and private universities. Therefore, academics with master's degrees are treated at the same level as academics with PhDs in this work.

Qualitative methods were used to collect data and document observations, including structured and semi-structured interviews, and I also spent time with academics in their departments, homes, and in public places. On campus, I spent time with interlocutors in their offices, at university cafeterias, and in libraries. I have also spent many hours attending lectures and during their office hours to observe how these academics live, teach, write, advise students, deal with administrative tasks, interact with colleagues, and run departments. The latter applies to those currently holding administrative positions like deans and chairs of departments. I spent time with my interlocutors in public places like cafés, restaurants, and parks; mingled with their families and friends, went on picnics, and observed their daily lives, which included getting to know their social circles, and accompanying them on daily tasks such as shopping and going to pick up/drop off their children at daycare centers, kindergartens, and schools.

With others, I experienced their social, intellectual, and charity-related activities off campus. These included visiting festivals, going to cultural centers to present and/or listen to lectures, participate in book group readings, and, particularly in Iraq and Jordan, many were heavily involved in teaching and helping Iraqi—and later Syrian—refugees in different capacities ranging from providing them with free classes to coordinating, collecting, and distributing necessities such as food, stationery, household items, and many other basic needs for refugee families. I became close friends with many academics who shared their future plans, writings, and their personal relationships with me. There are many memorable moments of academics reading their poems and drafts of researches to me as well as sharing their marital and social challenges. All these ways of living and being in their lives have been crucial in providing a qualitative and holistic understanding of the rhythms of their daily lives.

CHAPTER-BY-CHAPTER SUMMARY

Bullets in Envelopes is divided into two main parts. Part I includes Chapters 1, 2, and 3, which, besides telling the story of how this work came to life, cover the Ba'ath era up to the 2003 occupation of the country. Factors such as gender, class, and social mobility are examined throughout the book.

The Introduction, "The Story of this Story," outlines how my doctoral research gave birth to this work; the population studied and the reasons for choosing this population to tell the Iraqi story; my positionality as the author of this work; and details of the fieldwork and research methods I employed to collect materials for the book.

Chapter 1, "A Nuanced Understanding of Iraq during the Ba'ath Era," focuses on the complexities of the Ba'ath era and the silences about it, meaning all that is absent from Western discourse and propaganda, both prior to and after the occupation of Iraq. This chapter complicates our understanding of the period to show how Iraqi academics (and implicitly Iraqi people) lived, thought, and contributed to building their nation before the occupation.

Chapter 2, "The Ba'ath Era: Iraqi Academics Looking Back," examines the lives of currently exiled academics under the Ba'ath system and its higher education institutions. Using first-hand accounts, the chapter analyzes how academics functioned within the Iraqi state.

Chapter 3, "The UN Sanctions: Consenting to Occupation through Starvation," is dedicated to the 13 years of the UN sanctions (1990–2003), which many academics perceive as a period in which their suffering and struggles were due as much to the imposition of sanctions as to the Ba'ath party's actions. Many viewed the sanctions as a method used by Western powers to force people to consent to the later occupation of Iraq. These 13 years, for most of my interlocutors, were the most difficult and suffocating of their academic, social, and political life in Iraq.

Part II includes Chapters 4, 5, 6, and 7 and covers the post-occupation period and the lives of academics in exile and internal displacement. Chapter 4, "The Occupation: Paving the Road to Exile and Displacement," examines how Iraqi higher education institutions were destroyed, dismantled, and reconfigured after 2003. Based on what these academics (and other groups) suffered following the occupation, the chapter argues that the three major "cleansing" methods that best define the reconfiguration of power, and subsequently the reconfiguration of the role of academics in post-occupation Iraq, included assassinations and death threats, sectarian violence, and the notorious policies of "de-Ba'athification."

Chapter 5, "Lives under Contract: The Transition to the Corporate University," examines how exiled academics went from being vital actors with relatively stable jobs in Iraq before 2003 to living what I call "lives under contract," in Jordan and Iraqi Kurdistan. It closely examines the transition from public, state-funded, not-for-profit education into a more corporate, for-profit, private set of universities as being one of the biggest challenges faced by exiled academics. Under these corporate for-profit universities, academic lives are tied to annual contracts that may or may not be renewed, and to residency cards that can only be valid so long as their contracts are valid. The testimonies in this chapter show that the case of these academics is inseparable from the ongoing corporatization of higher education worldwide, which is driven by neoliberalism. The experiences captured speak to the ways in which transnational corporations and global powers imagine the "new state" and its "new citizens" in the world today. In a sense, this chapter reveals the intertwined relationship between the military–industrial complex and the refugee–industrial complex and how they work hand in hand in producing and benefitting from disasters.

Chapter 6, "Language as a Metonym for Politics," examines how the Kurdish language, for academics internally displaced within Iraqi Kurdistan, acts as a metonym for politics and significantly affects and shapes the lives and experiences of these academics. Given the historical, social, political, and cultural context of the Kurdish and Arabic languages in Iraq, internally displaced academics often struggle with the Kurdish language, which then becomes a tool determining identity and belonging. It also blurs and complicates the boundaries between home and exile. Such conditions force academics to live in what I call a "plan B mode of existence," where they constantly have to make alternative plans in case their contracts and residency cards are terminated or revoked.

Bullets in Envelopes concludes with Chapter 7, "Final Reflections: Home, Exile, and the Future," which in addition to summarizing the key points of the book, closes with a collage of Iraqi voices that concludes the work by letting academics share in their own words what they think about home, loss, and the destruction they and the Iraqi people have been enduring. They speak about their hopes, aspirations, and dreams for a future that is yet to be born. It is also a space in which I share moments from my final days of research in Iraq.

PART I

1

A Nuanced Understanding of Iraq During the Baʿath Era

THE CONVENIENTLY OMITTED NUANCES OF IRAQ'S STORY IN WESTERN DISCOURSE

Having lived the first 24 years of my life in Iraq, been educated in its schools and treated in its hospitals, and having traveled extensively around the country, I am sensitive to the nuances of the Baʿath era under which I lived for those years. Having experienced first-hand the wars that Iraq went through from the 1980s (the decade in which I was born) until 2005, when I left the country as a result of a death threat for "collaborating" with the occupiers (working as a linguist/cultural advisor with the Coalition Forces), I am well aware of the destruction that was caused, and the way the American occupiers saw Iraq and its people. Lastly, having lived and extensively traveled in Europe and the United States since 2005, I am equally aware of how Western propaganda works to produce malicious narratives about any nation or group of people dominant powers seek to occupy and plunder. This chapter sheds light on why the Iraq wars and UN sanctions were some of the biggest crimes against humanity of our time, and how we might prevent this type of vicious rhetoric from causing future wars or blockades designed to starve millions of innocent people.

From 1968, when the Baʿath party came to power, until the present, Iraq and its people have witnessed some of the most vicious internal and external attacks a nation has experienced in modern history. Since the 1980s, Iraqis have suffered multiple wars. This includes the eight-year war with Iran that caused devastating human and infrastructural losses for both countries, followed by the Iraqi invasion of Kuwait, which led to the First Gulf War in 1991 that destroyed the remaining infrastructure of the country. This was followed by 13 years of the most inhumane sanctions imposed upon a nation and its people in modern history by the United Nations Security Council (UNSC) (Arnove 2000). These sanctions had deeply destructive effects on the fabric of Iraqi society, institutions, identity, and politics. When Iraqis thought things could not get worse after the First Gulf War and the 13 years of the cruelest sanctions, they did. In 2003, the USA and its allies invaded Iraq, causing one of the most disastrous occupations in recent history marked by countless deaths, endless destruction, displacement, and ongoing sectarian and ethnic violence.

Most Iraqis I know from all ethnicities and backgrounds see the catastrophic US-led invasion as graphic evidence of how unjust this world is. They also know that the stakes for any so-called "third world" nation aspiring to be independent from the dominating superpowers have become more challenging in the neocolonial imperialist age than ever before. Neocolonial agendas hide skillfully behind a million masks and justifications to ensure that so-called Third World countries remain in that category—that the "developing" world remains in a permanent state of never really developing. If we take seriously Hegel's "slave–master dialectic" (Hegel 2006 [1910]: 70), or Edward Said's theory of Orientalism whereby the West defines itself by defining the rest (Said 1979 [1978]), then it follows that "developing" countries must be prevented from developing at all costs because, if they do, then who will the so-called "developed" world compare itself to and define itself against? If developing countries are truly allowed to develop, where will the "developed" world steal its resources from? Yet, the price of preventing these countries from being truly independent from the iron fist of the superpowers is costly. The price for those who happen to be considered as the "wretched of the earth" (Fanon 2004 [1961]) and who dare to say "no" and choose to challenge the colonial powers has produced millions of deaths and refugees around the world. We are at a point in history where the military–industrial cybernetics and the refugee–industrial complex are feeding, making, and, in some ways, in bed with each other.

To understand the stakes within the context of this project, a brief survey of Iraq's contemporary history is necessary. I challenge stereotypical assumptions, both scholarly and general, that blame Iraq's problems on the fact that it's an artificially created state produced by the colonial Sykes–Picot Agreement of 1916. Iraqi historian, Thabit Abdullah, theorizes the most crucial events in the contemporary history of Iraq by strongly opposing this "fashionable talk" about the artificiality of Iraq. He writes:

> Iraq is no more artificial than any other country with borders drawn as a result of a variety of reasons including wars, treaties, compromises, backroom deals, internal and external pressures, and plain chance.
>
> (Abdullah 2006: 2)

Therefore, the "sectarian divisions which today threaten the unity of the country are the result not of the assertion of 'essential' unchanging identities, but rather of the unraveling of national structures" (Abdullah 2006: 2). This point is crucial for this book because the story of Iraq's exiled academics speaks volumes about what happens to a place and its people when its national structures are destroyed and replaced with forms of governance and regimes of power that are aligned with the occupiers' agenda. Abdullah, like other historians before him, writes that far from being an "artificial" creation, the land known today as Iraq has for thousands of years had a sense of "economic and administrative unity" (Abdullah 2006: 2). After all, it was in ancient Mesopotamia—present-day Iraq—that humans "first established cities with laws regulating the increasingly complex relationships between the rulers and their subjects" (Abdullah 2006: 5). As such, the complexity of the political reality in Iraq is nothing new.

By the mid-nineteenth century, the Ottomans introduced a series of reforms and regulations to increase the power of the central state. Facing a growing danger from European colonial expansion, the Ottomans decided:

> to strengthen the military by organizing the country's resources more efficiently. Ambitious reforms were announced in 1839, beginning with the creation of a modern army and taxation system, moving, in later years, to areas such as secular education and the establishment of a constitution in 1876.
>
> (Abdullah 2006: 8)

Abdullah argues that Iraqi society has always been keen on fighting for its political and human rights. For example, challenging some of the post-2003 occupation narratives about the first "free elections" in Iraq, he writes:

Recently there has been much talk of the novelty of elections in Iraq. Yet as far back as 1908 and again in 1912, elections were held for a new Ottoman parliament as well as local councils in Baghdad and other Iraqi cities.

(Abdullah 2006: 10)

In fact, even the growing enthusiasm for embracing pan-Arabism in Iraq must be understood as an Iraqi reaction to the then Ottoman Young Turk government, which adopted a policy of "Turkification" to be applied to all the Ottoman-controlled territories. This policy, among other things, "enforced Turkish as the single official language of the empire. All over the Arabic-speaking parts of the empire this policy was met with stiff resistance, often in the form of cultural clubs which glorified Arab history and language" (Abdullah 2006: 10).

While responses to the Ottoman policy of "Turkification" varied in Iraq, they mostly stressed Arab unity and achieving the autonomy of Iraq. This resulted in the creation of many secret, underground nationalist organizations with nationalist goals:

The most important was the Covenant Society which included several Iraqis, usually officers in the Ottoman army, many of whom would later play a leading role in the formation of the modern Iraqi state. Many of these clubs and political groups were secular with a particularly high participation of non-Muslims. Other groups, especially those that attracted elements from the Shi'i community, sought to define the nationalist project in Islamist terms by emphasizing the need to protect Islamic laws and culture. This was also the time when foreign intervention intensified.

(Abdullah 2006: 10)

Political resistance in Iraq intensified even further after the discovery of oil, which made the then superpowers—especially Britain—even more determined to dominate the region. Britain's occupation of Iraq in 1920 caused significant resistance among different sections of the Iraqi society, leading to the famous revolt that united various elements of Iraqi society against the British invaders. While the revolution itself failed to end the British occupation, it did achieve two important goals: first, it enhanced national consciousness; and second, it forced the British to change their policy of "direct rule" (Abdullah 2006: 11–12). Indeed, at that time, the struggle against the British invasion became the most defining factor for Iraqi nationalism and national consciousness.

Between 1932 and 1958, Iraq was ruled by a monarchy that managed to implement important social and economic reforms, but nonetheless failed in building social support. This, once again, was an important moment in modern Iraqi history as:

A number of global powers vied to increase their hegemony over a country with a strategic location and rich resources. Britain was clearly in an advantageous position early on, but after the end of the Second World War and the onset of the Cold War, both the United States and the Soviet Union came to play more prominent roles. Throughout the period of the monarchy a number of developments were to sow the seeds for the turbulent political changes of the 1960s. Landed interests solidified their semi-feudal status through such draconian measures as the Rights and Duties of Cultivators Law of 1933 and the Lazma Law of 1952, both of which effectively bound the peasants to the land and gave landowners exemption from most taxes ... By 1958, about 80 percent of the peasants were landless, and only 1.7 percent of landowners owned over 63 percent of all cultivated land ... Most of the new [army] officers, who hailed from middle-level Sunni backgrounds, held strong nationalist views and deeply resented foreign controls ... Another important development was the rapid extension of education at all levels.

(Abdullah 2006: 16–17)

The story of education in post-independence Iraq is particularly important because it made education accessible to Iraqis from different classes and backgrounds. Access to education enabled unprecedented social mobility, which, in turn, had significant political, economic, and social implications for Iraqi society and the broader region. The result of an increasingly educated Iraqi population in the 1950s and 1960s had paradoxical effects, as Abdullah notes:

On the one hand, the state could justifiably claim credit for reducing illiteracy and establishing impressive colleges which were putting out an increasing number of professionals in all fields. On the other hand, it also produced a new generation with high expectations and an ability to articulate its demands and organize its activities ... The 1950s and 1960s were decades of revolutionary change throughout the Middle East and much of the world. The post-Second World War order was being challenged by a variety of nationalist and socialist movements directed chiefly against Western capitalist hegemony. In this sense, the revolutionary period which swept through Iraq was no different.

(Abdullah 2006: 15–19)

It is crucial to understand Iraqi nationalism and the pan-Arabist project within the context that produced them, namely as fierce reactions to the region's colonial domination by foreign powers. It was under these circumstances that the Iraqi Communist Party and the Ba'ath party were conceived and received strong popular support and admiration from many Iraqis of different sects, religions, and backgrounds.

The Ba'ath, which successfully seized power in 1968, considered itself a nationalist, socialist party advocating pan-Arabism and the unity of the Arab people from Morocco to Iraq. In Iraq and Syria, the Ba'ath saw itself as a secular party strongly opposed to regionalism, sectarianism, and tribalism as reactionary elements considered to provide a perfect recipe for dividing nations and allowing colonizers to "divide and conquer." In 1972, the Ba'ath took the popular step of nationalizing Iraq's oil, expelling exploitative foreign companies. In addition to the Ba'ath's great interest in modernizing Iraq, building a strong nation, particularly health, agriculture, and state institutions, it took a special interest in educating Iraqi society to produce Iraqi citizens who would be deeply aware of internal and external challenges to their country. The party sought to establish solid educational institutions that were strongly anti-imperialist, anti-colonial, and anti-Zionist. While the Ba'ath attempted to influence education with its own principles, many scholars along with many interlocutors in this book, convincingly argued that it is an oversimplification to assume that Iraqi educators and students simply took things at face value. The relationship between the party and its people was dialectical rather than top–down.

The Ba'ath party's agenda and vision for developing Iraqi society and institutions was not always in conflict with the aspirations of the majority of Iraqi people, especially regarding Iraq's education system. Iraqi academics in various higher education institutions worked hard to negotiate with the party in power as they sought to build a rigorous educational system on a par with some of the most advanced educational systems worldwide. Most Iraqis I know, including many interlocutors in this work, consider the 1970s and the 1980s, when the Ba'ath strongly supported education, provided fellowships to educate Iraqi students at the best universities around the world, and other reforms, as the golden years of Iraqi academia. This is especially significant when considering what the Iraqi people and society at large lost in the aftermath of the 2003 occupation. Dismantling and destroying Iraqi education was not just "collateral damage" from the occupation: it was part and parcel of the occupation forces' deliberate efforts to restructure the Iraqi state, society, and identity as many testimonies in this study make clear.

The Ba'ath party's many other important achievements in the 1970s and 1980s made it popular among large swaths of Iraqi society. In this regard, it is worth citing Abdullah at length:

Support for or acquiescence to the Ba'ath also came as a result of real gains made in a number of fields. Politically, the most important developments, though temporary, came early. An agreement with the Kurdish nationalist leadership to establish a self-governing autonomous Kurdish region was followed by the formation of the National Progressive Front with the Communist Party and a number of other political groups. In many ways, these two agreements were the culmination of the steady, albeit bumpy, progress of national integration which had started during the monarchy ... More impressive were the material gains. The most obvious was infrastructural development including electrification of the countryside, and wide-scale construction of dams, bridges, roads, port facilities, hospitals, schools, and family homes. The problem of social inequalities was vigorously addressed through guaranteed employment, a campaign to eliminate illiteracy and a general improvement in household incomes. Manufacturing industry grew by a healthy 14 percent between 1968 and 1981. Life expectancy rose with improvements in free universal healthcare and increased access to safe drinking water from forty-six years in 1960 to fifty-seven in 1980. Infant mortality declined from 139 deaths per 1,000 live births in 1960 to 76 in 1980. The most notable exception to this story of material progress was in agriculture which was gradually marginalized in favor of imported foodstuffs. Support for the arts resulted in a dynamic intellectual life which hastened national integration despite the strict limits set on freedom of expression. In 1978, new laws were passed which enhanced women's rights in areas of education, employment, divorce, child custody, and severely curtailed polygamy and child marriage. Perhaps the clearest sign of progress, however, was the rapid growth of a large, well educated, urban middle class of professionals, administrators, and businessmen.

(Abdullah 2006: 28)

These details are important to bear in mind for two reasons. First, they are precisely the kind of details that have often been downplayed or simply absent from the Western discourse on Iraq, especially the Western media narrative that paved the way for the Iraq invasion. Second, these details provide a sense of the losses Iraqis incurred as a result of the occupation, which this book traces through Iraq's exiled academics. Considering the consequences of the US invasion of Iraq, this book takes seriously the premise that Iraq's invasion resulted from the productive rather than the destructive aspects of the Ba'ath regime. This is not to condone the transgressions of Ba'ath party leaders in Iraq. It is rather a way to understand other often neglected and positive aspects that were equally important for Iraqis.

A MORE REFINED UNDERSTANDING OF THE IRAQI BA'ATH ERA

The three and a half decades of the Ba'ath years deeply impacted the lives of the Iraqi people. The upheavals during these years were not primarily the work of the Ba'ath or the Iraqi regime, but rather a combination of the regime, the war with Iran, the First Gulf War, and UN sanctions, which all culminated in the 2003 US occupation. In turn, Iraqi academics' struggles and relations with the institutions of power must be multilayered rather than simply explicated as a case of dealing with an authoritarian ruling party, as is commonly portrayed in Western narratives.

Many scholars writing about the Ba'ath era in Iraq agree that one of the party's main objectives was to create a "new Iraqi man" and a "new society" (Davis 2005: 148; and Sassoon 2012: 62). Eric Davis's book, *Memories of State*, provides detailed analyses of how the Iraqi Ba'ath engineered the state, institutions, culture, and intellectual life during its 35 years in power. Davis argues that the Ba'athist regime evolved through a number of phases. The first one (1968–1973) "was characterized by a belligerent anti-imperialist and anti-Zionist rhetoric, support for Arab unity, and overtures to the Iraqi Communist Party to form a united front" (Davis 2005: 153). The second phase started shortly after the successful 1972 nationalization of the Iraq Petroleum Company and continued until the end of the Iran–Iraq War in 1988. During this time, and despite the war, "there was a slight opening of cultural expression during the early 1980s, during which some nongovernmental presses were allowed to function and publish material that had previously been forbidden" (Davis 2005: 154). The third phase started at the end of 1988 during which the credibility of the regime started to be challenged: "Economic pressures caused by falling oil prices and war debts fueled public discontent at the regime's inability to enact the new policies that it had promised would follow the war's end" (Davis 2005: 154). While there is more nuance and complexity to the way Davis describes the sequence of these phases, they are useful to map out the trajectory of the lives of Iraqi academics during the Ba'ath years.

According to Davis, nearly all cultural, intellectual, and scholarly production of that period was "state-sponsored" (Davis 2005: 170). He divides the intellectual production in Iraq during the Ba'ath era into three main categories. The first is what he calls the "ideological tracts, such as speeches and essays by Saddam and works by Ba'thist thinkers such as Michel 'Aflaq, Ilyas Farah, Shibli al-'Aysami, and Fadil Barak, to name a few" (Davis 2005: 170). The second category is one that "encompassed works explicitly designed to use culture to promote the state's political and ideological objectives" (Davis 2005: 170). The third category included "intellectuals who produced scholarly works" (Davis 2005: 170).

Regarding knowledge production during the Ba'ath era, Davis suggests: "To argue that all state-sponsored publications during the Ba'thist rule were ideologically biased and instrumental is simplistic and shortchanges much serious scholarship" (Davis 2005: 212). By surveying a wide selection of academic texts, publications, and different types of scholarly productions during that period, Davis concludes that the Ba'athist attempts to influence society were less successful in scholarly works and it "seems to have only superficially entered the educational curriculum at the secondary school level" (Davis 2005: 224). Such conclusions shed significant light on the role of Iraqi academics in negotiating with the regime to shape their own society. As he notes at the end of his survey of Iraqi knowledge production under the Ba'ath, especially as regards texts produced by academics, Davis emphasizes "the always open-ended quality and intellectual ambiguity of state efforts to impose hegemonic thinking" (Davis 2005: 225–26). These conclusions are significant considering that a "large number of talented and educated Iraqis played a major part in maintaining the country and the system in spite of the widespread destruction of the First Gulf War" (Sassoon 2012: 277).

As such, it's hardly surprising that the Ba'ath era had different meanings for Iraqis from all walks of life, depending on: the decade examined; the individuals involved (their class, political, religious, and sectarian affiliations); their relationships and ties with the ruling party; and other factors. During the 1970s, for example, the Ba'ath started putting its vision, reforms, and plans into action after it took power in 1968. This explains why it was considered to be a "golden decade" in which many Iraqis found themselves involved in a huge state-building project emphasizing institutions and society, and producing a new type of decolonized Iraqi citizenship and identity.

The stories and testimonies of Iraqi academics in subsequent chapters show that creating a "new citizen" and a "new society" was not simply rhetoric trumpeted by the Ba'ath. Many Iraqis genuinely believed in the need for such a plan to undo the damage of centuries of colonial rule in their country. Wresting control of national resources, especially oil, from exploitative foreign companies in the 1970s significantly increased the state's budget and allowed more revenues to be allocated to vital public services, education among them. The National Campaign for the Eradication of Illiteracy was so successful that Iraq was awarded the United Nations Educational, Scientific, and Cultural Organization (UNESCO) prize for eradicating illiteracy in 1982.[1] Iraqi higher education institutions became among the best in the Middle East, attracting huge numbers of Arab and foreign students.

At the same time, given the Ba'ath's animosity toward and competition with what had traditionally been one of its biggest political rivals, the Iraqi Communist Party (ICP), Iraqi academics who were affiliated with or were sympathetic to the ICP relate rather different experiences during this era. Many ICP members were directly or indirectly subject to persecution, demotion, and imprisonment, depending on the scale of their political activities. Some were co-opted; others were forced into exile.

Despite the war with Iran, for many Iraqis in the academy, the 1980s saw a continuation of flourishing in many walks of life. Still, several of my interlocutors also told me that they viewed that decade as the beginning of the deterioration of Iraqi higher education, with the state redirecting its resources to the war with Iran, at the expense of vital sectors like health and education—not to mention the hundreds of thousands of lost lives which gave rise to the common saying that "almost every Iraqi individual has lost a loved one in the war with Iran." One of the unintended consequences of that war was a serious shortage of professionals in most state institutions, which presented countless opportunities for Iraqi women to take on an active role in every sector of society and strengthened their negotiating powers with the state. In 1979, there were only four universities nationwide and, by the time of the 2003 occupation, there was at least one university in each of the 19 Iraqi governorates. The structure of the Iraqi educational system was so strong that it allowed Iraqi students to be competitive at an international level, even after the 2003 occupation.[2]

Most of the interlocutors in this book view the 1990s, particularly following the Kuwait invasion and the First Gulf War, as the most devastating decade for Iraq, primarily as a result of the harshest economic sanctions ever to be imposed by the "international community" on a modern nation state. To combat the ensuing brain drain, the Iraqi state prohibited academics and professionals from leaving the country, although many found ways to do so in search of work in other Arab or Western countries. Besides the loss of hundreds of thousands of Iraqi lives, the UN sanctions also caused irreparable damage to the fabric of Iraqi society. Rather than holding the Ba'ath party or Saddam Hussein's regime responsible, many academics viewed the UN sanctions as a tactic by the international community to pave the way for weakening and later invading Iraq. One academic I interviewed at length put it succinctly: "They thought a hungry nation would receive the occupation with cheering and flowers!"

2
The Baʿath Era:
Iraqi Academics Looking Back

I start with the stories of the communist Iraqi academics for two reasons: first, because of the decades-long and fierce rivalry between the Iraqi Communist Party (ICP) and the Baʿath before the latter came to power in 1968; and second, and consequently, because Iraqi educators (and professionals) who belonged to or were aligned with the ICP were particularly disadvantaged and struggled more than most other groups during the Baʿath years. I first learned about the complexity of the struggle of Iraqi academics who were communists, in summer 2013, when I was doing fieldwork in London. The first accounts I heard came from an academic couple, Sameer and Siham, who were not communists themselves but whose long experience in Iraqi higher education had provided them with unique insights on this issue, and also, through the Council for At-Risk Academics (CARA) and the Iraqi Cultural Centre in London. Over time, I made connections with other academics, who had left Iraq at different times because of the persecution they faced for their political affiliations. In some cases, they were individuals who suffered simply because their spouses or other members of their families had such affiliations.

As I started connecting with more Iraqi communists and leftists in London and others who still live in Baghdad, three specific elements emerged from their stories. First, the majority were fiercely opposed to Baʿath rule. Second, the Baʿath attempted to neutralize communist and Islamist academics who threatened its vision of nation-building by transferring them from educational jobs into other industries and sectors so as to limit their ability to spread communist or Islamist ideas in the classroom. Third, even those who managed to leave Iraq were not totally immune from surveillance by Baʿathists abroad.

* * *

It was a beautiful summer day in London, in June 2013. I was already late for my first interview at a top university to meet with a renowned Iraqi professor of political science, Sameer J., who agreed to share with me his lifelong experiences in teaching and higher education administration in Baghdad. Sameer who looked to be in his mid to late sixties was dressed professionally and reminded me of my professors at the University of Baghdad during my undergraduate years. His "office" was just a modest cubicle in an open space. Despite the modest cubicle provided to Sameer at the department where he worked as a part-time lecturer teaching a few courses and volunteering to support the research of Middle East scholars in his discipline of political science, it didn't take long to realize that I was in conversation with an important scholar, educated both in Iraq and the UK, who had published extensively in his field and had held high-level academic positions at the University of Baghdad for over 30 years. Now his life was reduced to a cubicle and teaching classes on a part-time basis.

During my time in London, Sameer and I had multiple meetings and long conversations in his office and later at his home. He started first by discussing the 1970s when the Iraqi government began sending many students abroad on fellowships and scholarships to create Iraqi expertise rather than rely on foreign expertise. Most academics I met viewed these fellowships as one of the most important steps taken by the Iraqi state to allow Iraqis to manage their own country. In the late 1970s, Sameer said, many students returned from Europe and the USA with doctoral degrees in different fields essential for "building the nation and society." These scholars started new PhD programs in public Iraqi universities to decrease reliance on foreign know-how, and to create "new citizens" able to "build Iraq with Iraqi hands." Many academics agreed that, if it were not for these Iraqi experts, they would have never been able to rebuild a destroyed Iraq after the First Gulf War in 1991. This, to them, was strong evidence to support the critical role academics play in any society because they train everyone else to build it. Sameer was one such person, "though I paid for my education abroad from my own pocket," he said to remind me that he did not benefit from Iraqi state scholarships at that time.

Sameer noted that relations between academics and the state did not always go smoothly because scholars sometimes "took different political routes and ideologies" that were opposed to the Baʿath vision and commitments. Particularly troubling for the party at that time were the communists, who also called themselves "leftists," and Islamists. Sameer said he was neither a communist nor an Islamist and that such academics, once identified, were not necessarily killed or imprisoned but were "punished" by being transferred to "non-academic jobs, where they still maintained a comfortable life, but were no longer able to spread their ideological vision to students in classrooms." However, despite some "foolish steps," Sameer said, the Baʿath continued to support good research and "objective knowledge and academic analysis" in many other ways and in most academic fields. Further, the regime "did not insert its own ideologies in the topics taught at the political science department," where Sameer taught for many years, save in one course called "*al-thaqafa al-qawmiya*" ("National Culture"). This topic was taught in every university department nationwide. The course was designed to introduce the history of Iraq and the vision, philosophy, and teachings of the Baʿath to all students, regardless of their majors. Another "foolish step" the party took in the 1990s that affected the quality of research was to introduce "The Committee for Intellectual Soundness," a body that was meant to monitor the "quality of PhD dissertations prior to final approval by faculty" and to "make sure that dissertations did not contain anything inimical to the ruling party." During our last meeting, as he drove me back to the tube station near his home on the outskirts of London, he took a deep breath, sighed, and said:

> I actually got an academic job offer as soon as I obtained my PhD here in Britain back in 1970. I could have easily stayed here permanently, but I decided to return to serve my country, and perhaps it was a mistake on my part. I have not known a day of peace ever since. In 2008, due to the horrific consequences of the occupation, I finally had to decide that it was time to leave.

Sameer said this with an ambivalent tone similar to what I sensed throughout our meetings about the pros and cons of the Baʿath era and how all the latter's offenses can easily fade away in comparison to the occupation and its consequences after 2003.

*   *   *

I was advised to frequent the Iraqi Cultural Centre in London to meet other exiled Iraqi academics and intellectuals. On my first visit there, I encountered a number of them who were attending a poetry reading night. The discussant of the event was Farah S., a former academic with a sad and compelling story. Farah holds degrees in English literature and translation from Baghdad and London. She is also a playwright and taught drama in Iraq in the 1970s. Her problems with the Ba'ath started in 1977 when she taught one of her plays that was critical of the party. She was "harassed" in her department and transferred multiple times to different places and cities. She eventually quit teaching to work for the Iraqi airlines but was unable to flourish there because her passion was teaching drama and playwriting.

After winning a national award for one of her plays, she returned to teaching and was assigned a teaching job in one of Baghdad's poorest neighborhoods. In her new department, the chair was "very Ba'athist" and she was asked repeatedly to join the party. "I refused because I wanted to maintain my creativity and independence," she said, adding that she had realized:

> they had been recording some of my lectures to make sure that I started every lesson with praising the party. Very Big Brother stuff. Later, along with three other female academics, we were approached by some men from the intelligence service. We were dragged by our hair and kicked out of the building.

Although Farah was not a communist, her husband was and she was the one who "paid the price" for his politics and anti-Ba'athist activities. Initially, they hounded her husband, who first hid in the countryside and was later aided by shepherds to cross the border into Syria. Once he left, they went after her and, in 1979, Farah decided to join her husband in Syria. Like many others who sought to leave Iraq during those years, Farah had to change her passport-listed occupation from "academic" to a "housewife" (men generally changed it from "academic" to "freelance worker"). Farah left for Syria where a long journey and many years of suffering awaited her.

In Syria, she found that her husband had joined the Palestinian Liberation Organization (PLO), which "helped the Iraqi opposition a lot in those days." After spending some time in Syria, Farah and her husband had to leave once again, and they headed to Lebanon, despite the then ongoing civil war there:

I was given a Palestinian ID to cross the border to Lebanon under a different identity. In Beirut, the situation was quite harsh. I was told about the possibility of working as a teacher at a refugee camp in Ba'albek through the United Nations Relief and Works Agency [UNRWA] ... We stayed there for a year. The manager of the camp was a Palestinian who had lived in Iraq, so he was sympathetic ... After that, I was told about teaching opportunities in Algeria, but I didn't have my transcripts because they never gave them to educated Iraqis leaving the country at that time. We went to Algeria anyway, without any documents. Life there was also extremely hard; they didn't even give hotel rooms to Iraqis.

Farah and her husband endured extreme hardships in Algeria. In those days, "many people slept and bathed at the public baths because they didn't have any other place. We, like many other Iraqis, slept in parks." She tried to support herself by teaching but was unable to do so since she did not have her transcripts to prove her qualifications. However, after multiple visits to the Ministry of Education in the city of Algiers, Farah was hired to teach. They simply trusted her:

I worked as a teacher in a high school. We lived with a family of a well-known poet ... We then moved to a small and modest hotel, with little or no amenities. Even after I was hired, I had no money, because I wasn't paid for the first few months. Life was so hard in that overcrowded hotel. The place was extremely cold in winter. My mother visited us in Algeria. She brought us clothes, blankets, and some food from Iraq. Later, the Ministry of Education gave us a small apartment, but with no amenities whatsoever. We all slept in one bed.

Farah gave birth to her two children in Algeria, but soon after, her husband was arrested for doing illegal work to earn extra cash. They were deported to Syria and were back to square one. After multiple failed attempts to make a living in Syria, and with no hope of returning to Iraq, Farah and her family moved to Yemen where she got a teaching post in a remote part of the country:

We went to a tiny village in Yemen. There were more goats there than people ... People, however, were so friendly, though the place was unbearably backward. Yemen then also had some political upheavals and we had to live through that. I taught there. I always taught English language, plays, and theatre because that was my passion ... We lived this life for six years ... More political upheavals followed in Yemen, so we couldn't stay longer ... I went to the UK Embassy in Yemen and asked for a visa to study English in the UK and, to my surprise, was granted a visa! We came to the UK in 1991 and life those days was better for the newly arrived immigrants. We applied for asylum within a week and were accepted as political asylees.

Farah told me she is half Sunni and half Shi'a but she emphasized that it was not one's sect or religion that mattered under the secular Ba'ath regime. What mattered was whether one was with or against the party: "The notion that Sunnis ruled under the Ba'ath is a myth. I know many well-known Sunni families who opposed the party and who paid a high price," she added.

At another time, Farah and I took a nice walk in one of London's parks near Kentish Town. We then decided to sit down at a table to have a cup of tea. A few minutes of silence followed. As she started sipping on her tea, I could see so much depth and sorrow in her amber-colored eyes, which were further amplified by the kohl she wore. Looking at her, one could see that her eyes had seen so much, they had shed many tears, and were perhaps withholding many more stubborn tears of dignity. Farah talked about her love for Iraq and about missing home. When I asked her how she could miss Iraq after all she had gone through, she said, "I suffered from the political atmosphere, not cultural, social, or any other atmosphere in Iraq. This is why I will always love it and miss it." I then asked, after all these years of struggle and exile, how she defines "home"? She said, she will tell a real story to make the point:

You know how overwhelmingly rejuvenating the scent of Iraqi roses is? I have never smelt any roses like Iraqi roses. Ever. I always missed them here in London. When my sister died, I went to Iraq in 2003 to attend her funeral. I took a quick visit to my late mother's old house now occupied by other family members. I saw lots of roses in her garden. I decided to cut a few branches to bring them and plant them here in London to remind me of home. I hid them well and managed to get them past security points in airports. I planted them in my garden here. When they bloomed, to my disappointment, they still didn't have that strong scent. They smelt like any British-grown roses. This is "home," my dear Louis.

I told her this was such a touching and deep story and that if she did not turn it into a poem, I would. She promised she would write the story and she did. I was so pleased to see it published in a magazine a few months on from our meeting. Farah continues to be politically and culturally active in London. She continues to write in Arabic for progressive left-leaning magazines and journals. She still participates in all types of literary and intellectual events related to the Iraqi diaspora in London. Speaking about the resistance of many Iraqi communists, she noted in reference to the US occupation that Iraqis had always resisted injustice in one way or another and did not need anyone to do it on their behalf.

*   *   *

The story of Yousif N. captures how academics can find themselves trapped within multiple regimes of power. It shows how communist academics who left Iraq were still not fully safe abroad, given the fact that the Baʿath and the Western regimes saw communism as a threat during the Cold War era. Yousif was on a promising academic path working at the Nuclear Institute in Baghdad from 1969 to 1975. I first met him at a picnic with a group of leftist Iraqi academics on the outskirts of London. Yousif started narrating his story by noting the academic and scientific rigor that existed in Iraq in the 1970s, which he said gradually eroded. He came to the UK in 1977 on a fellowship funded by the Nuclear Institute in Baghdad to study applied radiation. In 1980, while in the UK, his passport was confiscated by the Iraqi Embassy.

According to him, his trouble began when he started becoming active with a group of leftist Iraqi students in the UK who "voiced their dissatisfaction with how the Baʿath had started suffocating certain freedoms." Things had been smooth up to the mid-1970s, but then the party became more aggressive and higher education became more politicized. "Many students who got scholarships from the government were Baʿathists," he stated, although this was denied by some of my other interlocutors. If true, did it mean that Yousif was also a committed Baʿathist since he was sent to the UK on a fellowship? In all likelihood, he, like millions of Iraqis, had to join the lower ranks of the party just as a formality. Upon confiscating his passport, the Embassy asked him to return to Baghdad immediately. He realized that in doing so might cost him his life. In 1980, not only was Yousif without a passport but he was also assaulted twice by "regime thugs":

> I used to see cars waiting for me next to my accommodation ... I returned to the labs to avoid the situation. This was psychologically harmful. The UK government would not take adequate action against such threats because they were on good terms with Saddam's regime at that time. All these things delayed my studies, although my name as a scientist was already established ... I lived a very difficult life until I was forced by the UK government to apply for asylum in 1984.

Yousif's narrative reveals two key points: first, how far the Ba'ath went in hounding and persecuting Iraqi communists or individuals who posed a political and ideological threat to the system; and second, how even being on foreign soil like the UK was no guarantee for Iraqi dissidents. As Palestinian author and journalist Said Aburish wrote, "Even Saddam was allowed to murder in the middle of London when his government was following policies friendly to the West" (Aburish 1997: 367). Sassoon's analysis of Ba'ath documents makes clear that the "activities of the Student Union, another organ dominated by the party, illustrate how the Ba'th attempted to control students' activities not only in Iraq but also when they were studying abroad" (Sassoon 2012: 272). Sassoon cites a report by the Scottish Union of Students from the University of Strathclyde that accused the Iraqi Student Union of "harassing Iraqi students who opposed the regime and even of using physical violence to intimidate them" (Sassoon 2012: 273).

But there are other explanations for the Ba'ath's monitoring of its scientists abroad beyond questions of political dissent or opposition to the party. Scholars have noted that Saddam Hussein was "always in awe of scientists, because of his belief in their vital contribution to building a strong modern Iraq, scientists were continually honored and rewarded by the party" (Sassoon 2012: 78). However, after the "Israeli air force had destroyed Iraq's initial nuclear reactor, Osiris, in 1981 and had assassinated some of the scientists who were considered part of Iraq's nuclear weapon's program" honoring and rewarding scientists took a different turn (Davis 2005: 198). The Iraqi state became ultra-cautious by further surveilling its scientific academics, particularly those studying physics or biology abroad, which further complicated the relationship between academics in the sciences and the regime.

This point was confirmed in October 2015, when I met with Iftikhar A., an internally displaced academic currently residing and teaching in Iraqi Kurdistan. Iftikhar holds advanced degrees in physics from Iraq and the USA. She first recalled her "beautiful days" in the USA between the end of the 1970s and early 1980s, where she was on a fellowship doing her PhD in physics:

> At that time, there were no anti-Islam sentiments as they now have in the USA. People there were even nicer than Iraqi people. I loved every minute I spent in America … They admired Iraqi people and the standards of our education … They also thought of Iraqis as open-minded and smart people. They did not think of us as they think of Saudis. I was not veiled in those days as I am now. I remember one American professor who mocked Iranian women and told me "imagine, if you were totally covered like them!" This was the time of the Iranian Revolution.

Iftikhar's narrative sheds light on how alliances, and consequently discourse on a group of people, shift depending on politics. It shows how the friends of yesterday suddenly turn into the enemies of today. In fact, it also sheds light on Islamophobia that existed in the USA during the 1970s against the Iranians for political reasons related to the overthrow of the Western-friendly Shah government by the Islamic Revolution in 1979.

After obtaining her PhD and returning to Iraq, Iftikhar worked as a researcher for many years at the Iraqi Atomic Organization. Remembering those years, she said:

> We did not work on a nuclear bomb … We only did research on certain aspects of nuclear energy. However, our research was secret because they did not want the scientific information to be stolen. When the place [Iraqi Atomic Organization] was bombed in 1991, one missile fell on my office … We were part of the reactor that was installed by France in 1981. We were extremely advanced scientifically. I did not even feel the transition from the USA to Baghdad.

Given the nature of her experience under the Ba'ath, I wanted to understand how Iftikhar felt about doing research at such a sensitive place. She responded:

> The Ba'ath did not interfere in our work and scientific research. People were treated very well. The state appreciated good expertise and good research. They cared about merit and qualifications more than anything else. However, when sending scientists abroad for workshops, further education, training, buying resources and machines, and so on, they would always send someone with the scientists to "protect them."

After a short pause, she added, "we also had many women doing research there" because "they always recruited the top students from all scientific fields and most of these top students were usually women." Iftikhar vividly recalled the American bombing of the facility in 1991.

> We were sent home before the bombing. We did not have any nuclear bombs—of course—but they had to lie about it to destroy Iraq, because we were very advanced scientifically ... They had to destroy us for the sake of Israel.

Other academics who spoke to me also felt that Israel had had a big hand in destroying Iraq. Some of them went so far as to say that many US policymakers who supported, pushed for, and indeed caused "the Iraq War" were neoconservative Zionists who were more loyal to Israel than to the United States. When I asked Iftikhar about whether one had to be a Ba'athist to do the kind of research she did, she said that given the sensitive nature of their work and research, one had to be somehow affiliated with the party, or at least to have no known anti-government activities:

> However, one could manage with a low rank in the party, which, as you know, was merely a matter of formality. I have also known a few people here and there who were independent and still managed to work there because their skills were in high demand. The point was not to be or not to be in the party; the main criterion was that one was not against or a threat to the party. With our work, they also didn't allow people with foreign spouses to work there, although I have also heard about excep-

tions to this rule, so I can't say for sure how strictly it was applied ... After the 1991 bombing, they dismantled our place and redistributed us to different places. Most people were sent to work for Military Industries, which was just a fancy name for rebuilding Iraq after it was almost totally destroyed by the First Gulf War ... I worked there for a few years and then looked for an academic post to teach physics. It was hard to move from hands-on scientific work to just teaching. It felt like a huge gap between theory and practice.

Iftikhar's narrative shows another angle of why the Ba'ath took extra measures to surveil or, in her words, "protect" its academics both inside Iraq and abroad. Based on these narratives, we see that the Ba'ath, especially under Saddam Hussein, was particularly aggressive toward communists, Islamists, and indeed any parties or individuals that posed a direct political or ideological threat to the party and the regime. But these stories equally show that many of these academics were far from passive. They resisted and insisted on not compromising their intellectual and political beliefs both inside and outside of Iraq. The Ba'ath's animosity toward communists can be explained through the fact that the ICP remained one of the most active rivals of the Ba'ath ideology from the time of ICP's inception in 1934 until Saddam Hussein came to power in 1979. In his study of the history of the ICP, Johan Franzén writes that the ICP was "one of the most prominent and influential political parties in Iraq. At certain moments during this period, the ICP attracted a mass following making it arguably the largest and most important communist party in the Arab world" (Franzén 2011: 1). Franzén also calls it the most important political party in Iraq that never officially held power.

Because the Ba'ath was a secular, non-sectarian party, rather than targeting any Iraqi religious, sectarian, or ethnic groups per se, it primarily went after opponents of the party/regime—even when that opposition came from Sunnis. This is important because it challenges the common misconception that Sunnis were exclusively privileged under the Ba'ath. This aspect explains why academics from diverse backgrounds were affected by the party's policies, while other equally diverse groups were not. It all depended on their positionality within the state, whether they actively posed a threat to the regime or not, and on the ways in which they negotiated the obstacles on the ground.

Some studies have attributed the animosity between the ICP and the Ba'ath to the latter's lack of "intellectual depth" compared with the ICP (see Sassoon 2012: 222; and Franzén 2011: 5–33 and 185–245). Yet, the assumption that Marxism, born in Europe, is intellectually superior to other ideologies is a rather arrogant and colonial view that privileges Western ideologies and political movements over those shaped elsewhere. Likewise, to assume that believing in the Ba'ath philosophy made people more indoctrinated than believing in other ideologies, like communism or capitalism, is equally arrogant and dismissive of ideas and visions coming from non-Western environments. Such analysis, therefore, must be challenged and decolonized. In fact, many of the early visionaries of Ba'athism started as communists or had sympathies with Marxism. They only abandoned it after it became clear to them that Marxism did not fully account for their struggles and problems in the Arab region, after they felt betrayed by European communist parties.

Despite some of the horrific experiences of communist and Islamist academics under the Ba'ath, the testimonies of the communist and leftist academics provide only one perspective, albeit an important one, and they do not necessarily dovetail with what many other Iraqi academics in this research shared. Communists and Islamists in Iraq espoused ideologies that sought to wrest power from the Ba'ath, and the remainder of this chapter captures other academic voices and testimonies to provide a more holistic picture of the period.

CURRICULUM, FELLOWSHIPS, AND FREEDOM OF EXPRESSION

While discussing the lives of academics during the Ba'ath era with Sameer J. (cited earlier), he, like others, emphasized that the Ba'ath in many ways encouraged academics to be critical and to teach students about different ideologies and political challenges around the world. "Our curriculum was designed to provide an in-depth understanding of the Cold War era and the decolonization movements to rid countries of colonization and imperialism," he stated, "topics taught and researched even at top higher education institutions in the West." He noted that academics were allowed "great freedom" in designing their curricula with a view to graduating "well-informed students."

We taught about every continent around the world. The Palestinian case was an important part of our studies. The committee at that time also put a special emphasis on Latin America, Africa, Arab and Islamic thought. The materials on the history of international relations were revised and in fact decolonized to go back in time and include histories prior to Europe. They also brought back political sociology after it had been removed earlier. Later in the 1980s, we the professors, decided to add public opinion to the curriculum.

Sameer's words are confirmed by Eric Davis, a scholar and a political scientist in training, who writes: "In 1980, the Baghdad University Department of Political Science was a sophisticated academic unit with a well-developed curriculum similar to that found in Western universities" (Davis 2005: 221). Through analyzing university curriculum during his time in Iraq, Davis writes:

> Of interest in terms of the presentation of its subject matter was a comparative politics text, *al-Mushkilat al-Siyasiyya fi-l-'Alim al-Thalith* [*Political Problems in the Third World*], written by the chair of the Political Science Department, Dr. Riyad 'Aziz Hadi.
>
> (Davis 2005: 221)

Davis seems to equate an "advanced curriculum" with Western education, which is a colonial way of evaluating other academic systems. Nevertheless, his point illustrates that Iraqi curriculum was not only on a par with Western standards but some of its best references were authored by Iraqi academics. During our conversation, Sameer emphasized that by sharing this information he sought to give me an idea of how Iraqi academics played a pivotal role in choosing their own academic materials and directions of teaching. Many academics, according to Sameer, were invested in countering the Western domination of knowledge production, hence the choices made in revising the curriculum.

One of the most ironic and sad things for Sameer was the way that many academics who were on good terms with the former regime—"some even dedicated their dissertations to Saddam Hussein"—had become "vicious critics" of the old regime and "attained high-ranking positions in the new Iraq." He sighed and added:

These people will always be around. I still feel sad about that, because they always distort history for their own benefit. They have no concept of morals and ethics. They are simply waiting to clap for the winner to turn any situation to their own advantage.

Sameer then talked about how the regime had strict filtering on certain educational institutions, but its grip varied from one institution to another, from one college to another, depending on their function. For example, colleges that graduated teachers or individuals who were going to work in national security related areas were strict about party memberships, this included colleges of education, physical education, and military and intelligence academies. However, Sameer wondered, "is there a country in which this is not the case? Though it may be done in different ways." The Iraq scholar, Joseph Sassoon, documents an interview he had with a senior Iraqi military officer at al-Bakir University (a military academy). The officer was responsible for the university in the late 1980s, and later taught there as a professor of strategy and national defense. Sassoon writes, "the officer assured me that the party did not get involved in setting the curriculum of this university or the military colleges, although all candidates had to go through 'political guidance' sessions" (Sassoon 2012: 136).

I then asked Sameer to speak about how certain groups like Kurds and the Shi'a were treated in academia. He said that groups like the Kurds, for example, were not banned from pursuing education and higher education, but there was something called the "security background check" that had to be obtained to make sure that the person in question "had no history of actively being against the party." He noted that minorities like Kurds were expected to change their ethnicity in their national IDs from "Kurd" to "Arab."[1] Further,

they were expected to bring a document proving that they were at least at the rank of *nasir* [supporter] in the party, which, frankly, was a formality only. There is no graduate from any Iraqi university who did not have to be at least a *mu'ayyid* [sympathizer], and this, of course is not to condone it, but rather, it is pointed out as a negative aspect of the party.

It must be noted that *mu'ayyid* (sympathizer) and *nasir* (supporter) were the lowest two ranks in the hierarchy of the Ba'ath and most Iraqis, including at schools and universities, held one of the two ranks. In fact, the party considered each Iraqi to be a *mu'ayyid* by default. Many academics told me that sticking to these low ranks meant that people were not necessarily interested in politics or the party. For many, this was just a symbolic title to avoid institutional hurdles and bureaucracies. Those who wanted to reach higher up administrative positions had to advance in the ranks of the party. However, Sameer said that when it came to academic standards, the party was always interested in skilled people with expertise.

* * *

Much of what Sameer told me in London in 2013 was reiterated in summer 2014 in Amman, when I met another political scientist. Tall, handsome, well-mannered, and fiercely anti-occupation, Badir A. was in his early forties with a PhD in political science. He had taught in Iraq before the war with a master's degree. After 2003, he went on to pursue his PhD, obtaining it in 2006 under what he described as "the most difficult circumstances."

When I asked Badir how he had experienced academia under the Ba'ath, he responded that one of the hardest things for academics like him was the accusation of being "pro-Ba'ath" or of justifying the party's transgressions when highlighting the positive aspects of academia at that time. He then spoke about "freedom of expression" noting that, although the office of the president was a "red line" not to be crossed, it was "nothing" compared to the many "red lines" and taboos that have surfaced since the 2003 occupation, adding that at least seven academics in his department had been "independent," politically speaking. Badir noted that he strongly opposed any "academic red lines" whatsoever, be it in Iraq or elsewhere, and offered the following compelling perspective:

Last year I presented at a conference in California and it was nice that one could criticize Bush, Obama, and everything without any red lines. But then, in America, they have other red lines, like Zionism. I know people in America who lost their jobs for criticizing Zionism … [In Iraq,] we did have people of different politics and beliefs at our college, but they simply wouldn't attack Saddam directly … Going back to my department, the dean of my department for two rounds whose name was Riyad 'Aziz Hadi[2] was not a Ba'athist. Some people belonged to the party, but others did not. The claim that the Ba'ath only sent people from the party on fellowships is a big lie ... I know many people in my department who went on fellowships to the USA and the UK who weren't Ba'athists.

The issue of "red lines" that cannot be crossed in different countries is important; political systems have different written and unwritten rules about them. The problem becomes even more serious when the "red line" is precisely what needs to be crossed in order to change societies for the better. Under such circumstances, academics and intellectuals may find themselves in a situation in which writing, scholarship, or any other work they do becomes a distraction from doing what really matters to change the status quo.

During a later conversation in his Amman office where he works as a political consultant, Badir shared that he liked Ba'ath "thought" but was deeply critical of the practice of certain individuals in power. He called Ba'ath philosophy "the thought of prophets" and noted that the party had managed to build strong and good institutions for Iraq, and that they could have done better if the system hadn't been infiltrated by many "opportunists" who cared about "power" more than the party's original teachings as envisioned by its key thinkers such as Michel 'Aflaq. Badir's words echo those of many academics who for a long time believed in Ba'ath thought and purpose, if not practice. In fact, I met several academics who, for many years, sincerely adhered to the party's principles but turned their back on the Ba'ath after witnessing the abuses of its leaders.

* * *

Issa D. is exiled in Amman. He teaches management and holds advanced degrees in the field from Iraq and France. He worked in Iraq from 1984, when he returned with a PhD from France, until 1996 when he left because of the UN sanctions. His PhD dissertation was unique at the time because it was a comparative study of strategic leadership in France versus the Arab world, which Saddam Hussein had expressed personal interest in. "I wished we had an institute in Iraq to prepare strategic leaders to be administratively good, experts in their fields, and care about nationalism but not in a fanatic, narrow-minded way," he told me. Issa's statements made me wonder about his connection with the Ba'ath, and when I asked him, he said that he wanted to provide an "honest testimony for history":

I was a Ba'athist for 25 years—from 1965 to 1990. My other parallel line with my academic life is my political life. I joined the Ba'ath in 1965, when I was 16 years old. I worked for the party continuously until 1990, when Iraq invaded Kuwait. The latter event was the biggest mistake, in my view ... That was a turning point at which I cut my relations with the party. In the Ba'ath ideology, you do not unite countries by force. Invading Kuwait was contrary to the principles of the Ba'ath. I found all kinds of excuses to distance myself from the party. I used the sanctions and the difficult life conditions as an excuse to stay away from activities, meetings, and so on.

Issa said, despite the many valuable ideas in Ba'ath philosophy, the problem was its practice, which is why he quit. That was the only form of resistance he could perform at that time. Based on his academic and political experience, however, Issa views the political and the academic aspects of life as inseparable and intertwined in any system, no matter how tenuous the connections may appear to an outsider:

Academic and political lives are inseparable. Anything academic in Iraq during the Ba'ath era was influenced by the party. The reasoning was to keep education uncontaminated by other ideologies and agendas. The academic became the tool to implement this plan. Rare are those academics who weren't connected with the Ba'ath in some way. This means even the so-called "independent" people were connected in different forms like committees or were surrounded by others who would prevent them from bringing in "destructive thoughts" to the system. The system worked like a cycle in academia: you couldn't become an academic without an advanced degree, you couldn't get an advanced degree, especially a fellowship to go abroad, without somehow being in the system. You were necessarily part of the system if you were to become an academic at all. I do not understand how people can claim that they were not Ba'athists as academics.

After a short pause, he added:

Let's look at the big picture: no country in the world, to maintain control and get consent from its peoples, would give up on such sensitive places as academia, the justice system, military, and so on, and let them be ruled by so-called "independent" people. No country would allow you to be in the system if you were really against that system. We need to be honest about this matter. So, this wasn't just a Ba'ath "flaw" in the system, it's something you see worldwide in variations and with different degrees of compromise.

Issa made some convincing points on the role of an institutionalized academic within any political system, especially regarding how hard it is not to compromise one's intellectual life and freedom, at least partially, in order to succeed. During another conversation with Issa, as he was driving me home after spending the day on his campus on the outskirts of Amman, he said that experience had taught him that many of us come into the massive machine of the system full of life and ideas hoping to change it from within once we "get in." However, we discover that the huge bureaucratic machine and the processes in place are there precisely to kill our intellectual dreams and creativity: "You discover late in the game that it was much easier to adjust yourself to the system, to become what it wants you to be, than to change it from within. This is what I have learned."

WOMEN ACADEMICS UNDER THE BA'ATH

Another pattern that emerged during my interactions with academics was the issue of Iraqi women during the Ba'ath years compared to post-occupation Iraq. Sura M. is currently living and teaching in Amman, where she chairs one of Jordan's top architectural engineering departments. She left Iraq in 2005 after receiving a bullet inside an envelope that was slipped under her office door in what became a classic method of threatening Iraqi academics in post-occupation Iraq. When Sura opened the envelope, she found a bullet and a short note telling her to leave immediately or be killed. She did. While sitting at her beautiful and well-organized office in Amman, she described the academic atmosphere under the Ba'ath in the 1980s with more gender-specific details. Like previous interlocutors, she talked about the dynamics of how state fellowships were awarded for academics to pursue higher education abroad. She said that despite the need to have at least a low rank in the party to get these fellowships, they still tried hard to make them merit based. She also noted that even though Ba'ath members had a quota of academic jobs, "even those [Ba'athist] academics, for the most part, were qualified and decent people." Sura emphasized the importance of not having a sectarian regime. She spoke particularly about her experience as a woman academic under the Ba'ath:

> As women under the Ba'ath, we were not oppressed. We had a lot of freedom within what Middle Eastern societies allow. I started working from the 1980s during days and evenings. The society accepted that. During the war with Iran, society depended highly on women. They became ubiquitous: in health, education, ministries, banks, and so on. Men were either on the battlefield or hiding from going to the battlefield. Women had a big influence on the society. Even the civil law codes were revised under Saddam in ways that protected and advanced women's rights. Women were never obliged to wear certain things or behave in certain ways.

Despite this freedom, Sura said that the post-1990 period was more regressive because Iraq was attacked, and the country was cut off from the world. She was particularly disappointed in the so-called "Faith Campaign," which Saddam Hussein launched in the 1990s to win over some tribal and religious figures from within Iraq and from certain Arab regimes. Spreading religiosity, in her view, was just a façade. Sura lamented:

> I think the "Faith Campaign" of the 1990s paved the way for all the oppression of women that followed, especially after the occupation. Saddam, it seems to me, started it to ensure a "next stage" in society after he was gone, and he implemented his plan masterfully.

This statement echoes what other female academics told me. Each of these women provided different experiences to emphasize two things: first, that the Ba'ath highly supported women as it needed them in different walks of life; and second, that Iraqi women strategically sought to make as many gains as possible by welcoming any additions to their rights and freedom.

With most testimonies from female academics, there was a pattern indicating that the relationship between the regime and women was dialectical. The gains made were not "free" or without sacrifices and hard work. Therefore, such gains could not be considered as charitable acts by the Ba'ath.

Rather, they were inseparable from Iraqi women's long battle for gaining their rights. Yet, women academics agreed that Iraqi women's gains were significantly undermined following the 2003 occupation. Siham S. is an exiled academic in London, specializing in international relations. She has taught in Iraq, Ireland, and the UK. She noted that Iraqi women were now "caught between the 'democracy' of the occupiers and the concepts of 'humanitarian interventions,'"—the topic of the book she had just published when we met. Before leaving her house, she gave me a signed copy of her book and said, "we will never stop fighting to save Iraq for what was done to it."

* * *

Mayada W. is an academic in the field of languages and literature who teaches at a British university two hours north of London. A few years earlier, while still living in Baghdad, her book documenting the daily death and violence in occupied Iraq had been published in the UK. Mayada was reluctant to meet with me at first. I emailed her several times while in London and, when she finally responded, her response was curt and brief: "I can't meet in person. Please send me a questionnaire to fill out, if you'd like." That was better than nothing, but I did not want to give up on the opportunity of speaking with her in person. As it happened, another academic, currently working at a British news outlet told me that she knew Mayada well and that she was unwilling to meet with me because of her traumatic experiences in Iraq, especially after the invasion and that if she asked on my behalf, Mayada might honor her request, since they were "good friends." A few days later, I received Mayada's phone number. After exchanging several text messages, we finally agreed to meet. By the end of that week, I was sipping a cup of tea with her in the cafeteria of the campus where she now teaches.

Educated in Iraq and Scotland, Mayada is currently a lecturer in literature and taught at an Iraqi institution for a few years under the Ba'ath after obtaining her MA from the College of Arts. She witnessed what she called "the ugly transition from the previous regime to an occupied Iraq" while teaching in Baghdad from 2001 to 2007. When we started talking about her experiences prior to 2003, she, like other female academics, lamented the freedom that Iraqi women had lost as a result of the occupation, providing a glimpse into her family life to emphasize the status of women in Iraq during the twentieth century:

I come from a Shiʿa family. My grandmother, born in 1908, was a head-mistress at a secondary school. She retired in the 1950s. My mother was born in 1933. She was a pharmacologist, with a PhD, a free woman in every way you can imagine. Mom and Dad obtained their PhDs from Scotland and Ireland. My mom did her PhD during the Baʿath era. She left Iraq freely with no limits or restrictions on her freedom.

Mayada continued telling me about her own life in Baghdad. She stated:

I have written a book about my experiences of being a woman in Iraq during that time. In brief, I drove a car, I worked late hours at a news-paper with no problems whatsoever. I dressed as I wanted, within the social norms—jeans, T-shirt, and so on. We had lots of friends from both sexes. The only limitation was that politics was treacherous. There were taboos to avoid, like the party and the president. If you did not talk about these, nobody would hurt you. We had friends from all types of religions and beliefs. People of different faiths and backgrounds mingled and even intermarried.

Mayada continued, "I was always a rebel, by the way. Do you want to hear a funny story about my first academic interview in Baghdad during those days?" I nodded. She narrated:

When I got hired for my first academic job, I was invited for a meeting with the president of the University of Baghdad. On that day, I was wearing a shirt and a pair of jeans. He told me during the meeting: "I am not backward or anything, but it is not appropriate for an academic to wear jeans!" He then said I had to be a good example for other girls to follow. I told him: "this is a new pair of jeans. I wanted to wear the best of my clothes to impress you!" He said my sense of humor reminded him of another woman who was a big rebel and who had formerly worked at the university. When he mentioned that woman's name, it was my mother!

Scholars have argued that women were important to Baʿath ideology, par-ticularly in its early years, as a means of implementing its vision and policies in shaping the society.[3] Some scholars have argued that these women's expe-riences (those like Mayada) are not representative of all classes in Iraq.

Furthermore, the Ba'ath support of women's causes, especially during the 1980s, was a "tactic" to gain the support of women during the Iran-Iraq War, as most men were fighting and dying on the battlefield. Women were desperately needed to fill the gap (Al-Ali 2007: 109–46). As such, this "tactic" was a form of "state feminism" referring to the "state's active promotion of women's rights and attempt to change existing gender relations" (Al-Ali 2007: 146).

These analyses are important but inadequate for two reasons. First, the struggle of Iraqi women for their rights is as old as Iraq's history itself; the Ba'ath era was just one chapter—though a long one—in that struggle. During the twentieth century alone, Iraqi women's struggles have been ongoing both before and after the country's independence from the Ottoman and later the British rule. Mayada's narrative above already captures a few generations of women fighting for their freedom (her grandmother, her mother, and herself) as an ongoing battle. So, to look at their gains under the Ba'ath as merely a charitable crumb granted as a "tactic" by the regime is unfair to their long-standing struggle and negotiating powers. It is also dismissive because it does not acknowledge significant advancements made during the Ba'ath era.

Second, even if we assume that the Ba'ath simply capitalized on women to fill the gap left by men on the battlefield, the unintended consequences that resulted from such a move were still significant. This in no way means that Iraqi women did not have their own strategies to accomplish these gains. In a sense, rather than seeing this is as solely a state "tactic" to capitalize on women, it is more useful to see it dialectically, as a transaction that was constantly negotiated and revised in ways that benefitted both sides. Opportunities were not just "given," they had to be snatched by women. Many stories I heard from female academics demonstrate that Iraqi women both before and during the Ba'ath have fought hard for every single one of their accomplishments over the years, both inside Iraq and even abroad, as will be clear in the next interlocutor's story.

* * *

Hiba S. is one of the most prominent Iraqi academics and scholars of media and journalism. She has published many books and articles over the years, attained the rank of a full professor at the University of Baghdad, and chaired the department for several rounds, including once after 2003. Her academic experience in Iraq extends from the mid-1970s until 2006, when she received a death threat, which resulted in her immediate escape to Jordan. "A number of students attacked my office screaming 'she is a Sunni! She is a Ba'athist!' ... the truth is I am neither a Sunni nor a Ba'athist. I come from a prominent Shi'i family from the city of Najaf," she told me. Hiba said that although her writing and academic work had always focused on interference in Iraqi affairs, as well as anti-Zionism, she was not a Ba'athist. "My academic work simply focused on how Iran, Israel, and other global powers use the media to conduct vicious psychological warfare on Iraq and the Middle East." Following the death threats, Hiba had to be smuggled out of her department—something she found humiliating—with the help of her students who had apparently confirmed that she was now blacklisted.

It was clear to Hiba that some political actors were on a mission to get rid of her to "replace me with someone of their own people more aligned with the post-occupation Iraq agenda." As we went back in time to the 1960s, Hiba spoke about how hard she had worked to reach her goals. "I worked tirelessly for every single achievement." Shedding light on an important period in the history of Iraqi higher education, Hiba's remarkable story demonstrates how Iraqi academics were educated and prepared both inside Iraq and abroad. She emphasized that the state took the mission of educating Iraqi society seriously and did a great job at it:

> I was sent to the Soviet Union to pursue my bachelor's degree ... I arrived there in the late 1960s, very young and fresh from high school ... After finishing the Russian language preparatory year in Moscow, like all students then, I was put through so many tests, including psychological tests ... The Soviets had a high regard for psychology. They used such tests to determine what the best field of study is for each student, where their passion lies, and where they may succeed. Based on these tests, it was determined that I should pursue medicine. This made me miserable. I absolutely hated it. Unlike most people in those days, I knew first-hand that being a physician was not the good life that most people thought it was. Having had a few doctors in my family, I knew the misery that came with such a job. They practically had no life ... I went to an Iraqi friend in Moscow, a woman who was older and much more experienced than me. I

told her that I was not happy. She told me that I was born into this world to study journalism. I still remember her words: "You become a doctor? No big deal! There will be a lot of women doing medicine. If you do journalism, you will become one of the pioneering Iraqi women in the field!" And so it was!

Although I did not ask her about her marital status, Hiba volunteered that she was not married, and never would be as she "believes that a good scholar can either take care of family and children or of their scholarship. Chasing both wasn't something I wanted to do." She continued:

> Living in Moscow and learning to accept Soviet culture was hard at the beginning. But, with time, I learned to love it. I learned how smart, hardworking, and meticulous the Russians are. I must say that I do not agree with those who say that Iraqi institutions were designed to be like the Soviet ones. We were neither like the Soviets nor like Western institutions, simply because our culture is very different from both. We have our own traditions, work ethics, for better or worse. We have our own style, and pace of life, and it would have been impossible for us to fully adopt the Russian or the Western ways of life. Yet I think Russian education and institutions have deep roots and spring out of great traditions and experiences, unlike Americans. To be precise, Russians are nationalists and that is important to them. Americans are patriots. The two concepts are different and they bring with them different consequences.

Hiba then talked about her fight in Moscow to switch from medicine to journalism:

> I was determined to abandon medicine in favor of journalism. I went and asked to be transferred, but my request was denied. After I asked for an appeal, Moscow State University asked me to appear before a committee to justify my request. The committee was to make the final decision after that meeting. In front of the committee, I was shy and timid ... One committee member, an older woman, asked me whether I had read a memorable story in my life that I could share with them to convince them of my wish to transfer from medicine to journalism. I still remember it like it was yesterday, I recited an old Russian short story by a Russian

47

author ... When I started reciting the story, I totally forgot where I was and who was sitting in front of me. It was as though I had left the real world and gone to another one. I even started quoting parts of the story, especially by the heroine who was a woman challenging the world with her love. As I finished, I looked at one of the committee members to see tears flowing from her eyes. She told me: "I had read this story several times but never was so touched by it like hearing it from you. You will certainly make a great journalist, and best of luck to you!"

But teaching in Iraq also was not easy, Hiba went on. Working in media was frowned upon, in those days—the late 1960s to the late 1970s. For that reason, Hiba decided to go into teaching, but getting hired as a journalism instructor was also arduous because of gender bias and the notion that such jobs were reserved for men. She met all the criteria for the job (age, degree, and experience) but only managed to get her foot in the door thanks to working some connections (*wasta* in Arabic). "Taking that job was a big deal because it was a job that even men did not want to do those days. It was a hard job with vicious politics involved," Hiba said. To further buttress her credentials, Hiba was a reporter for a local newspaper from 1967 until 1970. The life of a woman journalist in Iraq at the time was hugely challenging: staying up all night to write stories, being sexually harassed by male colleagues, and not being given the same opportunities as men. As she began writing about the challenges, the powers that be wanted "to shut me up" but then she was admitted to a university in Moscow to pursue a PhD in media and public opinion which she obtained in 1978.

Hiba's story captures the treacherous ground Iraqi women had to tread in order to advance, and illustrates the complexity of the status of women academics under the Ba'ath. Rather than viewing it as "state feminism," as many scholars have done, I argue that this period was feminism in constant negotiation with the state. The state was in many ways genuinely invested in supporting certain causes, like educating Iraqi women and involving them in all walks of life, even prior to the war with Iran, but the gender bias toward men was also real. Both the Iraqi state and women needed each other to keep society functioning. In brief, rather than thinking of these gains as "state feminism," we should see them as feminism negotiated with the state, or in some cases, feminism despite the state.

RELIGION AND SECTARIANISM UNDER THE BAʿATH

Religion and sectarianism constitute an important topic for all the inter-locutors I spoke to, especially when comparing the Baʿath years with the post-2003 occupation period. Many academics recalled nostalgically the absence of sectarian violence during the Baʿath era, lamenting the institu-tionalization of religion and sectarianism as primary forms of governance in post-2003 Iraq, a situation that has forced millions of Iraqis into exile and internal displacement. Both political and religious players have employed sectarianism to reconfigure the academic space in Iraq, according to my interlocutors. Mayada explained that the Baʿath party did not tolerate:

> anyone with different political orientations, especially those who favored Iran ... Anyone active politically with a party other than the Baʿath, was treated ruthlessly. If you were neutral with no political activities or no anti-Baʿath opinions, nobody would care to hurt you.

Mayada stressed that the Iran–Iraq War had made the Baʿath especially defensive and that this would have been the case in any country in the world which had undergone what Iraq did in that war. But she added that many Iraqi exiles in the West had "exaggerated the problems with the Baʿath" helping create distorted images of and notions about Iraq which ultimately "led to our destruction." Mayada says that many people who had left Iraq as presumed anti-Baʿathists were in fact wanted by the Iraqi state. "I am not saying that the party was one of innocent angels," she added.

> There were indeed many transgressions. But many Iraqis also misrepre-sented reality. In my big extended family, for example, 43 people were executed or punished by the party! After the toppling of the regime, many members of my family finally admitted that those punished actually had ties with Iran through the *Daʿawa* party.[4] So, this means that the Baʿath had good reasons to punish them. This is my opinion.

Coming from a Shiʿi academic, this is a controversial statement to make. Regardless of whether one agrees with Mayada that the Baʿath had good reason to suspect and punish individuals it views as suspect, such a narrative raises broader questions of morality. The dominant discourse concerning the

Ba'ath is that it consistently eliminated "innocent" people. But who defines "innocence" when analyzing different political systems around the world? Does the definition of "innocence" change from one country to another and from one era to another? Are the "criminals" of today the "innocents" of tomorrow (and vice versa)? These questions are important but are beyond the scope of this book and deserve special attention and further research.

*   *   *

Another story that provides a glimpse into how academics experienced these issues is that of Tamara L., currently residing in London. Tamara holds a BSc. from the University of Technology, Baghdad (1983). After getting her degree, she enrolled at the Civil Aviation Institute to obtain another degree that qualified her to teach at the same institute. Upon graduation, she became a lecturer at the Civil Aviation Institute before eventually moving to London in the early 1990s.

On one occasion, Tamara invited me to their house in the outskirts of London. Since her academic experience in Iraq was mainly during the 1980s under the then ongoing Iran–Iraq War, she shared experiences that shed light on the intersection between religiosity and women academics at that time. Her position was that, despite the harsh measures the Ba'ath took to suppress religious fanaticism and sectarianism in the society, the advantages of this approach far outweighed the disadvantages. This position was strongly felt by many female academics and professionals. Tamara spoke about how the Ba'ath dealt with religion in the 1980s when she lectured at the Civil Aviation Institute:

> During the war with Iran, there was a rising tide of *Hizb al-Da'awa* [Da'wa Party] which made a few female academics and staff decide to wear hijab at work. I remember our boss at the Aviation Institute met with us after three women started wearing the hijab. He said that if he sees any women wearing hijab, he will shave their heads and have them walk around to be shamed publicly: "If you don't like it, go to the Ministry of Religious Affairs and complain," he said in the meeting. So, religiosity was very different during those years. Women had many victories, especially during the 1980s. Manal al-Alousi, the president of General Federation of Iraqi Women, suggested that polygamy was not acceptable according

to Islam. She challenged religious beliefs in Iraq, something that had not been done in other Arab countries at that time. As far as you go back in our family's history, my mother, grandmother, we had education, worked, and were independent women. My mother for a long time wrote and presented special programs for *al-Jamaheer* Radio in Baghdad. She was the first woman who presented a special program for women in the 1960s. In the 1950s, the Minister of Education was a woman. Iraq has long been very diverse and accepting of diversity. My husband's mother was born in 1912 and she was driving in the 1940s. This has yet to happen in Saudi Arabia. [Rural–urban] migration restricted some freedoms because some of the newcomers [to Baghdad] were more conservative, especially in the mid-1970s.

Tamara's narrative is hardly unique among the class of educated and professional Iraqi women. I noticed how female academics who spoke about religiosity and sectarianism in Iraq during the Baʿath years consistently connected it to women's freedom. For them, the less religion and sectarianism the better. Tamara was careful to emphasize that her experiences were based on life in Baghdad and might not be applicable to other Iraqi cities:

My responses could be biased in the sense that they represent Baghdad more than the rest of Iraq. My aunt studied in Babel in southern Iraq. Women there were still honored and respected, but they dressed and behaved more conservatively compared to Baghdad. Mind you, even neighborhoods within Baghdad were not all the same. Practices were different, depending on people, their level of education, economic status, and many other factors.

The testimonies of these interlocutors on how the Baʿath handled religious and sectarian fanaticism raises questions similar in nature and complexity to the arrests, torture, and executions of "terrorists" and "radical Muslims" in the West's "war on terror." What is the difference? Is the West's treatment of those perceived as "terrorists" or "radicals" who "hate our freedom" or who pose a danger to our "national security" any different than the people punished by the Baʿath because they were also perceived as such? Neither of these cases is justified, but they demonstrate that the struggle is political rather than religious. Religion and sectarianism in this context become political tools to eliminate the "unwanted," as was the case in Iraq after 2003. These complex situations raise serious questions about how "terror," "radicalism," or "sectarianism" are applied by different powers at different times in the most selective and problematic ways.[5] They become different forms of governance and disciplining practiced by different political systems. The fact that the Baʿath eliminated people for their sect or religiosity and that the post-occupation Iraqi sectarian governments have been doing the same shows some disturbing connections between secular and religious regimes worldwide.

In this context, it must be remembered that the Baʿath in Iraq (and Syria) was a secular party strongly opposed to three elements: regionalism, sectarianism, and tribalism. These elements, as seen in the party's philosophy, were considered backward in providing a perfect recipe for dividing nations and allowing colonizers to interfere by using the "divide and conquer" rule. Yet this made the Baʿath in Iraq and Syria fall into some contradictions because, as Nikolaos Van Dam argues, on the one hand that the Baʿath "disliked the idea of exploiting sectarianism and other traditional social loyalties which they considered as being backward and contrary to the ideal of secular and egalitarian Arab nationalism" (Van Dam 2011 [1979]: 138). On the other hand, it would not have been possible for the party to implement its vision and plans without "dependence on those same loyalties" (Van Dam 2011 [1979]: 143). This explains why the Iraqi Baʿath, particularly under Saddam Hussein, had a love–hate relationship with these elements. This relationship is best articulated by the academics in this study who are critical of the way the Baʿath quashed religiosity and sectarianism but also recall with appreciation an academic environment free of religious and sectarian divides and tensions. Indeed, many Iraqis—academics and others—believe that the occupying forces capitalized on religion, sectarianism, and ethnicity to get Iraq to where it is today. Therefore, for many Iraqis today, freedom basically means freedom from the grip of religion and sectarianism.

The Baʿath's relationship with religion and sectarianism was far from static. For example, in its early years, the regime took strict measures against anything tribal and religious because they were considered backward and reactionary.[6] Yet, tribalism, like religiosity, was brought back in when the regime was blockaded and isolated by the UN sanctions and needed more internal support from Iraqi tribes as well as external support from certain Arab regimes in countries like Yemen and Libya. Here, as we see in Mayada's narrative earlier and as some scholars have argued, the Ba'ath was not threatened by Shi'ism only. It was threatened by any religious activity deemed potentially radical or threatening to the regime, even if coming from radical Sunni traditions like Wahhabism (Sassoon 2012: 224). Eric Davis writes,

> the regime's decline was most evident in the reintroduction of tribalism as the basis for Ba'thist rule. When it first seized power, the Ba'ath vowed to eradicate tribalism, which it condemned as a reactionary vestige of imperialism. Still, tribalism was always a core component of Ba'athist rule.
>
> (Davis 2005: 238–39)

In practice, however, the party continued to act promptly and ruthlessly against any religious or tribal acts that promoted fanaticism, radicalism, or simply posed a threat to Iraq's unity. It is precisely why many Ba'athists, especially those genuinely loyal to the party's principles, continue to have a strong animosity toward these three elements. This approach was the exact opposite of what the occupying forces revived in Iraq after 2003. Some academics gave me the impression that while the Ba'ath, for the most part, forced Iraqis to "forget" their differences, the occupiers forced them to remember them to divide the country into smaller, weaker, and more manageable territories to control.

3

The UN Sanctions:
Consenting to Occupation
through Starvation

The long and harsh 13 years of the UN embargo on Iraq started when I was in primary school and ended with the invasion of Iraq in 2003, when I was still an undergraduate studying English language and literature at the University of Baghdad. I vividly remember many of my high school teachers and university professors who profoundly shaped my personality and my outlook on the world with their diligence and perseverance, despite getting almost nothing in return, and it is to them that I attribute my decision to write this book. One of the most memorable images in my mind is my high school math teacher who used to scream in the classroom every time a student misbehaved or failed to prepare their homework. On one occasion, he said: "You all should stop making our lives harder than they are. Do you realize that our monthly salary is barely enough to buy two kilos of tomatoes?" Like many teachers and professors, the math teacher was forced to do other kinds of jobs to survive during the sanction years.

Another image that sticks in my head was when I was returning home from visiting a friend on a cold winter evening. On the way, I noticed a small kiosk adjoined to a house and wanting to find an excuse to warm myself inside for a few minutes, I pretended that I was there to buy a piece of gum. I was shocked to see that the owner of the kiosk was my math teacher who was being forced to sell gum, cigarettes, and a few other "convenience items" to sustain himself during those years. He was at first embarrassed to see me but then immediately smiled and gave me a piece of gum for free (Yako 2015a).

A similar memorable experience of academics' suffering during the UN embargo years was with my grammar professor at Baghdad University's College of Languages, who spoke flawless English fast and expected us (students) to catch up with her to improve our listening skills. The way words came out of her mouth in the classroom resembled bullets shot from a revolver. I used to walk with her and chat after class. Her footsteps were steady and fast just like the way she uttered her words. Since the UN sanctions and the international blockade imposed upon Iraqi people had made it impossible for us to get new books, magazines, literary journals, and newspapers from abroad, she used to lend me her old 1980s copies of *Reader's Digest* to help me practice reading American English, and learn new vocabulary and idioms beyond the canonized classics in English literature. She told me once,

> we used to get copies of all types of English magazines and literary journals from different English-speaking countries before the embargo. They were very helpful for reading modern English and staying up to date with what is happening in the literary world. Though these are old *Reader's Digest* copies, you can still learn from the vocabulary and the modern forms of writing in them. Please do return them when you are done reading them.

By the end of my second year at the university, she shared with me that she had accepted a new teaching post at another university in Baghdad but she would make sure to come visit me in the future. As soon as the war erupted in 2003, I lost all contact with her (Yako 2015a).

These are just some memorable stories out of many that demonstrate some of the key issues that emerged from discussing the period of the UN sanctions with academics in my research. Based on what most academics shared about this period, their vision can be summed up as: rather than considering the Iraqi regime solely responsible for these sanctions, many exiled and displaced academics believe that the UN bears the main ethical and human responsibility for the damage the embargo caused for Iraqi people and society. Many academics saw these sanctions as the UN's method to obtain the consent of Iraqi people to the 2003 occupation through starving and weakening the people, as well as destroying Iraq's strong institutions and infrastructure.

This finding is significant as it changes how we understand that period. Many academics insist that they were fighting an intellectual, human, and economic embargo caused by internal and external powers at once. Scholars and analysts typically analyze the Ba'ath's 35 years in power as based on getting "consent" from many Iraqis through its complex system of rewards and punishments, as well as the productive aspect of the regime. Yet, in this chapter, the academics extend this notion of "consent" to be applied to how the colonial powers sought to get what some called "consenting to occupation through starvation" by imposing the UN sanctions on Iraq. For many academics, the UN embargo was the most damaging technique the imperial powers used to destroy Iraqi society and institutions. Many interlocutors argued that while these sanctions destroyed the Iraqi people and society, they also empowered rather than weakened the regime. This is important when we consider how economic sanctions work in other countries (e.g., Iran and Syria, at the time of writing).

In 2015, internally displaced academics in Iraqi Kurdistan shared many stories about the effects of the sanctions. Nasreen A. is a Kurd from Iraqi Kurdistan. She was raised, educated, and lived most of her life in Mosul. Nasreen had to leave Mosul in 2014 because of ISIS. She is currently a researcher and lecturer of chemistry in Kurdistan. When I asked about her experiences during the sanctions years, she recalled many impoverished academics and students. The salaries of academics, as many of them have confirmed, ranged from US$3–6 per month. It was barely possible to survive one week on such meager salaries. Nasreen said she had to be honest that she did not suffer as much as many academics did, despite her embarrassingly low salary. That was "because my husband was a physician and made good money. I wouldn't have made it without his salary on my own." She remembered how during those years not only were academics deprived of every possible basic need to teach, do research, and live with dignity, but also many couldn't even afford to buy food and clothes. She said she often secretly handed down clothes or extra food to her colleagues in the department. They accepted her help because they knew she would not tell anyone about it to embarrass them. Nasreen said,

> even as a mother, I felt how other children going to the same school as my children suffered. I often intentionally packed extra sandwiches for my children to share with their friends who were unable to bring a sandwich to school.

These stories are just the tip of the iceberg of what many Iraqi people from all walks of life suffered during the years of the inhumane UN embargo. Before sharing more testimonies, it is important to contextualize this period.

DOCUMENTED FACTS AND CONSEQUENCES OF THE UN SANCTIONS

The UN imposed sanctions on Iraq from 1990 until the occupation in 2003. After Iraq invaded Kuwait, the UN Security Council (UNSC) declared a full financial and trade embargo starting on August 6, 1990. The UNSC banned anything that could be construed as being useful to the production of military technology. In practice, the banned goods included the most basic human need items, severely affecting millions of Iraqis' access to food and medicine. The effects of the shortages in food and medicine continued to affect Iraqi people causing many direct and indirect deaths, malnutrition, and shortages in electricity, clean water, and countless other items and services. It took five years, following widespread condemnation of the effects of the embargo on Iraqi people, before the UNSC enacted the so-called Oil-for-Food Program with UNSC Resolution 986 of April 14, 1995, although the implementation of the program did not start until December 1996. Those who fully supported and highly contributed to the war and sanctions on Iraq, like the Zionist neoconservative, Douglas J. Feith, claimed that the sanctions significantly curtailed Iraq's military capabilities (Feith 2008: 193).

The humanitarian impacts of the embargo were so harsh that multiple UN officials resigned in protest. Denis Halliday, the UN Humanitarian Coordinator in Baghdad resigned in 1998, after working for the UN for 34 years. Halliday resigned not only to protest the inhumane sanctions regime but also to have the freedom to criticize the program and expose it. "We are waging a war through the United Nations on the people of Iraq. We're targeting civilians. Worse, we're targeting children ... What is this all about?" he said in an interview with investigative journalist John Pilger. "I am resigning ... because the policy of economic sanctions is ... destroying an entire society. Five thousand children are dying every month. I don't want to administer a program that satisfies the definition of genocide," Halliday added (Pilger 2004). Hans von Sponeck, Halliday's successor, also resigned in protest. After calling the sanctions a "true human tragedy," Washington and London accused Sponeck of "siding with Iraq" (Plett 2000).

The studies on the number of deaths caused by the sanctions vary widely depending on the time when they were conducted, the methods used, and, predictably, the political agendas of those who funded and conducted them. Some studies estimated that upwards of 500,000 children died as a result of sanctions.[1] Others have dismissed these figures as inflated despite the plethora of evidence suggesting otherwise (Spagat 2010).

The New Zealand scholar of human rights, Ramon Das, concluded that it was the UNSC and not Saddam Hussein who bore primary responsibility for the human rights violations of civilians in Iraq over the last 12 years of sanctions (Das 2003). Das went further to conclude that the evidence at hand "seriously undermines the claim that the UNSC's motives in administering the 'Oil-For-Food' Program since 1996 have been (primarily) humanitarian" (Das 2003: 26). Citing Halliday, Das also concluded that the "Oil-For-Food" Program was designed to:

> stop further deterioration in Iraq at a time when famine conditions prevailed ... It has maintained quasi-famine conditions for many Iraqis now for over six years. So we've nothing to be proud of—all we've done is stave off mass starvation.[2]

Das's conclusion in fact supports the arguments of several Western and Iraqi academics and intellectuals that the sanctions had little economic or humanitarian consequences for the Iraqi regime itself, punishing the Iraqi people and destroying their society more than anything else (for example, see Arnove [2000]; and Richards [1999]).

Lastly, but not insignificantly, the harshness and suffocating effects of the UN sanctions have been captured in several literary works that have vividly and poignantly depicted how Iraqi people lived through those times that destroyed the fabric of society. A notable work in this regard is *Ghayib* (*Absent*) by the Iraqi novelist Batūl Khuḍayrī, which centers on the suffering of Iraqi women during the sanction years (Khuḍayrī 2004). Another autobiographical novel, which may be more pertinent to this work and remains unavailable in English translation is *Idha al-ayamu aghsaqat* (*If the Days Turn to Dusk*) by the Iraqi academic, translator, and author Hayat Sharara, which captures the struggles of Iraqi academics during the UN embargo years (Sharara 2011). Many of the details and observations in Sharara's novel are also articulated and confirmed by many interviewees in this book. Although it is a work of literature, the novel captures many historical facts and events. Sharara's depiction of Iraqi academics during the sanctions period brings to mind Carlos Fuentes' words: "Art gives life to what history killed. Art gives voice to what history denied, silenced, or persecuted. Art brings truth to the lies of history" (Fuentes 1990 [1981]: 62).

BLOCKADED ON EVERY SIDE

When I asked Sameer, introduced in Chapter 2, how he experienced the effects of the embargo as an academic, he said:

> We suddenly found ourselves unable to get any new resources like journals, publications, books, and scientific sources. They deprived us of all of that under the pretext that any academic/scientific resources could potentially be used to "manufacture weapons of mass destruction." The reality is that they were destroying the masses with this embargo to pave the way for their invasion in 2003. They had to set the ground for a weakened society with damaged institutions and damaged people so that the agenda of the occupation would go smoothly ... It was crucial for the occupiers to come to a demoralized population to do whatever they wanted with them.

Although it was terrible for their morale, Iraqi academics resorted to having scholars and students from other Arab countries smuggle more current academic materials into Iraq. As noted earlier, the UN sanctions paved the way for the most serious brain drain in Iraq's contemporary history and it was during those years that even the academics who had been educated abroad and returned to play a vital role in educating future generations started to leave the country.

Mazin B. is a computer scientist who teaches at al-Nahrain University (formerly Saddam University), one of the best and most rigorous universities in Iraq. Mazin still lives and teaches in Baghdad. I was introduced to him by one of my Kurdish friends and we had multiple Skype conversations in 2014 and 2015. In one conversation, Mazin noted that the most humiliating effect of the embargo was the devaluation of the Iraqi currency, which turned professors' salaries to between "$4–6 per month." As mentioned earlier, the state banned academics from leaving the country in order to stem the brain drain and many academics not only had to change their occupation on their passport, if they were fortunate enough to get one, they also had to leave the country without their academic transcripts, which were sequestered by the authorities for the same reason—to avoid the loss of academics and professionals with advanced degrees. Mazin said "because you couldn't get your original transcript, many academics I know had to forge credential documents to get employment abroad."

This statement is at once shocking and paradoxical. Academics who wanted to leave Iraq in search of other opportunities had to forge a document that was "equivalent to" their original one such that the "fake" degree was at once fake and real. When it comes to the relationship between academics and power, I see this as the quintessential irony—that one must forge what is already real to survive and get out of the grip of the system. Equally paradoxical is how the "real" can lose its meaning and value depending on the power that grants it. Seen from a different angle, "forging" the real degree withheld by the authorities becomes a form of resisting power by individuals trapped in those circumstances. Yet, this is also a case in which academics have been subjected to a multilayered intellectual embargo. The first layer was imposed by the UNSC and the second by the Iraqi state that wanted to hold on to its brains to keep the society functioning. In this case, the second layer is indirectly caused by and an extension of the first one. In others, the boundaries and the relationship between these two layers are hazy and slippery at best. Academics are sandwiched between the push and pull of external and internal forces, and, like ordinary citizens, become a battlefield in which these forces confront each other. One last irony on forging real degrees is that, in post-occupation Iraq, many had to forge degrees that did not exist just to escape the war and its consequences. In both cases, forging becomes a necessary method for survival.

* * *

Ghanim B. is a communist academic from a Shi'i family who still resides in Baghdad. He identifies as an atheist. I connected with him through another exiled Kurd academic currently living in the Netherlands. Ghanim and I connected in 2013 by chance, and we have stayed in touch ever since, exchanging many rich conversations.

Ghanim holds an advanced degree in architectural engineering from the University of Technology in Baghdad. He is currently a Senior Lecturer in Baghdad, having resigned from the same position three different times over the years to protest "wars, sanctions, oppression, and occupation," he told me. Since the 1990s, he has had to leave Iraq a few times in search of job opportunities elsewhere in the Arab world but always returned because he missed Iraq in spite of everything. The last time he left was after his wife was diagnosed with cancer and he could not find good treatment for her in Baghdad. She received treatment in one of the Arab Gulf states and is still in remission. He told me he would remain in Baghdad as long as his wife was in remission and as long as he could bear it.

When I asked him about the embargo years, he noted that the impacts of the sanctions on Iraqi people, society, and institutions aimed to destroy two of the most important components of any modern society, physical infrastructure and, more importantly for him, "human infrastructure."

For Ghanim, physical infrastructure is not as much of a problem because once the causes of its destruction are over, it can be rebuilt, but human infrastructure takes many generations to repair. And, if not fixed, human infrastructure can continue to undermine the entire society, as has been the case since the 2003 invasion. Majeed, also introduced earlier, echoed Ghanim's words regarding human infrastructure:

Millions of Iraqis were transformed. Their lives, their ethics, their hopes, and views of the future were diminished because of the sanctions. As an academic, I could notice the impacts on many of my students ... We, academics, couldn't pressure students to do things beyond their means. It was a difficult period filled with anxiety. The future seemed very dark and this affected most academics ... Many people were planning to graduate and leave to places like Yemen, Libya, and other Arab countries that we would never consider inhabiting in the past. I was not immune from this pressure. I often considered looking for alternatives, including quitting academia altogether ... Students weren't clear about what to do with their education. Many Iraqis were welcome in the 1970s and 1980s in Arab countries, especially Gulf countries, but this changed after the 1990s. Fewer countries were accepting Iraqis like Libya and Yemen did ... We were struggling with circumstances and lack of knowledge exchange with the rest of the world ... I often asked friends living abroad to send me books, but many academics and students didn't have this option ... We often got materials very late, after they had become outdated.

In spite of these challenges, the embargo "helped in showing the determination of the Iraqi people ... especially when it comes to keeping infrastructure and institutions running, despite all difficulties," Majeed added. This was a view widely held by other academics I worked with.

Ghazi F. is a chemist and an academic, currently displaced in Iraqi Kurdistan. He holds advanced degrees in chemistry from Basra University and the UK. His research focus is theoretical organic chemistry. I met with Ghazi several times during my time in northern Iraq. When I asked him about the sanctions, he echoed Majeed but provided a slightly different perspective based on his work in the sciences rather than the humanities:

> In the period of the UN sanctions, and right after the First Gulf War, we had so many places rebuilt with Iraqi expertise. Some experts, including many academics, were able to dismantle factories and equipment, hide them, protect them from bombing, and reassemble them after the bombing was over. They were able to read manuals written in different foreign languages like English, Russian, French, and others. This was all done with Iraqi hands.

Ghazi noted this as an example of the way that academics continued to play a pivotal role in maintaining society and institutions despite the brutal effects of the First Gulf War and the subsequent sanctions.

Hazim H., who I met in Amman in 2014, has advanced degrees in Education from Iraq and the UK and specializes in education technology. He too articulated what Ghanim and Majeed had said, providing important numbers gleaned from his experience working at the Iraqi Ministry of Education. He cited the advances that Iraqis had made during the 1970s and 1980s and insisted that the 1990s should be framed as the "UN's crimes against the Iraqi people." Despite the devastating consequences of the UN sanctions, he noted that one could not ignore the degree of self-sufficiency Iraq attempted to reach during those years:

> For example, we used to print about 42 million copies of school textbooks every year. Imagine the cost of having to do this by relying on foreign companies. Also, don't forget the opportunity and access of free education to every single Iraqi, even during the sanctions ... We were blocked from the world for 13 years, without internet, mobile phones, and so on.

This was not the fault of Saddam's regime. These things were banned by the UN. In fact, Iraq worked for years to prepare itself for bringing in mobile phones to the country but was never given the permission to operate them.

For Hazim, the sanctions and the occupation combined, were nothing less than the occupiers' attempt to "reconfigure Iraqi consciousness." Hazim's insight extends this analytical framework to argue that in doing so, the aim was to create malleable citizens and later rewrite Iraq's history from the occupiers' standpoint. This point, which deals with the consequences of the occupation, will be elaborated in Chapter 4.

WOMEN ACADEMICS DURING THE SANCTIONS

Zeynep C., an Iraqi Turkman from Kirkuk recalled both pros and cons of the Ba'ath era from her vantage point as a female lecturer in Fine Arts. For example, despite the restrictions on certain political freedoms and the pressure on minorities like her own, Zeynep noted that the party was supportive of creative academics and intellectuals, regardless of their backgrounds and social class. She described her years studying Fine Arts in Baghdad as the most creative and rewarding of her life. I asked her to speak about how she experienced the sanctions since she taught art during those years before eventually moving to Turkey at the end of the 1990s and later emigrating to a Western country. Zeynep first said that upon "turning the page of the Iran–Iraq War" most Iraqis had been hopeful about a new start, but the invasion of Kuwait and the subsequent harsh sanctions felt like "a car suddenly breaking after it was going 120 kilometers per hour." She talked about the sanctions and how after an active artistic life filled with art galleries and intellectual gatherings in Baghdad, she had to return to Kirkuk upon graduation and look for a job in teaching art at an institute under the most difficult circumstances:

> People were hungry, starving, and dying from lack of medicine. Can you imagine what art meant to people under such circumstances? Yet I loved art and I had to work in the field no matter what. My parents were both retired state employees getting meager pensions. I had to support myself. It was very hard and intellectually suffocating.

I asked Zeynep to share a memorable story from those days:

> During the sanctions, teaching was in a sad state. Teaching art was particularly hard due to shortages of art supplies that students needed. There was a serious shortage of notebooks, pens, coloring materials, you name it … I once asked my students to bring materials into class, but most were unable to buy them. I will never forget a female student who was supposed to bring a piece of cloth for art work purposes, but she couldn't afford to buy the proper one, so she cut a piece of cloth from her father's underwear and brought it into the class. When I asked her why she did so, she did not answer. She just started crying.

Despite the sanctions, Zeynep said that the quality of Iraqi education and standards remained relatively good, though not what they had been in the 1970s and 1980s. She remembered how sad she felt because people started to care less and less about art or anything artistic. "A disintegrating society has no need for art, literature, or even philosophy," she added sorrowfully. Still, she loved her job despite the embarrassingly low salary, which she spent mostly on transportation.

Eventually, like many Iraqi women during those years, Zeynep reluctantly accepted a "loveless" marriage offer from an Iraqi expatriate "just to exit that hell." She did so even though she was far from ready for marriage. Like many other women told me, female academics wouldn't have been able to survive on their salaries if they didn't have certain social networks of support to lean on, such as spouses and other family members. In fact, one academic told me that she remembered several women academics who did not have any support and were forced to leave academia and find different avenues to make a living. For Zeynep, this was not just a "brain drain" but an "internal hemorrhage" within the body of Iraqi society.

Many female academics in this research confirmed what anthropologist and gender scholar, Nadje al-Ali, has found in her research on Iraqi women, particularly middle-class women, living under the sanctions. Al-Ali writes: "The breakdown of the welfare state had a disproportionate effect on women, who had been its main beneficiaries" (Al-Ali 2007: 186). It equally confirms al-Ali's findings, as we see in Zeynep's marriage story, on how family and gender relations were severely affected by the sanctions (Al-Ali 2007: 195–208).

One female academic who had direct experience not just of the effects of the sanctions but also of the actual UN sanctions inspections teams, provided intriguing details on those years. Israa K. holds a BSc. from Pharmacy College, Baghdad University, and a PhD in biochemistry and photochemistry from the UK, obtained in the early 1980s in the context of Iraq's state scholarships at the time. After advancing in the tenure process as an associate professor, Israa was due to apply for full professorship in 2006. However, despite her many publications in the field and her long and excellent teaching experience in Baghdad, she was denied the full professorship due to sectarian reasons at which point she found herself forced to leave the university and escape to Jordan. This happened right after her husband had been kidnapped and released only after she paid a huge ransom from selling most of their possessions in Baghdad.

When I asked Israa about those years, it became evident that Israa and her family had suffered greatly due to the sectarian tensions in post-occupation Iraq. Upon first meeting, she immediately said, "I am a Sunni, let's be clear about that and get it out of the way because I know people are obsessed with evaluating everything we say based on sect rather than honest and objective facts on the ground." Israa said that the sanctions presented the perfect opportunity to debunk two big myths about Iraqi people and society: first, that Iraq's Sunnis benefitted from the Ba'ath regime disproportionately; and second, that Iraqi academics benefitted from the system in place. The harsh years of the sanctions and the way "many Iraqis held hands to get through these hardships discredit these absurd claims," she said in an agitated tone, elaborating further as follows:

> Those who say that we Sunnis are "angry" with the current situation because we benefitted from the previous regime, I respond to them with this: first, we need to define what is the meaning of the word "benefit"? If by that we mean getting education, getting jobs, and advancing academically or in other fields of work, then these opportunities were not only granted to Sunnis. I do not think anyone would disagree with the fact that these opportunities were available to all Iraqis, regardless of religious or ethnic backgrounds. Everyone accessed these state privileges under the same conditions. If by benefitting they mean the salaries, then everyone can confirm that all academics were seriously disadvantaged, especially following the Kuwait invasion when living expenses were very high and

academics were paid next to nothing. So, what was the benefit we got more than any other Iraqi working next to us and doing the same job and amount of work? Surely, there were people who wanted and needed to make more money to survive, and those had to teach private lessons, do extra research, teach evening classes, and so on. But again, these opportunities were available to anyone who wanted to go that route.

Israa added, "many Iraqis will confirm to you that their suffering during the sanctions was the harshest thing they had ever experienced." She insisted that, in her academic discipline, she was free as an academic to do any type of research she wanted and she never felt academically suffocated until the UN sanctions were imposed. She provided an important testimony on this point:

The only party that suffocated our academic freedoms was the UN delegations and inspection officers who came to Iraq to inspect during those years. Just to give you an example, at our labs we used growth hormones to grow tissues, and the UN interfered even with that. In such cases, bacterial overgrowth sometimes happens, so the inspectors thought we had been working with tissues related to biological weapons. In reality, I would discard any samples in which such bacterial growth occurred, considering them simply as contaminated hormones. They did not like it whenever they saw any growth of microorganisms. They photographed everything in our labs, classrooms, including every single blackboard where we simply wrote information for students. They were frightened by Iraqi minds.

Like many Iraqis, Israa believes that the "international community" represented by the UN was bent on "disabling" Iraqi minds and aspirations for a strong and self-sufficient country not subjected to direct or indirect colonial agendas. She added:

The UN did everything they could to hinder Iraqi academia, research, and academic freedom with all sorts of restrictions on so many materials we needed to work with in our labs to teach students. In doing so, they were seeking to create a state of total desperation and humiliation for Iraqi people to later invade the country. In many ways, they succeeded in their goal.

Israa's narrative about the UN inspection teams shows how academics were caught between different powers that seriously undermined their ability to function. At the time, the Iraqi regime and the UN were each trying to make the other "look bad," using Iraqi people and society as a battlefield to make the point. The Iraqi regime consistently tried to remind Iraqis that their suffering was caused by the UNSC, which was controlled by the superpowers and driven by a Zionist vision for the Arab world. The UNSC was similarly trying to persuade Iraqis that their suffering was solely attributable to Saddam Hussein's policies and actions. This Catch-22 is important because it will resurface in later chapters as a more serious issue in post-occupation Iraq. Although most academics I met in researching this work strongly blamed the UNSC, several were also mindful of the Iraqi regime's contribution to what happened.

ACADEMIC VOICES CRITIQUING THE IRAQI REGIME

While they were aware of the external factors that contributed to their suffering, academics I met with viewed Iraq's internal problems, including the regime, with a critical eye. Sameera S., an exiled chemist in Amman whom I met in 2014, spoke about both factors during those years. Sameera received her BSc. and MSc. in chemistry from Baghdad University in the late 1970s–early 1980s and went on to obtain her PhD in chemistry, focusing on photochemistry from the same institution. She left Iraq in 2007, after receiving a bullet in an envelope with a death threat telling her to leave her academic post and the country immediately.

While having dinner with Sameera and her husband at their home in Amman one evening, Sameera articulated the central idea of this chapter, namely, that Iraqi academics were caught between two power centers: the UN on the one hand; and the Iraqi state attempting to protect itself from the international blockade, on the other. She found disturbing similarities between the measures the Iraqi regime took to "protect our national security" during the sanctions and those taken in the USA after 9/11. The UN prevented almost every academic resource, whether materials or equipment, from entering Iraq. They even banned lead used in the manufacture of pencils (I remember how unaffordable pencils were for most students, in those years, when I made sure to be careful so as to prolong the life of my pencil as long as possible).

Like others, Sameera noted that academics were banned from going to conferences, publishing internationally, and so on. She said that in many ways it was a vicious circle: the Iraqi state banned most academics from attending conferences abroad, and the UN banned everything that could help them do good research and teaching from entering Iraq, leaving academics to rely on materials, labs, and resources that dated back to the 1970s and 1980s. As for the Iraqi state restrictions,

We could not even talk, correspond, or interact with any foreigner. If I talked to any foreigner at a conference, they would always send someone with me to watch me. I remember at a conference in Amman, an American academic in my field came up to me and asked how I was doing, how life was under the embargo, then she handed me her card and asked me to contact her if I needed any resources. The Iraqi government official accompanying us immediately took it away and ripped it up!

[Likewise], the UN banned even something as simple as uranium acetate from entering Iraq. This is a very simple material that all chemists need to do lab experiments. I personally protested this and wrote a letter to the UN, but of course it was nothing but, as we say in Arabic, a holler falling on deaf ears.

Sameera emphasized that it is a common mistake to think that Iraqi academics did not criticize the regime during those years:

I know many academics in my department who strongly criticized certain steps taken by the state, but an academic can only do so much. We really should not exaggerate how much our criticism can change things. The Ba'ath did not kill or imprison those who criticized things. They simply sent warning letters or had them summoned to "have a talk." In my department, I know several professors who wrote letters protesting the low salaries, the militarization of academics when they tried to train us to bear weapons to presumably protect ourselves from the invasion, and many other things. Many of my colleagues, including me, refused to attend any party meetings in protest. Frankly, even the party did not take such meetings seriously at that point. It was just a formality. I have seen some academics during those years cursing the president of our university to his face to protest what was going on. The point is, we did resist on both fronts, but mostly, I am sad to say, in vain.

Another way the UNSC sought to achieve "consent through starvation" during the sanctions years—as a means to pave the way for the occupation—was articulated in the testimony of Issa, the management specialist introduced in Chapter 2. For him, besides their economic effect, the sanctions were a form of psychological warfare. This was best reflected by the way that academics had to resort to all kinds of menial jobs just to survive.

Many academics, including Issa, drove taxis, worked as car mechanics or ran small convenience stores just to survive and maintain their dignity. Others went astray by asking students for bribes, intentionally lowering their teaching standards in public universities to teach students privately on the side for more money, asking students for all kinds of petty favors from packets of cigarettes to getting new tires for their cars. Issa went as far as stating that both the First and the Second Gulf Wars did not affect Iraqi academia and society in general as much as the sanctions did. "The effects of the sanctions on Iraq were greater than all the wars combined," he told me. For Issa, the sanctions also contributed to the Iraqi regime seeking to militarize all sectors of society, including academic institutions. In this regard, he noted:

Saddam failed to understand that the sanctions would become his graveyard. Iraq, or any country, does not fail because of bombs, but because of economic sanctions that kill society's value system. When you are hungry, there comes a moment when you break down and give up your values in order to survive. The embargo did just that. It was the seed that turned Iraq into the most corrupt country in the world.

Issa insisted that the genealogy of the current state of corruption in Iraq should be traced to the traumatizing economic and human effects of the UN sanctions on the society.

Kareem, a professor of media and journalism currently living in Amman, said that the first couple of years of the sanctions were bearable but, as time passed, their effects became increasingly intolerable to bear. For him, the saddest thing was being forced to sell many of his books in al-Mutanabbi Street, Baghdad's famed booksellers' market, because he was unable to sufficiently provide for his family.[3] He showed me his diary from 1996 with multiple entries about having to sell books from his collection. Looking through the diary, my eyes fell on the January 26 and a short entry stating, "Went to al-Mutanabbi to sell more books." Kareem, like many intellectuals, writers, and academics I know, was forced to sell his books for bread. During one of our conversations recalling those years, Kareem shared that besides the economic suffering it caused, the embargo was unfortunately used by the state to further restrict academic and general freedoms. But he understands that the state had its own reasons for doing so. He noted that any state, under such dire circumstances as those Iraq found itself in, would have done the same, citing what the USA has been doing in terms of curtailing freedoms since 9/11 as a case in point.

PART II

4

The Occupation:
Paving the Road to Exile
and Displacement

RESTRUCTURING STATE AND SOCIETY
THROUGH CULTURAL AND ACADEMIC CLEANSING

In Part I, we were introduced to Hiba S., one of the pioneer Iraqi women academics and authors in the field of media and journalism, currently exiled in Amman. During a visit to her office in summer 2014, Hiba shared that the early days of the occupation in 2003 were the most difficult she had ever experienced. She recollected:

> I was sitting in my garden smoking when I suddenly saw a huge American tank driving through the street. I saw a Black soldier on the top of the tank. He looked at me and did the victory sign with his fingers. Had I had a pistol in my hand, I would have immediately shot myself in the head right then and there. The pain I felt upon seeing that image is indescribable. I felt as though all the years we had spent building our country, educating our students to make them better humans were gone with the wind.

Hiba's description carries strong feelings of loss, defeat, and humiliation. Also significant in her narrative is that the first American soldier she encountered in post-invasion Iraq was a Black soldier making the victory sign. This is perhaps one of the most ironic and paradoxical images of the occupation. A Black soldier from a historically and consistently oppressed group in American society, who, one might imagine had no choice but to join the military, coming to Iraq and making the victory sign to a humiliated Iraqi academic whose country was ravaged by war. In a way, this image is worthy of a long pause. It is an encounter of two oppressed and defeated groups of people—Iraqis and African Americans meeting as enemies in a warzone. But, if one digs deeper, are these people really "enemies" or allies struggling against the same oppressors? Do the real enemies ever come to the battlefield? Or do they hide behind closed doors planning wars and invasions while sending other "oppressed" and "diverse" faces to the battle-field to fight wars on their behalf?

Hiba then recalled the early months of the occupation at the University of Baghdad where she taught. She noted that the first thing the Coalition Provisional Authority (CPA) tried to do was to change the curriculum Iraqi academics had designed, taught, and improved over the decades. While the Americans succeeded in doing this at the primary and high school levels, Hiba believed that they did not succeed as much at the university level. Iraqi professors knew better than to allow the "Americanization of the curriculum" to take place. "We knew the materials we were teaching were excellent even compared to international standards," she said. "They [the occupiers] tried to immediately inject subjects like 'democracy' and 'human rights' as if we Iraqis didn't know what these concepts meant." It is clear from Hiba's testimony, also articulated by several other interviewees, that the Iraqi education system was one of the occupying forces' earliest targets in their desire to reshape and restructure Iraqi society and peoples' collective consciousness.

This harkens back to Hazim's comment, mentioned earlier, about "recon-stituting Iraqi consciousness." When I asked Hazim to elaborate further, he said that, in the education sector, changing curricula was aimed at getting rid of the "unwanted" and "inconvenient" academic voices who were opposed to the occupiers' agenda in Iraq. He added that spreading "fear and confu-sion" among Iraqis through the plethora of "supposedly local media" that mushroomed following the first few months of the occupation can also be understood through "cognitive dissonance theory." The post-occupation media, he noted, was funded by internal and external actors whose objective was to "spread more and more confusion in a war-torn society." Hazim, who holds advanced degrees in education and education technology from Iraq and the UK, felt strongly about how the occupiers and their supporters in the "new Iraq" sought to "re-educate, if not to say miseducate" Iraqi society after 2003, not least by stoking "sectarian violence." In post-occupation Iraq, people were too confused to understand the long-term effects of what was being done to them, he remarked, adding that this could "easily happen in every war-torn place." For him, Iraqis were not only confused, but were also caught in a vicious circle. "They always come back to square one," he said.

These two post-occupation testimonies provide a glimpse into how currently exiled and internally displaced academics understand the post-occupation reality, both of Iraqi society in general and of academia in particular. Part II of this book examines the different but intertwined realities of Iraq under occupation through the eyes of its exiled academics. This chapter focuses on how former Iraqi institutions were dismantled, "cleansed," and restructured. The experiences of academics captured here show that this was done primarily through three "cleansing methods":[1]

first, through direct death threats and assassinations of academics and professionals who were no longer wanted in post-occupation Iraq;

second, by igniting sectarian violence that significantly contributed to turning Iraq from a unified, central state with strong institutions in place, into divided zones run by militias and militant groups practicing "necro-politics," that is, who gets to live and who gets to die, who is saved by the powers-that-be and who is abandoned (Mbembe 2003)—in the case of academics in this work, the determination was who gets to stay in Iraq and who gets forced into exile; and

third, many academics were removed/cleansed through the notorious and controversial policy of "de-Ba'athification."

When I asked my interlocutors about *whom* they thought would benefit from cleansing Iraqi academics, many asserted that the plan was implemented by armed sectarian militias with the full knowledge and blessing of the occupying forces. Some academics cited the West and Israel as being behind the destruction of Iraq and its society, the objective being to turn it into a weak and divided country that would not pose any threat to their hegemonic aspirations in the Middle East. Others blamed Iran and the Iranian-supported Shi'i militants that mushroomed inside Iraq after the occupation. Some academics, particularly Shi'a, thought that Sunni insurgents caused these killings to destabilize the country because they were angry for losing the control they had before 2003. It was clear that each academic's positionality and background contributed to their view.

Statistically speaking, my research shows that Sunni academics have been disproportionately removed, threatened, and forced into exile. Yet, the more I asked, the more confusing this matter became. One thing many academics were aware of is that the parties arming, inciting, or supporting sectarian violence on either side had nothing to do with supporting Shi'a or Sunnis per se. Most of these sectarian groups have nothing to do with the sects they claim they are defending. They are political actors seeking to serve themselves and their own interests only. Although it was hard for academics to determine which parties might be behind the cleansing of Iraq's intelligentsia, I found that understanding the changes and challenges academics experienced on campus, in the classrooms, and in daily life, right after the occupation before they were eventually forced into exile or displacement was crucial. Understanding what went on in university classrooms in Iraq right after 2003 is an important indicator of the reconfiguration of both "state" and "academics" on the one hand, and consequently, the terms of the "contract" or relationship between the two parties on the other hand.

KILLINGS, ASSASSINATIONS, AND THREATS AS CLEANSING

One of the key ideas we learn from the French philosopher, Michel Foucault, in tracking the "genealogy" of events is that rather than focusing on how things are, we should pay closer attention to how they have come to be the way they are (Rabinow and Rose 2003). Therefore, as we examine the path that forced academics into exile, or even multiple exiles and displacements, we must understand how things started before they left Iraq. Most interlocutors I met in London, Amman, and Iraqi Kurdistan had either received death threats, survived assassination attempts, or had members of their families kidnapped, threatened, or assassinated. As we saw earlier, a classic means of threatening academics and inciting them to leave their academic positions (and the country) was by sending them a bullet in an envelope, oftentimes with a note threatening them with death if they did not leave. Those who did not act swiftly were indeed subject to assassination attempts, not all of them successful. The IraqSolidaridad group, part of the Spanish Campaign Against the Occupation for the Sovereignty of Iraq, reported that as of November 7, 2013, a total of 324 Iraqi academics from different disciplines had been assassinated in the country. Many of these murdered academics were prominent figures in their fields. The group, in collaboration with the brussells Tribunal, provides the names of and other information on each assassinated academic (CEOSI 2013).

Of the 63 academics I interviewed for this book, 20 were directly subjected to death threats, mostly by the bullet in an envelope method. Others were told by some "informants" on campuses where they taught that their names had been put on "death lists" and were advised to leave as soon as possible. Seven interlocutors had spouses and other family members threatened, kidnapped and released upon paying huge ransoms, or killed. Four interlocutors survived assassination attempts. A few had their houses searched and their academic work and documents confiscated by the US military and/or different militia groups that mushroomed in Iraq after 2003. At least one (Badir, previously introduced) was imprisoned because of his anti-occupation PhD dissertation in the field of political science. Most interlocutors kept the threatening letters and the bullets in envelopes they had received as evidence. Most were able to present them to me to corroborate their stories. Since the notes and envelopes included their first and last names, I chose not to include images of them in order to protect their privacy and lives. Many of the threatened academics were able to reach places like Jordan and the UK thanks to organizations such as Scholars at Risk (SAR), Scholar Rescue Fund (SRF), and Council for At-Risk Academics (CARA). Those who could not leave the country had no choice but to become internally displaced in places like Iraqi Kurdistan, as one of the few relatively "safe havens" available for them. What follows is a survey of some of the most chilling death threats and assassination testimonies shared by different interlocutors, some of whom have already been introduced in previous chapters concerning their experiences and lives in Iraq during the Ba'ath era.

* * *

Sameera S., introduced earlier, is an exiled chemist and academic in Amman whom I met in 2014. She was a recipient of a bullet in an envelope. When the occupation happened, Sameera was teaching in Yemen, but she returned to Baghdad in 2004. She continued to teach there until 2007, when her brother-in-law was kidnapped and killed. At that point, she and her family decided to escape to Amman. As she was unable to find a job to make a living there, she was forced to go back to Baghdad in 2008, where she taught for a year before receiving a bullet in an envelope. It looked like "an official university manila envelope used for interdepartmental daily correspondence," she told me. Sameera and her husband showed me the original envelope, the bullet, and the note that read in Arabic:

> Warning: you must, without further notice, leave the University immediately lest you lose your life with a silencer, Dr. [name omitted]. Do not underestimate this warning. Save your and your family's lives. We will act on this threat. You have been notified.

Sameera explained this threat in light of the sectarian violence that was at its peak in Baghdad at that time. She said, "I am a Sunni that's why I was threatened." Sameera went on to say:

> We thought so much about it, but we could not guess who would benefit from such a threat. I was liked by everyone. All my students and all professors in my department. ... It is very sad that I had to leave Iraq at that time because I was at the prime of my scientific and academic life. I was looking forward to making up for the sanctions' lost years to continue to research, read, and produce work that would make a difference. I loved chemistry and was so happy that the invasion would allow us access to new books and scientific resources. But it was all cut short ... I cannot describe to you how this threat affected me psychologically. My only solace after that was working with the Scholar Rescue Fund (SRF). It was hard for me to suddenly lose my work, my income, and become a housewife overnight after all these years of hard work.

From Amman, Sameera eventually applied for early retirement from her academic post in Baghdad and started working with the SRF on research related to energy and water treatment at a Jordanian university.

* * *

Abbas D. is an academic specializing in economics, with a focus on economic agriculture. He received his advanced degrees from Iraq and Bulgaria in the 1980s. Currently internally displaced in Iraqi Kurdistan, I first met him in November 2015. Before the invasion, Abbas moved around a lot, teaching at universities and institutes located near rural and farming areas in a variety of small cities and towns in the middle and southern parts of Iraq. Married and a father of four children, he was very much "looking forward to a fresh start after 2003," though he strongly opposed the occupation. He noted:

> The invasion was wrong. They could have gotten rid of Saddam, but they should not have destroyed state institutions, as they are also trying to do in Syria now. We should have changed the regime without destroying institutions. We still do not have real institutions functioning in 2015. We have gangs, militias, and political parties. That is it. We have criminals ruling us. Iraqi oil is being stolen and taken without any supervision. Most of it is going cheaply to Iran to support internal militias inside Iraq.

When I asked Abbas to describe the circumstances that forced him into internal displacement in Kurdistan, he said:

> In 2005, sectarianism worsened significantly and they started targeting academics. At the end of June 2006, I received an envelope with a bullet inside. I left the following day. Inside the envelope there was a note saying: "we want your house!" I first left on my own and came here to Kurdistan. My Kurdish friends welcomed me, and I stayed here for three months. They helped me get my current academic position … Two days after leaving my town on the outskirts of Baghdad, they came for my wife and daughters whom I had left behind. They told them, "leave the house or we will rape you." They left the house immediately and went to stay with some Kurdish friends in Baghdad. Once I was settled here, my family followed. My house was occupied by militias for five years. I tried hard to get it back … In October 2011, I got it back and sold it right away. The house was in horrible shape. They had destroyed my big collection of hundreds of precious books.

Abbas paused. His face looked sad. I saw tears welling in his eyes as he said, "these are very painful memories." He then shared how after 2003, Iraq was not a state but a space ruled by different militant groups. A place in which each citizen had to be loyal to one militia or another to survive. Yet, he added, there were no guarantees because "one could always end up in the hands of the wrong militant group."

*   *   *

The case of Sa'ed J. was one of the most shocking I had encountered in the course of doing this work. Before the occupation, Sa'ed had been a well-known and highly regarded physicist in Baghdad. He received his education in the 1980s from al-Mustansiriya and Baghdad universities, focusing on solid state physics, material science, and plasma spraying technology. He was forced to leave Baghdad and fled to Kurdistan in July 2005. When another academic in Kurdistan introduced me to Sa'ed in October 2015, he warned me that the man had had seriously traumatic experiences.

Sa'ed invited me for a walk on campus on the day after we were introduced. As we talked about his pre-2003 experience, Sa'ed told me that most of his academic work was research-related and he was forced into teaching after he was internally displaced because he had no other options. He remembered with great pain what happened before his forced displacement:

One day in June 2005, I went to see one of my friends, also an academic. While we were both walking in a street near my friend's house, four masked people suddenly came out of a car. They shot me from a very close distance. I was shot four times ... I lost consciousness. My friend was shot once in his leg. He was seriously injured. I had already received a note before that date saying that my name was on an assassination list, but I did not take it seriously. I should have acted immediately.

Sa'ed survived, but the price was high. He told me half-jokingly: "You see, I received one bullet in the head. I almost have no brain left in my head after that attack. I often space out and forget where I am or who I am. I want to forget everything." Sa'ed was fortunate to survive this attack. Many of the academics and professionals targeted, he said, were not so fortunate. After his recovery, he immediately took his wife and five daughters and came to Kurdistan, his only option for a "safe haven" in Iraq.

Although not sure who might have had an interest in killing him, Sa'ed believes that "the colonial powers with hegemonic interests in the Middle East have every benefit from depriving Iraq of its brains to implement their own agendas." Sa'ed was not alone in expressing such ideas. Although most of them recognized that they had no concrete evidence to support their claims, most academics I talked to believe that the actors interested in controlling the Middle East are behind Iraq's brain drain and the "cleansing" of its culture and heritage. Some went further, stating that these actors are interested in destroying Iraq and its culture and simply dismiss Iraqi people's explanation of events as "conspiracy theories."

* * *

Iftikhar, introduced previously, also a physicist, is currently displaced and working as a lecturer in Kurdistan. She is originally from Mosul, although she spent most of her adult life and academic career in Baghdad. She described the years after occupation in Baghdad as littered with "killings, bombs, car explosions, and other forms of violence." One of the most worrying factors for her family was sectarian violence that started rising after 2005. She had to act swiftly when the American forces started raiding and searching houses randomly in search of "insurgents" or "terrorists":

> The Americans searched our house multiple times. My husband and I were worried they would arrest my four sons … There was a time when a missile fell nearby. They knocked on our door. My son answered the door and was shocked to see American soldiers outside … They entered and claimed that the missile was shot from our house. We told them that the claim was absurd. We were academics and professionals and had nothing to do with it all. They insisted that the missile was from our house according to their satellites. On a different night, they broke into our house and came searching while I was sleeping. They asked so many absurd questions … We started to be very concerned … eventually, we had to leave in 2005.

Iftikhar and her family felt the humiliation of leaving home for internal displacement from the beginning. Right at the checkpoint to enter Erbil, Kurdistan, they were shocked to see that there were two lines of people: one for Kurds and another for Iraqi Arabs because "Arabs can't enter without a sponsor or a residency card." The family had to wait in line for many hours before they made it through the checkpoint.

For Iftikhar, separating Kurds and Arabs, supposedly citizens of the same country, into two different lines, is already "a sign that citizens are divided into different classes within the same country. American occupiers are the masters of segregating people," she added. In Kurdistan, she and her husband were able to find temporary academic jobs. Her husband died soon after. She has been living on short-term contracts to support her family since.

* * *

Latifa A. is an academic in the field of computer science. She received her undergraduate and advanced education from Baghdad University. She has been through multiple exiles, ending up in Kurdistan in 2009, after her contract as a part-time lecturer was not renewed in the UAE. She taught computer science in Baghdad for 22 years and left her academic position "empty-handed," without being able to apply for early retirement or to remain on leave until security conditions improved. She received a threatening note that had been thrown into her garden, which basically said leave immediately or be killed. "They claimed that my son had been working against the al-Mahdi Army. They said if I did not deliver my son to them, they were going to take my daughter. We left for the UAE immediately." When her contract was not renewed in the UAE, like Iftikhar, above, she went back to Baghdad despite the dangers. She had no choice. However, she found herself forced to leave once again heading to Kurdistan in 2009, after her husband died in an explosion while he was praying at a mosque. She recalled those days:

> I left the UAE at the end of 2009. At that time, in Baghdad, they said that people with service could return to their old positions within 72 days. I went back. They told me that I could retire. However, when I started working on the paperwork, they said I couldn't retire because I was not 60 years of age yet, and so while the university counted me as retired, the Directorate of Social Security did not consider me eligible for retirement. I called this university here in Kurdistan and it turned out they needed a lecturer. They, however, did not count my 22 years of academic service in Baghdad, partly because I did not get a letter from Baghdad that proves it, and partly because I did not have connections here—people with strong connections still manage to get things done for them. I did not have any connections.

Iftikhar is one of many interlocutors who told me that they lost credit for so many years of service in post-occupation Iraq. These are academics who had worked for 20–30 years and then were forced to leave the country without being granted retirement or early retirement. These academics felt bitter about this loss because their years are neither counted in Iraq to help them get a pension nor in exile where they can only work under precarious annual contracts; and their service in Iraq is irrelevant to the private institutions hiring them. In fact, even for those internally displaced in Kurdistan, their service was not counted because "Kurdistan has its own Ministry of Higher Education, separate from Baghdad. We are the only country in the world with two separate ministries for everything. Moreover, they are constantly fighting with each other, undermining and overwriting each other," one interlocutor told me.

* * *

Siham S.'s story is particularly difficult because she believes that it was she who was targeted but it was in fact her sister, who was close to her age and resembled her, that was assassinated. The assassins shot her sister while she was heading home in a car with her friend. Her sister did not die immediately but was in critical condition for five days after which she passed away at the hospital: "I could not carry on teaching after that. I could not bear to be on campus anymore." During that time, Siham continued to be chased, receiving phone calls from unknown individuals, and she felt like she was being watched on her way back and forth from the university. In the end, she realized that it was she who was being targeted and that they had killed her sister mistakenly: "Imagine, I must live with the idea that my sister died on my behalf for the rest of my life," she told me. Siham applied for a postdoctoral in Ireland. In 2008, she left Iraq with her husband, also an academic, and has never returned.

* * *

Mayada, introduced previously, was targeted in a similar way to Siham. During one of our meetings on the campus where she now teaches two hours north of London, she told me:

I was subject to kidnapping attempts twice: once in 2004, and then again in 2007. In 2008, I was also shot at by the Iraqi Army. I heard from a colleague of mine that my name was on an assassination list for being secular and for not believing in the sectarian nonsense. My father is Shi'i and my mother is Sunni, so I see the nonsense of both sides. The first kidnapping attempt took place when I was on my way to my lawyer's house to hand him some documents. One of my friends was with me in the car. When I went out, rang the bell, knocked on the door, two men approached me. One claimed to be the guard of the house, but I knew he was not. They tried to take me, but I escaped, my shirt was ripped, I ran to the car and drove away. It was like a movie. The second attempt took place when I went to a pharmacy to get medicine. I was followed by a car with four men inside. I kept changing directions to see if they were following me. After some time, it was clear that they were. I drove into a dead-end street where an official lived and ran to the bodyguards to ask for help. The car that was following me turned around and disappeared. Also, my husband was targeted by some militia groups. At that time, we decided to move out. We came to the UK through Council for At-Risk Academics (CARA). I am still in great shock and have limited my contacts with all Iraqis because of these traumatizing experiences.

As Mayada finished telling me about these two kidnapping attempts, she added, that none of it came as a surprise to her. "Iraqi academia has always been connected with the political situation. We are not independent of politics ... The university is not an independent entity; therefore, academic stability cannot be separated from political stability," she said.

* * *

In Amman, I met several exiled academics who believed that they had been targeted for sectarian reasons, specifically for being "Sunnis" under the now Shi'i-dominated government in Iraq. However, when testimonies and statistics are examined closely, there is hardly a clear pattern as to why these academics were targeted and eventually either killed or forced out. Upon close examination of the testimonies as well as the documented biographies of those who were assassinated, the picture that emerges is that academics from different sects, religions, backgrounds, cities, and disciplines were targeted. The only thing they have in common is that they were part of the former Iraqi state and institutions, and many were prominent in their fields. Therefore, the fact that they were targeted should be understood as a case of shifting powers and alliances. It is a case of "cleansing" academics from the former state and replacing them with new post-2003 actors more compatible with the new reconfiguration of power. I asked most interviewees to name or at least theorize whom they thought the primary groups or actors interested in killing and/or forcing them out might be. While most of them did not have any concrete evidence as to who the perpetrators were, they had some important insights, namely, that cleansing Iraq of its academics was part of dismantling the country's society, culture, and institutions. Many believed it was a way of erasing Iraqi identity.

My interlocutors' experiences and insights have been confirmed by recent research that documents the "cultural cleansing" of Iraq. One notable work is Naomi Klein's *The Shock Doctrine* (2007), which examines case studies for several countries around the world. In this book, Klein coins the term "disaster capitalism" to examine how the concept of "shock doctrine" devised by the Chicago economist, Milton Friedman, has been applied brutally to destroy many economies and countries worldwide. Klein defines "disaster capitalism" as the "orchestrated raids on the public sphere in the wake of catastrophic events, combined with the treatment of disasters as exciting market opportunities" (Klein 2007: 6). These disasters provide capitalists with "clean slates" to start over and impose their own terms on the countries involved, whether they are natural disasters as in the case of post-Katrina New Orleans, or disasters caused by war, as in the case of post-2003 Iraq. Klein dedicates considerable space to the case of Iraq to show that the occupation was not meant to achieve "nation-building" but rather "nation-creating" through the "shock and awe" doctrine to erase the entire country, provide a clean slate on which to recreate it. In the end, the author sees the case of Iraq, although extreme, as part and parcel "of the fifty-year crusade to privatize the world" (Klein 2007: 359). Yet, given the great failure of the USA in Iraq, Klein concludes that "Iraq had been blasted with every shock weapon short of a nuclear bomb, and yet nothing could subdue this country. The experiment, clearly, had failed" (Klein 2007: 374).

Important arguments in a volume edited by Raymond Baker and Shereen and Tariq Ismael also lend credence to what interlocutors have shared in this work (Baker et al. 2010). Central to this volume is what the editors call "state-ending" theory to show how the Iraqi state was ended and its culture and institutions, including academia, were cleansed. The editors convincingly argue that "mainstream social science has yet to come to terms with the full meaning of 'ending states' as a policy objective." And while much social science literature exists on the state, there is little about "state-destruction" and "de-development" (Baker et al. 2010: 3). The authors draw attention to the fact that there is no "development" without "de-development"; there is no "rebuilding" without "destruction," and within the context of this book, I argue, understanding exile cannot be separated or resolved without understanding everything that produced it. The case of Iraq, the editors stress, makes "unavoidable the recognition and analysis of state-ending as a deliberate policy objective." In their analysis, to "remake a state," as happened in Iraq, the state has to be "rendered malleable." Obstacles to this goal "included an impressive intelligentsia committed to a different societal model and the unifying culture they shared" (Baker et al. 2010: 6). And because the Iraqi intelligentsia had always proposed the culture of a "unified country," the occupying forces saw the "liberation" of Iraq as part of liberating it from its intelligentsia also.

SECTARIAN VIOLENCE AS CLEANSING

Badir, the professor of political science introduced earlier, was teaching in his field with a master's degree while completing his PhD in 2006. He was imprisoned because of his PhD topic, he said, sharing his arrest story:

> In 2006, I wrote the first dissertation in my field on the UN Security Council and the 2003 illegal occupation of Iraq. I was arrested just one day before my doctoral defense by a group known as "*al-Theeb*" [The Wolf Brigade]. The reason they cited for my arrest was "describing the Americans as occupiers in inflammatory ways." They knew about my dissertation topic because I had submitted the title and the abstract in 2004. They arrested me not only because of my dissertation, but also because of my first name, my last name, and the neighborhood where I lived in Baghdad [all disguised but indicating that he is a Sunni]. It was all for purely sectarian reasons. I had to pay a bribe to be released from prison. I was released in June 2006 and immediately took a cab to the airport and left for Amman. I had planned to leave for Amman anyway, but I needed

to be in Baghdad for my dissertation defense. ... They did not torture me, but I saw many innocent people in prison getting abused and tortured. It was a traumatic experience.

* * *

When describing the campus and the classrooms between 2003 and 2008, before she left Iraq for Ireland and later England, Siham, whose sister was assassinated, reported that classroom discussions became increasingly difficult. As students began aligning with political and sectarian parties, they adhered to these parties' thoughts and ideologies even in classroom discussions. In the field of political science, this was particularly disturbing, Siham said. "I often had to remind students that it was okay to make any arguments [they wanted] as long as it was supported with evidence." She provided one example when a heated and volatile discussion erupted when a student brought up the issue of "resisting the occupying forces." Another student who had lost his brother in a car bomb reacted by saying that it was "terrorism not resistance." The classroom suddenly split into two opposing groups, mostly males dominating and shouting, with one group insisting it was "resistance" and the other calling it "terrorism." Siham added, "Females, on the other hand, became so quiet and silenced after the war. I could not blame them. They started feeling unsafe."

Siham reported, as other professors also witnessed, that students would show up to exams with guns: "Some students holding high ranks in the Ministry of Defense wouldn't even bother attending lectures. They would simply send lower-rank soldiers or employees to attend lectures and take notes on their behalf. We had never seen such things before." With all these changes, Siham said, "we started to even doubt our students and feel that they may kill us, if they didn't like us." This feeling was further amplified because the government was not taking any serious measures to investigate the assassinations of many professors on and off campus. When I asked her who she thought might have been killing academics, she said:

We did not know who would be killed next and why. Many professors were killed regardless of their sect or religion ... It was random. When someone was killed, we would not know when or by whom. All we could do was to be confused and just try to make guesses like "perhaps he/she had an argument with student X the other day?" and other such guesses.

This sense of "confusion" is significant because it ties in with what interviewee, Hazim, shared earlier about how post-war Iraq became a space filled with "distress and confusion." Siham said that each time a professor was killed, threatened, or kidnapped, "we had to revise our guesses on why this was happening." With each case, they had to add yet another potential reason to the list of reasons for being targeted:

At the beginning, we thought it was because he/she was a former Ba'athist. When someone independent was killed, they said it was sectarian. When someone was killed by American soldiers, they thought it was to wipe out Iraqi minds, and on and on we kept guessing. American soldiers would enter classrooms without permission, when professors were in the middle of lecturing. The campus was raided by Americans many times and this resulted in an outrage. The Iraqi government never raised the issue. It was only after it received international attention ... that they mildly protested about these raids. Some said that there was an intentional move to push Iraqi professors into exile to use them for cheap labor in places like Kurdistan, Arab countries, and Western countries. Killing professors was random as was the killing of some of their family members. The Iraqi government still has not conducted adequate official investigations to see who is really behind this—not to mention all the threatened professors who received bullets in envelopes.

* * *

Majeed, who taught English literature at the University of Baghdad, introduced earlier, left for the USA. Like others, he pointed out that academic institutions had become sectarian zones, some predominantly in the hands of Shi'i militias (like al-Mustansiriya University), and others predominantly in Sunni hands (like Mosul University). More diverse institutions, like Baghdad University, became more difficult spaces to be in as the various sects vied with each other to impose their own symbols, rituals, and beliefs on campus. This included flags, political statements, and other sectarian activities that had nothing to do with knowledge and education.

Majeed remained in Iraq until 2005. During one of our long Skype conversations in 2014, I asked him to describe how he experienced academic life after the occupation. He said that within a few months,

> there was a huge transformation from a despotic and strong state into a country that made most people wonder whether it was even safe to go to a grocery store. This sudden change of state and governance is strongly tied to the change academics felt in their daily lives.

At the beginning, many academics were hopeful for change. After long years of sanctions and intellectual and physical deprivation, they were finally hoping to reconnect with the world and with academic research to get new books, research, and materials. However, at the same time,

> it was a situation of great irony. I was invited to different lectures, and we started to teach new political themes in Shakespeare's writings, for example, that we could not necessarily discuss directly in the past. But, in return, we were hearing explosions and deaths all over the place. We were under new types of danger if we refused to subscribe to the political thoughts of certain religious and political parties that multiplied after the occupation.

Majeed said that much money started to go directly into the hands of reactionary and religious forces:

> We were seeing a country whose institutions were hijacked by sectarian groups whose main concern was to empower themselves ... Many neighborhoods were taken over by certain ethnicities and sects [seeking] to cleanse other ethnicities and sects. These frames of thought started affecting the new generations of young people who started to think religiously, ethnically, and almost exclusively in sectarian terms.

The sectarian divides nurtured by the occupation were a recipe for death because people of different sects and beliefs who used to mingle, intermarry, and work together in the past were suddenly clashing violently with each other. In fact, some academics shared that even some inter-communal couples (Shi'a and Sunnis) were affected by sectarian violence. In this way, it was not only that the "contract" with the former state has been changed from a centralized system into a sectarian one, but even "love" or "marriage" contracts between people were severely affected. One Shi'i academic from Mosul, currently displaced in Kurdistan told me:

> I started having a lot more disagreements and arguments with my Sunni wife after the occupation. One day we both caught ourselves in a ridiculous fight over sectarian matters. We both calmed down for a bit and then vowed not to let sectarian issues come between us.

Consequently, the relationships between people changed drastically, including those between academics on one hand, and between academics and their students on the other hand.

Furthermore, Majeed described the new meaning of "freedom" and "academic freedom" experienced after 2003. Sometimes, it was fatal. On the one hand, academics could write and speak about issues that were off limits before. But, on the other hand, they could also be killed, if a certain militant group did not like their writings or teaching in the classroom. In this regard, Majeed provided a specific example:

> One could publish what one wanted, but they could kill you for doing so also. Both actions were done under the banner of "freedom" ... Anyone who refused to be under the protection of a certain militia or religious group was not protected and even targeted by all these reactionary groups that sprung up in Iraq after the occupation. I was told by some of my morning-class students, who had friends enlisted with political/religious parties and militias, that I, along with other professors at our college, were the target of some groups because of certain things we had said in lectures. These students, from different sects, cared enough about me and told me what they had heard, and they insisted on taking me home to protect me. This is so bittersweet. When I arrived in the USA, I learned later about some of my former students and colleagues who were eventually killed and assassinated because of their views, their sects, and their politics. There was a constant feeling of being targeted by this or that faction, if you say something that would dissatisfy one or the other. Many received threatening letters telling them to leave within 48 hours.

Majeed's narrative shows a new form of "governance" that is much more complex, slippery, and almost impossible to navigate than the previous political reality of a one-party, central, secular state before 2003. Some interviewees said that in the past at least there was one political party in place, and they knew what lines they should not cross or be careful about or to do so implicitly. After 2003, no matter which militia or religious/sectarian group one adhered to (or pretended to adhere to for the sake of their safety), there was always a chance of falling into the hands of the "wrong side" and paying one's life as a price for it. Majeed, like many others, confirmed that the rise of sectarianism on campuses was accompanied by the removal of any academics who had no sectarian affiliation with this or that sectarian group. This is a significant method that was used to cleanse higher education of many academics who did not operate on a sectarian basis. One academic said that "each university became like a mouthpiece for a certain sectarian militia or political group."

Moreover, others discussed how the increasing number of religious holidays has impeded teaching and class attendance. One interlocutor said: "Students found all kinds of ways to avoid classes using religious holidays as an excuse." Another female academic currently living in Amman told me that, on her campus, where Shiʿi religious holidays were imposed, women were expected to dress in black on Ashura Day.[2] "I didn't wear black when my father died, why should I be forced to do so for a religious holiday?" she asked.[3] Other academics noted that, given these new realities of politicized sectarianism, many students started to write entire theses and dissertations dedicated to or simply in favor of one sectarian group or another. Students were also pressured to dedicate their dissertations to sectarian militias to make sure they would pass their defense. This observation, confirmed by several of my interlocutors and by journalistic accounts (Abu Zeed 2016), is important because it is reminiscent of what was done in the Baʿath era when some students dedicated their theses and dissertations to the party or to Saddam Hussein personally. Today seems so much like yesterday, except with many more actors and players one must please in order to survive. "At least in the past we had only one party to deal with or to navigate," one academic complained. "Today, we have dozens of them. You can't please one of them without simultaneously angering most of the others."

Academics who used to teach in the northern city of Mosul, before being displaced into Kurdistan after ISIS took over Mosul, noted that they were less affected by sectarian violence than those in Baghdad and the so-called Sunni-triangle. Still, they were far from safe. Aboud R., a professor of linguistics currently displaced in Kurdistan, noted that the students themselves became "vicious and started using Machiavellian methods to force us to give them grades they didn't deserve. They took advantage of the fragile security. Some became extremely aggressive and threatening." He added that rumor had it that students were responsible for the "bullets in envelopes" phenomenon, which they directed at professors they disliked or those who did not give them high grades. However, for most people I spoke to, it was clear that the systematic assassination of academics was far too serious to be the work of disgruntled students.

One case that particularly captures the post-occupation realities that forced many academics into exile or internal displacement was that of Omer S., an academic in his late fifties or early sixties specializing in Middle Eastern history. Though originally from the city of Anbar, Omer, who was currently displaced in Erbil, in Iraqi Kurdistan, had been raised and educated mostly in Baghdad. Here is how he narrated the story of what he called his "multiple displacements" due to sectarian violence:

> I escaped from Baghdad due to sectarian violence and threats against me, especially because of my name. I left behind a big, fully furnished house, with a rare book collection. It was occupied by a Shi'a militia group and they destroyed everything in it. I found out that they even dismantled the window frames in the house and sold them. It was devastating. I then had to relocate and start over in Anbar at my age. I had to build another house from scratch. I even had to borrow money to build it. As soon as it was finished, before we even got a chance to take a breath, ISIS invaded, and we were forced to escape in the middle of the night to Kurdistan with nothing but our clothes and IDs. We lost that second house, too, and had to come here and stay at a hotel for one month before I had my paperwork done to be able to rent a place. I am still paying off the debt of a house that I never got to live in and probably never will. I do not even know what happened to it. I do not know if it has been demolished or is still in one piece.

For Omer, the Iraqi case of exile and displacement is unique because "it is not only people who are being displaced, but entire institutions." By this, he means that entire universities in areas that have witnessed sectarian violence, particularly those occupied by ISIS like Mosul and Anbar, as well as other parts of Iraq, were displaced. This is a case of human displacement combined with what can be termed as "infrastructural displacement." In fact, when Omer came to Kurdistan, he could not find a job at either public or private universities in the region. He was fortunate, he told me, because his former university in Anbar was entirely displaced and forced to relocate to Erbil. They had to rent a new space for their displaced faculty and some staff members. "This allowed me to continue to go to work at my new location of displacement. In other words, I couldn't go to my university anymore, but the university followed me all the way here!"

"Displaced institutions," as I learned from Omer and others in Iraqi Kurdistan, had what they call a "relocation order," allowing their employees to work at their new "temporary" offices in relatively safer cities like Erbil, Kirkuk, and Duhok, but even these "relocation orders" are subject to annual renewals, which means that internally displaced academics can only stay if their "relocation orders" are renewed. To theorize this point, internally displaced academics are surrounded by many death zones and fronts, in the form of militias, insecurity, and job precarity, making the task of searching for life, a task akin to searching for a needle in a haystack.

When I first met Omer, he was extremely nervous and distrustful. He was reluctant to speak openly at first, even though I was introduced to him by one of his best friends, an academic I know well. Despite the latter's assurances, it took at least half an hour for him to warm up to me. When we met for the first time in February 2016, I noticed he was nervously smoking one cigarette after another. His voice shook and his hands occasionally trembled. His eyes were dark like a veil with so much pain hidden behind them. We talked for the first half hour about my research for this book and about the mutual friend who connected us. I tried to reassure him that everything he said, including his identity, would be anonymized when writing. I also shared with him stories about my own family and journey to help him feel safe.

After Omer told me about his "displaced university," he said that he was anxiously waiting for his "relocation order" to be renewed in Kurdistan, otherwise he would have no place to go. He and his family would not be able to stay in Kurdistan because his residency status was tied to his employment at the university. He had recently tried to relocate to Baghdad, but his request had been denied by the Ministry of Higher Education. He attributed the denial to "sectarian reasons." Either way, he emphasized, going back to Anbar under ISIS "could cost me my life," he said. And given the ongoing sectarian violence, returning to Baghdad was hardly a safe option either.

I asked him about how he experienced sectarian violence in Baghdad before he was displaced, especially in 2005–2008 when it was at its peak. Omer confirmed that violence was certainly a method to cleanse entire neighborhoods, workplaces, and universities. Based on his experience, the larger objective of igniting sectarianism was to change the demographics of Baghdad—and other Iraqi cities—depending on the militia groups that ruled any given place. He told me that "many 'Omers' were killed in Baghdad" between 2005 and 2008, a reference to the Sunni casualties of the sectarian violence. Omer is a common Sunni name (its equivalent is Ali for the Shi'a). Of course, it is also true that sectarian violence has killed many "Alis." With the rise of sectarian violence, people were often murdered based on their name and its sectarian associations. Likewise, at the institutions where Omer taught, if a university happened to be dominated by Shi'a groups, someone with a name like his would immediately be targeted or threatened with death, or, if fortunate, simply harassed and/or dismissed. In fact, sectarianism was so prevalent, Omer said:

> When I visited any government office to do any kind of paperwork in Baghdad, I knew immediately whether I was dealing with a Shi'i or a Sunni employee. If he was kind, polite, and cordial to me, it meant he was a Sunni, and vice versa.

And this was just the tip of the iceberg. On our second meeting, one week later, Omer spoke even more candidly:

> At that time, I honestly had to use a different ID to survive. I could not have walked around the streets with an ID under the name "Omer." Fortunately, I had bought a new car and its previous owner had forgotten his ID in it. His name was a generic Arabic name, not indicative of either sect. I used that ID during that year. Sadly, and here is another twist to the story: I later learned that that person, who was also a Sunni, was killed for sectarian reasons. His forgotten ID saved my life, but not his.

Thus, in some ways, academics and other Iraqis endured sectarian violence if only in the sense of having to "forge" a fake identity to "pass" and to simply "stay alive." This is reminiscent of the academics under the Ba'ath who were forced to "forge" their original transcripts to leave the country because the state withheld their transcripts to prevent brain drain. In post-occupation Iraq, under much more violent circumstances, the issue had become more serious than brain drain: it was one of life and death.

* * *

In December 2015, while chatting with Sadiq T., a lecturer in English language and literature in Iraqi Kurdistan, Sadiq provided some analytical and real-life insights on the issue of sectarianism. Sadiq succinctly expressed what multiple interviewees and other Iraqi writers and intellectuals had articulated to me.

> There is a difference between theorizing sectarianism and thinking about its consequences on the Iraqi scene since 2003. We are a multi-ethnic and multi-religious country. We are weak politically and, therefore, sectarianism is a perfect recipe for disaster. When you have a strong regime in place, they can tailor the social fabric that people are going to adopt. If the regime is Sufi, the people will become Sufis; if it is Sunni, Ottoman, it will be as was the case in Iraq under the Ottomans; if it is secular socialist, the people will behave as they did under the Ba'ath party, and so on. This means that Iraq still has not adopted or specified its identity. It perhaps never will. So, it all depends on the coercion, means of governance, authoritarianism, or occupation to determine or even postpone any latent sectarian tensions. Sectarianism has always existed but was always determined by political stability, or lack thereof. The question of identity in such an old and diverse civilization will always be problematic. Imposing identity will cause such problems. If you talk to the Assyrian Christians of Iraq, they will tell you "we are the Indigenous people of this place." The Muslims will claim that they have culturally made everyone, and so on.

These issues, for Sadiq, are all matters to consider before getting into the nuanced details of what happened on the ground post-2003, which forced the exodus of so many Iraqis. As he added, sectarianism affected different groups differently.

First, the impact was not equal for all parts of society and state institutions … Some sectors are more fragile than others. Academics and middle-class people in general were disproportionately affected. For example, when they disbanded the Iraqi army, what do you expect happened after? A civil war, ISIS, al-Qaeda, a-Sadir, Fallujah, and on and on—I could go with the list of disasters that ensued. Why did this happen? Because essential parts of the society had been dismantled. What happened to the army personnel after it was dissolved? Some left the country, but the rest turned into guerrillas and militiamen. The weakest link in this was academics and professionals, most of whom represent the middle class, which had already been totally eroded. This class was already on the verge of destruction because of the UN sanctions that hit us hard. The invasion was the straw that broke the camel's back. Saddam had already caused much damage to the middle class, whether intentionally or unintentionally … Sectarianism was the final blow (…) destroyed the middle class. Totally, I mean it. So, the paradox is that the weakest class was the most important in so many ways because it consisted of academics who shaped society … Despite the damage caused by the Saddam era, he, toward the end of the 1990s, drastically increased the salaries of academics when the Oil-For-Food Program came into effect because he knew how important this category of people was for society. In fact, by the end of the 1990s, many started returning to Iraq and people felt a difference in their living standards. This made people start trusting the state once again. People started to feel that there is a state that is not only scary but also worthy of serving in terms of public sector jobs.

Sadiq's direct experience and analysis of sectarianism combined have been articulated by some Iraqi intellectuals and social scientists. One notable example is the late Ali al-Wardi (1913–1995), who extensively examined Iraqi society, identity, and history in books like *Wu'ath al-Salatin* (*The Sultans' Preachers*) in which he designates as "preachers" poets, religious figures, judges, and other civil servants, and examines their relationship to power (Al-Wardi 1995 [1954]).

Some recent scholarly works have argued that sectarianism is neither a primordial phenomenon nor purely the result of colonialism's "divide and conquer" policies. Rather, it should be seen as an expression of "modernity," or an alternative modernity that expresses human agency (Makdisi 2000). Under this view, sectarianism is as much an expression of modernity as is nationalism. In the case of Lebanon under the Ottoman Empire, Ussama Makdisi shows that sectarianism was born of the confrontation and contact between European colonialism, imperial Ottoman *Tanzimat* practices, and the desire of the local population for freedom and agency. "This encounter profoundly altered the meaning of religion in the multi-confessional society of Mount Lebanon because it emphasized sectarian identity as the only viable marker of political reform and the only authentic basis for political claim" (Makdisi 2000: 2). Makdisi emphasizes how sectarianism plays a significant role in shaping identity, a role that can far exceed that of religion itself.

More recent scholarship on post-occupation Iraq has sought to understand sectarian violence beyond certain mainstream oversimplified explanations. It shows that while it is important to acknowledge the existence of different sects and sectarian tensions in Iraq, we should avoid the tendency to "reduce almost every instance of conflict in Iraq to primordial sectarian-based animosity" (Tejel et al. 2012). Instead, we must pay attention to the "intra-Shi'i; different Shi'i groups, parties, militias or interests are fighting over the same turf, with nary a Sunni in sight" (Tejel et al. 2012: 64–71). Moreover, as many testimonies have already shown in this work, the idea of the "Sunnis" as the main receivers of the pre-occupation regime's privileges is itself a convenient construct, which has led to much violence, cleansing, and forced migration.

A close look and analysis of how the currently exiled and displaced academics experienced sectarian violence prior to leaving reveals two other issues particularly important when thinking about the relationship between academics and power. First, this shift from a "secular" state into a "sectarian" one has imposed new forms of governance similar to what Achille Mbembe calls "necropolitics" and "necropower" (Mbembe 2003). As noted earlier, this new state of existence in an occupied space run by sectarian militias is drastically different from the previous concept of a centralized, unified state. Therefore, it also changes the place, the meaning, and the role of vital yet fragile groups of people in the society like its intelligentsia. It simply turns a zone in which they once lived and taught into one in which they have to beg for "protection" from a certain group but may still die at the hands of another. Second, it is not a surprise that "sectarian violence" becomes a cleansing method that, rather than alleviating or ending suffering, shifts it from certain groups or actors to others. In so doing, it becomes one of the key producers of exile, dispossession, and forced migration. This is clearly seen in the case of Lebanon during its long civil war, as well as in Iraq and Syria today.

Sectarianism as a form of governance forces the society to operate based on a sectarian identity. In many countries around the world, sectarianism has significantly contributed to dispossession, exile, and displacement (Chatty and Finlayson 2010). Nabil al-Tikriti argues that, while sectarian identities have always existed in the Iraqi society, upon close historical examination, we see that they only lead to massive violence and displacement in very specific contexts (Chatty and Finlayson 2010: 249–73). This is precisely what the interlocutor, Sadiq, articulated earlier. Al-Tikriti argues that the Ba'ath regime suppressed any ethnic and sectarian divisions by making "membership" in the party the only measure of belonging (or not belonging). The occupying forces, on the other hand, "intentionally encouraged the breaking down of institutions supportive of national identity, which thus allowed sectarian actors to step into the breech" (Chatty and Finlayson 2010: 12). Al-Tikriti points out, as some of my interviewees have done, that the apparent "use of assassination to gain political control resulted in the flight of middle-class professionals by 2005." Moreover, de-Ba'athification and "the dismantling of the former economic state system then led to the dissolution of the secular system and the strengthening of sectarian organizations" (Chatty and Finlayson 2010: 12). This is in addition to the fact that even the subsequent interim Iraqi governments, after the CPA was dissolved in 2004, were formed based on sectarian lines. These realities significantly increased the need for "sectarian protection" for those who must exist in such spaces. They create zones of life and zones of death. Anyone who is not in either, must necessarily be forced into exile as the only "safe haven."

The case of Iraqi academics shows that this "sectarian protection" is in fact a double-edged sword: on the one hand, it can provide temporary protection through various practices of "necropolitics" and "necropower"; on the other hand, this "temporary protection" can expire or indeed become useless when the person is suddenly in the wrong place at the wrong time and in the hands of the wrong party. In this way, "sectarian protection" necessarily has a short lifespan. Therefore, in the long run, sectarian protection is certainly a cleansing method for those who do not subscribe to its tenets, as many academics in exile have clearly chosen in rejecting sectarianism as a method of governance in Iraq and its academic institutions.

Furthermore, as we will see in Chapter 5, exile and displacement, too, have what might be called their own "conditional protections" and "intellectual strings attached"—whether exiled academics are granted "life and protection" or that right is denied them through the non-renewal of their contracts. The right to exist safely in exile or internal displacement in places like Jordan and Iraqi Kurdistan resembles the "sectarian protection" in that it, too, is subject to abrupt expiration when the contracts of these academics are not renewed.

"DE-BA'ATHIFICATION" AS CLEANSING

Most academics I interviewed considered "de-Ba'athification" to be yet another post-occupation phenomenon that was used to accomplish the academic, cultural, and institutional "cleansing" of Iraq. De-Ba'athification policies were applied right from the start as part of the "disestablishment" of the Ba'ath party of Iraq.[4] The process was inaugurated by the Coalition Provisional Authority (CPA) on May 16, 2003 and rescinded on June 28, 2004—though it was continued by subsequent Iraqi governments. The idea of de-Ba'athification was first expressed by Ahmad Chalabi and the Iraqi National Congress, presumably inspired by "de-Nazification." Although officially implemented by Paul Bremer during his time at the head of the CPA, and later picked up by the subsequent Iraqi governments, some scholars and investigative journalists have shown that the process was designed behind closed doors at the Department of Defense (DoD) in Washington, DC, by the Office of Special Plans. Douglas Feith and Paul Wolfowitz, both Zionist neoconservatives, have been identified as the key minds behind it (Chandrasekaran 2006: 79). Indeed, it has been reported that prior to his arrival to Iraq in May 2003, Bremer met with Douglas Feith as he received his instructions regarding de-Ba'athification (Chandrasekaran 2006: 80). In a filmed interview in Charles Ferguson's award-winning documentary film *No End in Sight: Iraq's Descent into Chaos*, General Jay Garner notes that Bremer had shared with him that he was simply "given orders" regarding the application of the de-Ba'athification policies that were established by the DoD (Ferguson 2007).

De-Ba'athification consisted of 100 orders produced between May 2003 and June 2004.[5] A survey of these orders shows that they were designed to dissolve former Iraqi state institutions and liquidate many individuals of rank in the former Ba'ath regime, without taking into account the intricacies and the complexities of how and why many people had had to enroll into the party. Order 2, for example, titled "Dissolution of Entities," aimed at extending de-Ba'athification to include not just former party members but also all governmental institutions, entities and their subsidiaries, including freezing the financial assets of such entities and placing them under CPA authority to "support the recovery of Iraq."[6] The reckless and dangerous application of de-Ba'athification policies continued until Order 100 titled "Transition of Laws, Regulations, Orders, and Directives Issued by the Coalition Provisional Authority," in which the CPA transferred power to the "interim government of Iraq," which was to come into existence right after the dissolution of the CPA on June 30, 2004.[7]

While this last order makes the CPA no longer responsible for applying and implementing de-Ba'athification, it in fact made things even worse in the years to come because it simply transferred the job from the CPA into the hands of the notoriously sectarian and vindictive Iraqi governments that subsequently applied the policy in spiteful ways. Before analyzing how some scholars and investigative journalists have documented the enforcement, effects, and the aftermath of de-Ba'athification, it is important to start with how exiled and displaced Iraqi academics experienced de-Ba'athification. For many, this was one of the main reasons that forced them out of the country, "cleansing" many vital individuals in Iraqi society and institutions. De-Ba'athification rewrote Iraq's modern history by the occupying forces and their supporters from within.

In June 2014, I met with Dr. 'Ala H., a dean and a professor of computer science at the time at one of Amman's private universities. 'Ala, who had graduated with a degree in physics from Baghdad University in the late 1960s, pursued his advanced education in the UK. He then taught in Iraqi universities from the early 1980s until 2003. Like many academics, he was strongly opposed to the occupation. He was particularly dismayed by the way the de-Ba'athification process was designed and applied in post-2003

Iraq. He considered it one of the main factors that emptied the country of its "brains" forcing many into exile:

> The real purpose of such steps was to destroy the country. I have lived through lots of turmoil, revolutions, and upheavals in Iraq since 1958. In all but the 2003 occupation, Iraqi people mostly continued to do their work to keep the country on its feet. In 2003, it was clear that it was the people who were the primary target of the occupiers. And by the way, de-Ba'athification was selective. There were many people who were Ba'athists in high positions but continued to express interest in serving the occupiers. They remained in their positions and were not hit by these policies. It only targeted those who refused to cooperate with the occupiers, and with their new plans for ruling and shaping Iraq. I know personally of a Kurd who had a very high rank in the Ba'ath, who then went on to become a university president in Kurdistan. In a sense, the Kurds are wise for giving him such a position because they knew they would benefit from his expertise. What we needed was to get rid of the corrupt people rather than get rid of qualified Iraqi academics and professionals just because they belonged to the Ba'ath. Many joined the party, as is well known, as a formality only.

'Ala, like many academics I met in Amman and Iraqi Kurdistan, blamed the occupiers, the post-2003 Iraqi governments, and the sectarian militias for using de-Ba'athification as a pretext to destroy education, get rid of many qualified Iraqis, and also replace them with their own "loyal" individuals. It was simply a matter of "shifting loyalties," one academic told me.

* * *

Israa K., a professor of pharmacology exiled in Amman, introduced earlier, had a similar reaction to 'Ala regarding de-Ba'athification. She shared that, in her case, she was hit by all the post-occupation cleansing methods (identified in this book) that contributed to dismantling Iraqi society. As mentioned earlier, Israa continued to teach in Baghdad until 2006 when she was denied a promotion to the rank of full professor, despite her long record of publication and teaching excellence in her field. Moreover, she learned through close friends at the university that her evaluations for promotion came back favorably but she was nonetheless denied for "sectarian and political reasons." All this happened in 2005 and, despite feeling suffocated and pushed into leaving, she decided to "stay strong and keep going." However, she said:

> The straw that broke the camel's back was when my husband, who was also a researcher, pharmacist, and an academic was kidnapped. Although, to be clear, previously he had been a high-ranking official in the former Iraqi military, he never ever hurt any human being ... I learned that he was kidnapped by a group from Ahmad Chalabi's side and they asked me for a huge ransom in exchange for releasing him. Imagine, I had to remain strong and negotiate for his release with the kidnappers over the phone ... We had to pay the money to save his life ... Still, when they released him, they said that the release was conditional upon us leaving the country within three days. We had to leave everything overnight and depart the country. We left our jobs, our two houses, our relatives, and everything behind. We left for Jordan. My daughter was then in her fifth year at the Pharmacology Department in Baghdad and she insisted on going back to finish. She told me: "Mom, I will finish my studies. I will graduate from Baghdad even if the cost is my life." She did. I had to leave the rest of the family here in Amman and accompany her, hiding in different places in Baghdad until she graduated.

Israa believed that there was a plan to "gut Sunni professors from Iraqi higher education and institutions," without any legal protections, without any proof that such people were guilty of any wrongdoing. It was simply a change of tides. In fact, she noted that where she taught in Baghdad, the dean of her college, who was a Shi'a, was always nice to her but he, too, had to submit to sectarianism in the end:

> He started giving me a hard time when it came to days off. He declined my request to go on leave after my husband was kidnapped, although the entire department was aware of the problem and the immense psychological and emotional pressure I was under during those days ... Although all my students and most of my colleagues loved me and appreciated my work ethic and research capabilities, I realized that it was time for me to leave. I realized that that place was not for me anymore.

Interestingly, most academics who suffered from or spoke about de-Ba'athification as a method to dismantle Iraq and push academics out referred to it as the "so-called de-Ba'athification" and then, depending on their politics and background, went on to accuse the occupiers, Iran, Israel, and other external and internal powers of using it as a means to divide and destroy the country. Like Israa, numerous other interlocutors emphasized that one of the key differences between pre-occupation and post-occupation Iraq was that before 2003 academics and other professionals could exist and succeed, regardless of their sect, religion, ethnicity, and other factors, so long as they either proved to be loyal to the Ba'ath party or at least proved not to be a "threat" to it. In this way, many could live and function by staying away from politics or simply remaining in the lower ranks of the party just as a formality. After the occupation, many were punished, purged, murdered, and pushed into exile simply because of their sect.

What is critical here is that in the past one could easily pretend to be in the party or not be a threat to it; whereas after 2003, it became impossible for, say, a Sunni professor to pretend to be Shi'a. It was also impossible for an Arab to pass as a Kurd. In this way, the risks of sectarian and ethnic politics far outweighed what was previously experienced under having a secular, single political party in place. In fact, as many interviewees pointed out, many Shi'a and Kurds who used to hold high positions under the former regime continued to keep their posts after 2003 precisely because of the new ethno-sectarian realities imposed on Iraq. Previously, they were able to keep their positions by playing along with the regime. After occupation, they remained because of their ethnicity in the case of Kurdistan, or their sect, in the case of the Shi'a. This has been much harder for Sunni because they were traditionally seen as a "dominating" and "privileged" group before 2003—a far from accurate representation of reality. It was a "convenient construct" that served the new sectarian-based governance in Iraq. Moreover, precisely because Sunni Arabs could not pass as "Kurds" or as "Shi'a," the effects of de-Ba'athification on them were many folds harsher.

Ghadeer K., an exiled academic in Amman, who had remained in Iraq until 2007, also had to leave as a result of sectarian violence. Ghadeer had replaced a departmental dean in Baghdad who had been dismissed as a result of de-Ba'athification policies. Therefore, he could provide a more nuanced description of how he experienced this shift. Majoring in foreign languages, with a focus on German language and literature, Ghadeer had

had lengthy academic experience of both teaching and researching at Iraqi universities since receiving his PhD from Germany in the mid-1960s. He was one of the oldest academics I met while researching for this book. Born in the 1930s, he had witnessed many important events and upheavals in Iraq over the decades. Ghadeer told me that he had been through multiple exiles because of the constantly changing political circumstances in Iraq. He first left for Jordan in 1998 for economic reasons. He returned to Iraq a few months before the occupation took place in 2003. "Out of my bad luck, I was stuck in the middle of it all," he said. Ghadeer waited until after the war to see if things were going to improve before taking the next step. When he saw that things were only deteriorating, he asked the dean of his college to help him apply for retirement. Unlike most cases we have seen so far, Ghadeer was told that he should consider staying as there was a need for his expertise and service. He went ahead and did all the paperwork needed to reinstate his academic position at the College of Arts in Baghdad.

Here, Ghadeer's story took another turn because he returned to his post at around the same time the process of de-Ba'athification started and the axe fell on the chair of his department. "They asked me to replace him given my good academic 'record,' even though I was a Sunni," Ghadeer told me. Although he was reluctant to do so, after the dean and many professors told him to go for it, he decided to accept, though still uncomfortably. However, to finalize the process, they "required all kinds of approvals and background checks done by Shi'i political and religious parties. This included the approval of the *a-Sadir* group," he added. This was around the time militias had started targeting academics, particularly former Ba'athists (including Shi'i ones). It was also the time when the assistant to the president of Baghdad University, Nihad al-Rawi, was assassinated on July 26, 2007. Unlike most Sunnis in this research, Ghadeer believed that there was no evidence that it was the "Shi'a who killed the Sunni academics," although he believes, albeit without concrete evidence, that these killings were executed by "Iraqi hands."

> The Shi'i militias and student groups controlled the university and our college ... There was a tension between the student and militia groups at the College of Languages and College of Arts. This affected classes. Students missed many lectures. Professors started to leave the university for their safety ... The dean of the College of Arts and his assistant

visited me a few times. They complained about the behavior of militia individuals from the *a-Sadir* group. They had to be careful not to talk in front of the guards, since the latter were loyal to the *a-Sadir* group. The *a-Sadir* group didn't have any animosity toward me, although I refused their constant pressure to do illegal things like moving students from one department to another, approving scholarships for unqualified students, and so on. Sometimes they spoke to me with a threatening tone. They basically asked for all sorts of side-deals and illegal things to be done for them. They even started threatening girls in certain departments to pressure and impose their politics and sectarian vision. For example, they threatened a Palestinian female student at the French department to force her to leave the university. One day, as I was on my way to the university, I got a phone call and was told not to show up. It turned out that some students from the colleges of Arts and Education loyal to militias had come to our department, the guards had miraculously disappeared, and the former entered the department and threatened all Sunni professors to leave their positions. My assistant told me they came into his office and said: "Leave your position now or we will break this chair on your head!"

It was right after this incident that Ghadeer decided to exit Iraq for Jordan. It was "during that year [that] colleges lost most of their Sunni academics," he added. This is despite the fact that the president of the university phoned him, begging him to return to his position, and promised to investigate the incident. Ghadeer agreed to return temporarily but, at that time, he was determined to find an exit as soon as possible. After the university had conducted what was purportedly a "serious investigation" into the incident, Ghadeer was told: "We were finally able to name the people/parties responsible for this incident, but it was decided that we name them as an 'anonymous' group in the final report, to avoid any retaliation from militias." He was told that the incident was the work of a group affiliated with the *a-Sadir* militia, but they were too afraid to name them in the report. Ghadeer insisted that they provide guarantees to hold the *a-Sadir* group accountable if he were to return to his position. They promised to do so "off the record":

As soon as I resumed my work at the college, an official from the *a-Sadir* group came to me with a delegation and said: "We know who was responsible for the incident and we assure you that we are aware that you are fair and don't discriminate against a Shi'a or a Sunni employee in your department." They told me if anyone bothers me again, I should call a number and they would be there right away to take care of things. They were very positive ... Yet, sectarianism seemed to only worsen on campuses. At the height of the sectarian violence, we received an order from the president of the university asking that all sectarian slogans, flags, ads, and so on be removed from every wall and corner of the university. When I told the guards to implement it, they refused. They literally told me: "Let the president come and do it himself. We don't want to get into any trouble by doing this." In fact, the guards told me that I, too, should not do it, lest I get in trouble with the militias. You see, this means that sectarianism was so infiltrated and had the upper hand in things that people would not dare to separate it from academia or other institutions, even if they genuinely wanted to do so for everyone's benefit.

On top of these threats, increasing sectarian violence, and the overall deterioration of the situation, Ghadeer's son was also threatened while on a work bus going to his office one morning. He shared the story:

They wanted to take my son away from his work bus. They insisted that his ID was fake because there was no "tribe name" on it. The truth is we never used a tribe name in any of our IDs. They wanted to know whether he was Shi'i or Sunni to proceed accordingly. He worked at the Ministry of Trade at that time. I told him to go to his boss and ask him to create a temporary ID to avoid such situations in the future. He could have easily been taken and killed by militias—there were so many of them all over the place. This happened to him a second time while on the work bus heading back home. If it was not for the other employees who begged the armed men and assured them that he was one of their employees, they would have killed him. This made me very concerned. I was more worried for his safety than mine.

It was right at that time, in 2007, when Ghadeer decided to leave Iraq for Jordan for the second time. Some of his family members had already moved before he did for their safety. As for him, it was not as easy because he needed to make a living and send money to his family members in Jordan. After the threats to his son, he had no choice but to leave:

I simply could not be there anymore. They finally agreed and sent my retirement paperwork to the ministry, which took a very long time with their bureaucratic procedures. I waited from mid-2007 until 2010 to have my retirement approved. I lived all this time on my own funds in Jordan, and you know how expensive life is here. In 2010, I was told that some changes in the pension requirements had taken place and they asked me to reapply. There was a new pension law that paid much more than the old one—not to mention that the officers doing the paperwork took lots of bribes. When I went to reapply, they told me they would do it if I paid my first pension allowance to them, so I did and everything was done properly. The old pension law paid me about $400–500 per month. According to the new one, I get about $1,500–1,600. This is how I have been living in Jordan with my family since I had to leave Iraq for the second time. I am still the only breadwinner here because my sons were not successful at finding a job. The economy is harsh and the competition is fierce. The locals usually do not hire Iraqis who are not extremely qualified professionals or academics. Most Iraqis living here are either extremely qualified and in high demand, or they simply live on their money and pensions like in my case now.

Ghadeer's story, like others before, captures the destructive effects of de-Ba'athification that were applied under strictly sectarian terms on academics and society at large. In fact, to close, it is crucial to provide some statistics on some of the most destructive effects of de-Ba'athification on society in general. First, it is estimated that between 50,000 and 100,000 civil servants and public sector employees, including doctors and teachers, were removed from their positions as a result of de-Ba'athification (Ferguson 2007). This number includes more than 12,000 teachers as well as school principals who were removed from the Ministry of Education rolls. The impact was so detrimental that many areas—mainly Sunni—were left with no more than one or two teachers per any given school (Chandrasekaran 2006: 83). This is not because most former Ba'athists were Sunnis but, as demonstrated earlier, because de-Ba'athification was disproportionately applied to Sunnis in much more severe ways than others.

The Iraqi diplomat, Feisal al-Istrabadi, who had a role in drafting the Transitional Administrative Law of 2004, criticized Bremer's de-Ba'athification for capturing "a large number of people who were innocent of any wrongdoing by any objective measure and were deprived of the ability to earn a living and support their families," and which, in turn, fed insurgency. Al-Istrabadi criticized the fact that even though most Ba'athists were Shi'a, the Sunnis were disproportionately removed from offices and public sector jobs. He stated that it was "de-Sunnification" rather than "de-Ba'athification" (Al-Istrabadi 2008). Likewise, other scholars have pointed out the same. De-Ba'athification:

> came to be perceived as a "de-sunnization" of Iraqi institutions and society a collective punishment by the new Shi'i master and their allies, the Kurds. On the other side, opponents of the process were characterized as frustrated Ba'thists refusing to lose their grip on power and Iraqi resources.
>
> (Tejel et al. 2012: 191)

As for the direct impact on Iraqi higher education and academics in particular, de-Ba'athification and its effects can best be captured in the words of the American neoconservative, John Agresto, who served as a Coalition Provisional Authority (CPA) Senior Advisor to the Ministry of Higher Education and Scientific Research in Baghdad. Agresto saw the destruction of Iraqi academia and society after the war as "the opportunity for a clean start." He also infamously noted that, prior to going on his "mission" to Iraq, he did not know anything about the country and purposely did not read about it. As Rajiv Chandrasekaran wrote, Agresto:

> knew next to nothing about Iraq's educational system. Even after he was selected, the former professor didn't read a single book about Iraq. "I wanted to come here with as open a mind as I could have," he said. "I'd much rather learn firsthand than have it filtered to me by an author."
>
> (Chandrasekaran 2006: 58)

On the subject of such willful ignorance, Naomi Klein comments:

> If Agresto had read a book or two, he might have thought twice about the need to erase everything and start over. He could have learned, for instance, that before the sanctions strangled the country, Iraq had the best education system in the region, with the highest literacy rates in the Arab

world—in 1985, 89 percent of Iraqis were literate. By contrast, in Agresto's home state of New Mexico, 46 percent of the population is functionally illiterate, and 20 percent are unable do "basic math to determine the total on a sales receipt."... Yet Agresto was so convinced of the superiority of American systems that he seemed unable to entertain the possibility that Iraqis might want to salvage and protect their own culture and that they might feel its destruction as a wrenching loss. This neocolonialist blindness is a running theme in the War on Terror.

(Klein 2007: 338)

Agresto wrote a book about his experiences and the "failure of good intentions in Iraq." Besides the many lines in which he clearly articulates a neocolonial, superior, and misinformed tone about Iraq, its people, and its education system, Agresto consistently uses the word "liberalize" when describing or explaining the actions and decisions he took to restructure Iraqi higher education. In one instance, he writes: "Working with the CPA legal office, our office cobbled together what amounted to a Bill of Rights to the universities" (Agresto 2007: 88). He then writes: "The Bill of Rights declared that the goal of higher education was to promote a broader capacity for thinking, accepting the opinion of others, and encouraging the search for the truth" (Agresto 2007: 88). Here, one is prompted to ask, do Iraqis lack the "capacity to think"? Think like whom? Do they lack the capacity to "accept the opinions of others"? Whose opinions? Search for "truth"? Whose truth? The answer is unwittingly provided by Agresto on the same page as he writes about the impact of this "Bill of Rights" that led Iraqi administrators in higher education to feel "empowered to enforce academic freedom" (Agresto 2007: 88). This statement contains a shocking linguistic oxymoron: How can one "enforce" any type of "freedom"? Doesn't freedom cease to be so, when it is "enforced"?

Finally, another scholarly work on "de-Ba'athification" and its effects on Iraqi academics and higher education is a chapter titled "Writing the History of Iraq: The Fallacy of 'Objective' History" by Johan Franzén (Tejel et al. 2012). The work is relevant for this book and acts as a good response to Agresto's book. In it, Franzén looks closely at how the CPA devised and implemented the cleansing policies of "de-Ba'athification" as a way to rewrite Iraq's history and to "transform the recipients of this 'new history' into malleable pro-Western youngsters ready to accept 'democracy' and American liberalism" (Tejel et al. 2012: 32). While this has already been confirmed by many interlocutors, Franzén's work is important because it provides insights into how post-conflict regimes deal with history, and therefore it emphasizes the relationship between academia and politics as a global rather than simply an Iraqi dilemma. The author provides brief comparisons between the Iraqi case and others, like Rwanda, post-apartheid South Africa, Bosnia, Northern Ireland, and others. In doing so, he shows that, in all these cases, the "common denominator is that education, and above all history teaching, has been seen as a vehicle to achieve political objectives" (Tejel et al. 2012: 33).

Although the Baʿath regime, like the post-occupation regimes, did attempt to rewrite history during its own time in power, Franzén reminds us that history education "serving nationalist objectives is not a novel concept—it pre-dated the Baʿthi regime by many decades, and it is a familiar phenomenon in the wider Arab world. Rather than viewing it as a cunning scheme to dupe the young generation," Franzén argues that "it is necessary to nuance the picture somewhat and recognize some of the positive effects of nationalist education for an artificially created state" (Tejel et al. 2012: 35). While this point is valid, it must be taken even further by acknowledging that, Iraq is no more an "artificial state" than, for example, the USA, the UK, Australia, Canada, Switzerland, or any other country. If we look at the history of any nation, no nation is "purer" or "less artificial" than another. In this way, every state is made up and all borders are artificial, but that does not negate the geographical, historical, and social connections that bind people either within the current so-called artificial borders, or even beyond these borders in neighboring areas. As such, it is important to understand that to "'de-nationalize history teaching entirely more or less equals going back to square one as most history instruction in Iraqi history has been nationalist and anti-Western" (Tejel et al. 2012: 43). This project of post-occupation history rewriting was done in the most problematic way. For example, Franzén writes, "Fuʾad Husayin, who headed the post-invasion textbook revision team, admitted that he had been instructed to consider anything anti-American found in textbooks as propaganda and these passages were subsequently removed" (Tejel et al. 2012: 44). Franzén sees that these practices ironically are similar to what the Baʿathist regime did in the past, and since the Iraqi historical memory was always anti-imperial and therefore anti-American, such practices, rather than solve the problem, will complicate things further.

All of these factors matter when we think about de-Ba'athification as a cleansing method that forced many academics and other Iraqis into exile. They matter because they show that the occupation and the subsequent governments it put in place paved the way into exile for many Iraqis who refused to play by the rules of the new game. It shows that "exile" cannot be understood separately from the power relations that produce it in the space from which exiled people come from. It also cannot be separated from the new power relations under which they now exist in their new locations. Exile is not just the location where exiled people are today, it is also everything that happened before arriving at their current destination.

5

Lives under Contract:
The Transition to the Corporate University

EXILE STARTS AT HOME

Before the end of my first week in Duhok in Iraqi Kurdistan in September 2015, one of my relatives offered to introduce me to an academic whose positionality is unique, as she told me:

> He is fluent in Kurdish, but he is an Arab from Kurdistan. He was educated in Baghdad and lived and taught in Baghdad and Amman before he eventually had to move back "home" when his contract was not renewed in Jordan.

I learned that this individual knew almost every displaced academic at the university where he taught, and so he could introduce me to many more.

Within a few days, after some phone calls, I was sitting in the office of Sattar D., an academic in the field of computer science, who was also serving his last days as the coordinator for his department at the time. When I arrived, he was sitting with another Kurdish female academic, Sheelan, from the same department. They were conversing in Arabic, even though they were both from the Kurdistan region and were fluent in Kurdish. That was because Sattar had been educated and had lived for many years in Baghdad and later in Jordan. Sheelan had studied and lived in Mosul. I greeted both and sat down, listening to the conversation already in progress. Sattar was about to finish his term as a department coordinator and hand his responsibilities over to Sheelan. They had been meeting for him to train her. They spent the next half hour jumping from one topic to another: the state of private education in Duhok and the Kurdistan region in general.

112

They discussed how their children are better off being in public high schools because the quality of education "is still better in these schools than in private ones." They talked about how private education is a "scam" just to drain people's wallets without providing "quality" or any promise for better jobs in the future.

After Sheelan left the office, Sattar and I talked about my research for this book. He was delighted to hear about it: "This project is almost about my life story," he said. He promised to do everything possible to help introduce me to many internally displaced academics he knew in his department, his university, and even in other nearby private universities in Duhok. "This university is filled with internally displaced academics. There are even more of them in private universities. They basically carry most universities in this region on their shoulders." He then joked by using an Iraqi expression that indicates the high quantity of something, "If you throw any stone randomly on any campus in Kurdistan, it would probably hit an internally displaced academic."

In the following two hours, Sattar shared part of his journey from Baghdad, to exile in Amman, and then back to Kurdistan: "I have been through all the cycles of exile and displacement you are looking for in your work." Sattar holds a BSc. and MSc. in computer science from Baghdad University obtained between the end of the 1970s and the early 1980s. Despite not having a PhD in the field, he has authored and co-authored a few books, which he proudly displayed in his office. He said that he knew many academics who have been through multiple exiles and multiple displacements. Many, he emphasized, rotate from one to the other in endless cycles. Sattar's journey between Jordan and Kurdistan was helpful to map out the key themes and patterns in the lives of this population in post-2003 Iraq. In fact, much of what he described were issues I had discovered during my summer field research in Jordan one year before. Moreover, I had noticed many of those issues during my first week in Iraqi Kurdistan.

First, I was struck by the similarities and differences he shared about his experiences in Jordan versus Kurdistan. His narrative showed that the boundaries between exile and internal displacement overlap in significant ways. Sattar spoke at length about how exiled and displaced academics in both sites have one thing in common: their lives are tied to precarious annual contracts that may or may not be renewed each year. Consequently, their residency status, crucial for them to stay safe in these places, is also tied to the renewal of these contracts: "No contract, no residency. Without residency, you have few if any options left for your safety." Such academics as those displaced from Mosul, under ISIS at the time of research and writing, would have no place to go to if their contracts were not renewed. Therefore, not having a contract renewed is akin to a "death sentence," if they do not immediately find another contract. It is like the sectarianism described in Chapter 4, in the sense that it is yet another form of "necropolitics" that determines who lives and who dies, who stays and who leaves. The "contract" is essential for living. It is a constant source of fear and sleepless nights. This, Sattar said, is precisely what had happened to him after ten years of hard work in Jordan, after which they did not renew his contract and so he had to leave.

The second issue that is critical for Sattar was struggling with language as a metonym that seriously shapes the lives of these academics and their families in these spaces. He is an Arab from the Kurdistan region. It may sound like an oxymoron, "but we have always existed in this region," he told me. Although he speaks Kurdish fluently, and therefore his suffering with language is less intense, very few displaced Arab academics speak the language. In fact, in this entire research, I have only met one other displaced academic who spoke Kurdish fluently. Still, in Sattar's case, he struggles because of his Arab identity: "I look a bit darker than average Kurds, so I get profiled and interrogated at checkpoints often when I go from here to Erbil. Once they hear me speak Kurdish, they leave me alone. It still hurts." Many interlocutors (especially Arabs) in Jordan and in Kurdistan shared with me the fact that being in Jordan feels less "foreign" and "alienating" for them than being in Iraqi Kurdistan. In this way, the exile feels more like a "home" for these Arab academics than internal displacement within Iraq.

As I got to know Sattar over time, I learned that one of the biggest challenges for these academics is not simply the exile or the internal displacement but, more importantly, the new academic conditions that come with them. Sattar spoke about how the Iraqi academic, who previously lived and functioned under an academic system within a central secular state is now having to cope with mushrooming private and greedy for-profit universities. "This makes the effects of exile much worse and more alienating than they would otherwise be." This transition comes with significant new pressures, complexities, and new academic and social challenges. Jordan, where he lived and taught from 1999 until 2009, was the beginning of his experience with exile before even returning to Kurdistan.

Sattar initially chose Jordan over Kurdistan because of the language and the cultural factors but eventually had no choice but to return "home." Returning "home" in his case was a less desired option. During our last visit together, while driving in the streets of Duhok on a rainy day, Sattar said that he couldn't wait to retire and leave the region for another Arab country where he could feel "less alienated." Speaking about his ten years in Jordan, Sattar said that living under an annual contract that determines one's entire life and existence,

> you feel a constant economic and job insecurity ... I often felt like a weak man with no will. When I went to an official institution to do paperwork, I needed to change my manners and ethics so that I did not upset the officials or natives of the country who could easily deny my residency.

At the same time, it makes academics work extremely hard, "almost to the point of exhaustion and collapse lest you lose your contract." Still, after ten years of living like this, his contract in Jordan was terminated. All the compromises did not guarantee renewal. Sattar explained how contract renewals in Jordan worked,

> the university where you work has to give you its blessings, send your paperwork to the Office of Civic Services, then to the Directorate of Labor, then to Intelligence Services. All these filtering parties must review your paperwork and approve it for that contract to be renewed. Just for one more year.

In the end, Sattar was lucky that one of his best friends could help him get a job in a public university here in Kurdistan. Yet, the suffering has not ended, it has simply changed colors. "It used to be an academic struggle in Jordan, now it is both an academic and a social struggle here. It is hard to be an Arab in this region," he emphasized.

Sattar's narrative is hardly an individual case. In fact, it captures the most central issues that emerged in my research in summer 2014 in Jordan and later in Iraqi Kurdistan. As such, it is critical to examine closely these key challenges, particularly what I call "lives under contract" and the transition of exiled Iraqi academics into the corporate private universities to understand how the post-2003 academics live in these new spaces and how their "contracts" shape their social and political existence. I argue that rather than just viewing these as entailing precarious economic conditions, they are also significant political tools that seriously undermine the freedom of living, teaching, and writing for these academics. The issue of living under contracts becomes ever more crucial when considered in connection to the increasing contingent and insecure academic jobs in neoliberal and corporatized university systems in Western countries. To keep academics insecure and under precarious contracts is guaranteed to silence their intellectual freedoms in writing, teaching, and thinking.

In Jordan and Kurdistan, academics are forced to deal with the shift from formerly public Iraqi universities prior to 2003 to mostly private universities that hire them under short-term contracts. Here we must ask: what do Jordan and Iraqi Kurdistan have in common when it comes to this shift from public to a private, for-profit higher education? Both sites have Western-friendly regimes that have adopted the current Western neoliberal market models as a form of governance in many walks of life, including higher education. This factor is precisely what connects the experiences of academics in both sites. While the situation in Jordan is slightly better in some ways, academics in both locations expressed great concerns about the privatization and corporatization of higher education.

Given my direct experience with US academia, I saw that many of the issues raised and shared in the testimonies included in this chapter are inseparable from the neoliberal corporatization that has been taking over worldwide, which has spilled over into the Middle East. The Iraqi case, however, captures how the corporatization of the university creates more severe and precarious conditions for countries and areas experiencing war, violence, and occupation. Furthermore, many interlocutors who have also studied and researched in different countries in the Middle East and the world noted that the decline of academia is a global issue rather than a problem limited to the Iraqi or Middle Eastern context. Many said that, nowadays, even Iraqis who return after obtaining their higher education in the USA and Europe are not half as qualified as they used to be in previous decades. Interviewees attributed this fact to the worsening standards of education even in the West because of the corporatization of higher education.

It goes without saying that a plethora of literature on this subject has been produced in the West.

Just within the context of this work, a survey of case studies on the status of academia in the Middle East reveals alarming challenges. These challenges are especially relevant when it comes to silencing intellectual freedoms of writing, teaching, thinking, and social mobility. It is critical to consider the hardships experienced in academic settings in the Middle East as part of the suffocating effects of neoliberal and corporate forms of governance coming from the West itself. Likewise, curtailing academic freedoms of Middle Eastern academics hired as contingent labor is inseparable from the lack of freedoms experienced by Western academics hired as contingent labor at different universities. After 2001, the market-driven commercialization of knowledge became a key factor in the reconfiguration of higher education in America, particularly suppressing knowledge related to Middle East issues (Doumani 2006).

As some researchers have shown, the changes sweeping the academy worldwide are generally imposed by the US academy, which is an "imperial university." As such, in "all imperial and colonial nations, intellectuals and scholarship play an important role—directly or indirectly, willingly or unwittingly—in legitimizing American exceptionalism and rationalizing US expansionism and repression, domestically and globally" (Chatterjee and Maira 2014: 6–7).

In an edited volume produced by multiple interdisciplinary higher education experts from different Middle Eastern countries titled *World Yearbook of Education 2010*, the contributors sound alarm bells about the destructive effects of this trend on academia in many Arab countries (Mazawi and Sultana 2010). Notable chapters in the volume include "Going International: The Politics of Educational Reform in Egypt," by Iman Farag in which he examines how the "internationalization" of higher education in Egypt has seriously undermined the mission of the university. Farag shows how higher education, which was made a social and political right for Egyptian citizens to advance in society following the 1952 anti-monarchist revolution, is now being turned into "a negotiable relationship between the student and the State; it is no longer a systematic commitment of public institutions towards students" (Mazawi and Sultana 2010: 29). This dangerous shift, the author argues, significantly undermines the university's mission in alleviating class differences or allowing social mobility for the disadvantaged.

In "American Dreams of Reinventing the 'Orient': Digital Democracy and Arab Youth Cultures in a Regional Perspective," Omar al-Khairy uses the notion of "smart power" to capture the:

> synergetic interaction between ideological and armed combat and its interface with broad notions of education, as identities and modes of being. Such a relationship suggests that while "there can ultimately be no military solutions to political wars," violence is nevertheless "not only still a viable option, but also necessary one."
>
> (Mazawi and Sultana 2010: 32)

Khairy shows how "predatory capitalism" that effectively combines the "welfare state" and the "warfare state," works as a method to attain "benevolent supremacy" (Mazawi and Sultana 2010).

In "Palestinians, Education, and Israeli 'Industry of Fear,'" Nadera Shalhoub-Kevorkian examines the Israeli–Palestinian conflict, focusing on its impact of delivering education in militarized zones from the perspectives of the dominated and the displaced populations. With unsafe and militarized conditions, the author argues that the spaces in which these people receive education are far from "neutral havens." Indeed,

> education becomes a highly politicized and political project, one that provides fodder for the creation of an "industry of fear" and "terror," racializing Palestinians as people to be feared. Such constructs generate modes of racism that effectively exclude access to schooling in the interests of "security considerations."
>
> (Mazawi and Sultana 2010: 32–33)

The author argues that Israel's presumed "war on terror" becomes a "convenient umbrella that obfuscates and camouflages atrocities, including the obstruction of access to education precisely because education grants Palestinians the intellectual tools required to liberate themselves from oppression" (Mazawi and Sultana 2010: 32–33). Based on these factors and conditions, Shalhoub-Kevorkian maintains:

> In the face of the loss of land and the cumulative loss of rights and dignity, education becomes a central factor in shaping, reproducing, and repre-

senting Palestinian identity as well as a key source of hope for the future, both individually and collectively.

(Mazawi and Sultana 2010: 32–33)

The issues above are crucial not only because they come up frequently in the testimonies of exiled Iraqi academics throughout this chapter, but also because they show the serious consequences and the precariousness of the neoliberal policies governing today's corporate universities worldwide rather than just in the Iraqi or Middle Eastern context.

LIVES UNDER CONTRACT: THE CORPORATE UNIVERSITY IN JORDAN

In May 2014, I was on my way to Amman, Jordan. I had to jump on three different planes to reach my destination. I was excited to go to Jordan because since leaving Iraq in 2005, that was the second closest I had been to Iraq. In 2013, I had gone to Turkey to see my parents whom I had not seen for seven years and it felt good to be close to home, even if I was not quite there. Jordan was going to be a similar experience. I felt that life was playing tricks on me by bringing me as close as possible to Iraq, but never quite to it. On the long flight from Washington, DC to Dubai, I thought how the lives of exiled people are like being on a flight. They are up in the air, between land and sky, not knowing when and whether they will ever land somewhere. In Dubai, I had a few hours of transit. Once again, I thought how transits are like the lives of many dislocated people like myself. The storyline from my experience often goes like this: a disaster befalls the place you call "home." You leave for another place hoping it will be just a temporary wait. Sometimes, the second destination is so harsh and unforgiving that you think of it as a "temporary transit" and keep looking for a "final" station that can grant you at least the basic human rights with some dignity. Over time, the temporary becomes permanent. But, deep inside, your feelings, senses, and existence may not cooperate with your new permanent reality. And so, you may find yourself in a state that can be best described as "permanently temporary." You become divided and torn deep inside constantly hearing two voices: one voice tells you that it is all temporary no matter how long it takes; and a second voice tells you not to believe the first one as this is your permanent destiny.

Going through these phases, the most difficult thing I have discovered, as some of my friends in similar situations have also shared, is to meet people who downplay or outright dismiss the significance of that "home" you still hope to reconnect with one day in the near or distant future. When I asked many interviewees about their biggest difficulties in exile, they shared that the problem for exiled people is that they did not sign up for it. They did not choose it. It was never on their agenda or their radar, not even in their wildest dreams or nightmares. One academic once told me: "Generally, Iraqis love traveling but not immigrating. This is why many of us find it hard to cope, let alone reconcile with migration and exile. We never asked for it. It happened to us against our will." Of course, "exile" and "displacement" are by definition against one's will. When they are no longer so, wouldn't they cease to be called so?

When I arrived in Amman, the dark curtain of the night had already covered the city. The shining lights of the distant houses on the way from Queen Alias International Airport to the city were like stars—far away, twinkling, and impossible to capture with my hands or eyes. I was exhausted and barely awake. The taxi driver from the airport was a Jordanian of Palestinian origin. I wondered then whether it is always my destiny to bump into exiled people everywhere I went. The driver quickly knew I was an Iraqi from the Arabic dialect and started:

> You know, there are more Palestinians in Jordan than Jordanians. And now, with all the Iraqi, Libyan, and Syrian refugees, we are officially not a country, but simply one big refugee camp. This place is really a big concentration camp for many refugees now. Stupid Arab regimes thought this was only a Palestinian problem. They did not know that each Arab country was on the list to be turned into the next Palestine.

Taxi drivers are some of my best friends in every city I visit. I wish to write a book on my encounters with taxi drivers in the Middle East one day. They see so much. They encounter all kinds of people. They learn to interact with people of different politics, backgrounds, gender, views, feelings, and even accents and dialects. In a sense, they are exposed to people in ways that any novelist, poet, anthropologist, or journalist would love to be. They are usually some of the best guides that hold the keys to the hidden secrets, especially the "dirty secrets" of the cities where they live and work. Throughout that summer in Jordan, I found that most taxi drivers were of Palestinian origin. They are poor and always looking for the slightest chance to earn an extra Jordanian dinar. They are usually well informed about the politics of the region. Many would welcome me upon hearing my Iraqi dialect. However, I discovered over time that it was not an unconditional welcome.

Many Jordanians, particularly of Palestinian origin, had favorable views of the former Iraqi Ba'ath party. Many people in the street loved Saddam Hussein and saw him as a hero who had done so much for the Arab world and was eventually killed by "traitors." In fact, in some taxis, I saw pictures of Saddam Hussein displayed on dashboards. In certain places outside Amman, I saw Saddam Hussein's picture in small kiosks and cafés. One day, on my way to a private university on the outskirts of Amman, I was surprised to see a roadside café named "Martyr Saddam Hussein's Café." On another occasion, when I was on a university bus heading to yet another private university on the outskirts of Amman, the bus driver had two framed pictures on his dashboard: one of King Abdullah II of Jordan and the other of Saddam Hussein. The reaction of many Jordanians of Palestinian origin to an Iraqi depended on whether the Iraqi was deemed favorable to Saddam Hussein. If not, their tone would change, they would become a bit distant and, sometimes, stop the conversation altogether. In Iraq, people usually are careful about what they say in front of taxi drivers because they are widely considered "informants" working for the intelligence services.

After some searching around the Amman neighborhood, the taxi driver from the airport helped me find the exact location of the place where I was going to stay, gave me his phone number in case I needed him, and disappeared in the dark. Within a few days, through a friend, also an academic, I connected with a few exiled academics living and teaching in Jordan. By my third day in Amman, I was on my way to a private university to meet with Kareem K., an academic of media and journalism introduced previously. On the way to see Kareem, I looked at Amman's streets and views. It is a beautiful city and the weather was still mild at the end of May, although the spring grass and wildflowers were almost totally dry. The scenery, the vegetation, particularly the cypress and pine trees, the hilly nature of the city, the mountainous areas outside of Amman, reminded me of northern Iraq. The gardens of many houses reminded me of Baghdad's meticulous and well-kept gardens. The neighborhood where I stayed, *Um Uthaina*, had a significant number of exiled Iraqi families, mostly professionals and people with some wealth allowing them to live in houses rather than in refugee camps. Even exile comes with variations of privileges for the rich and the poor. Even "loss" can be more comfortable for some classes of society than for others. Other things in Jordan reminded me of Iraq, including the old neighborhoods and the bazaars in and around the city center, and the taste of fruit and vegetables. There were many Iraqi restaurants and neighborhoods with a great number of Iraqi families in Amman. One academic who had lived in northern Iraq before said that Amman looks like some parts of Iraq, except the difference is that Jordan suffers from a shortage of water. I met a few academics whose job in Jordan was doing research on water conservation. One of them told me that she had an opportunity to choose between an academic job in Jordan or in Iraqi Kurdistan, but she chose Jordan because of the language factor. "I went to Kurdistan for a few visits and it was more foreign and alienating there because of the Kurdish language. Being an Arab there is an abomination," she said.

Many interlocutors told me that they loved being in Jordan because of its geographical proximity and resemblance to some parts of Iraq, which makes them feel more "at home." I heard almost the exact same words multiple times. "Here, I feel I can keep an eye on Iraq," was a common sentiment that was expressed, indicating how geographical proximity makes Iraqi exiles feel more engaged and involved in what is happening on the ground in Iraq. Some took solace in the fact that in Jordan they can still teach exiled Iraqi students, which reminded them of their lost academic and social lives in Iraq. Some said that the short distance between Jordan and Iraq allowed them to find different ways to stay informed about the political developments in Iraq, or to have their family and relatives come visit them in Jordan. In a way, Jordan allows many exiled Iraqi academics and professionals to practice a form of "long distance nationalism" (Schiller and Fouron 2001) by allowing exiled people across the border from their homeland to continue to participate in the academic, political, economic, social, and religious affairs in their homeland, if at a remove. They do so while at the same time making important contributions in Jordan.

Being on the border makes this much more possible than being too far away from it or being inside where they could be killed. Having been living in the USA for nearly 15 years, I know how far and disconnected it feels from what is happening in the region. By the time I wake up in the USA, the day is almost over in the Middle East. The events of the day have already unfolded. I wake up to simply learn about "what happened" rather than engage—or participate—in events *as* they are happening. I feel punished by "time" and "space" every day.

Despite the geographical proximity of Jordan to Iraq, the situation of Iraqi academics and professionals in Jordan remains painful because of the political, economic, and social ramifications. This is a vital population of Iraqi society being held hostage so to speak across the border without being able to make its full contributions to their society. Their contribution to Jordanian society, while vital, is constrained. When I met the former Cultural Attaché at the Iraqi Embassy in Amman, Sabir N., he furnished me with useful figures that add a quantitative layer to the qualitative aspects of this complex dilemma. He said on our first meeting:

> Here in Amman we have many professionals and Iraqi academics who could otherwise really help Iraqi society stand on its feet. To give you an idea, toward the end of my time at the Embassy, we had 325 exiled academics. Ten percent of them were jobless because there is no demand for their specialties. Here, they hire based on demand in terms of specialty ... Also, the priority is naturally given to Jordanian citizens. This is fair. But because most of the Iraqi academics here are trained in the USA and Britain, universities do like to hire them to benefit from their expertise. In Jordan, there are 10 public universities and 21 private ones. The policies of the former differ somewhat from the latter. The difference is in such things as standards, attitude, and the quality and make up of faculty. Not all universities here have the same level of excellence. Some are known for their good standards, like the German Jordanian University, which is a public university. The University of Science and Technology in Irbid and the Jordanian University are also highly respected. In private universities, the issue is different. The level of excellence varies from one university to another and from one department to another within the same university. Besides the academics, we have about 75 doctors. Most doctors here cannot practice. They live on pensions. The same is true of academics. The new pension law in Iraq for academics is attractive and pays about $2,500 per month, if you have a service of 25 years or more.

Sabir's statistics are important because they show that a significant number of exiled academics are not able to get jobs, and for them to be able to stay in the "safe haven" of exile, they have to live on their own pensions and savings. When considered in connection with how many of them were threatened to leave Iraq and are unable to get jobs in Jordan, this becomes a case of what can be termed as "disabled academics," whose academic lives have been cut short. Many interviewees, as demonstrated in the following testimonies, raised this issue.

* * *

When I arrived at Kareem's university, he met me by the guarded gate and walked me to his office. Right outside it there was a framed image of Arabic calligraphy that read: "Our dreams wouldn't have died had we not watered them with procrastination." I took a special interest not in the meaning of the phrase, but in how it was worded. At a private, for-profit university, this seems like a pessimistic way of putting it. I thought if this was displayed in a private, corporate setting in America, it would have been phrased in a more "optimistic" way—something like "Water your dreams with hard work not with procrastination." However, there was something sad in the suggestion of defeat in this framed image. The writing is in the past tense. The dreams have been watered with procrastination. They were already dead. The writer of the phrase is just wishing that this was not the case. Languages, in many ways, are living cells in cultures. They are like DNA storing traces of what happened, what is happening, and what could have or should have happened.

In the office, Kareem welcomed me warmly with a piece of baklava and a cup of tea. He then introduced me to some of his staff. Many academics and students in his department were exiled Iraqis, which made it an ideal setting for me during that summer. His office was spacious and well furnished. There was a big desk with a comfortable-looking chair behind it and a vase with plastic flowers in it. He had his own secretary, a friendly and cordial young Jordanian woman whose dream, she later told me, was to visit the USA one day to pursue an MBA. On the wall, right behind the chair where Kareem sat, there were three framed pictures: on the right, one of Crown Prince Hussein bin Abdullah; in the middle, the picture of his father, the current king, Abdullah II of Jordan; and on the left a picture of King Abdullah's father, the late King Hussein. These pictures were displayed in every institution, office, or public office in Jordan. They reminded me of Saddam

Hussein's framed pictures displayed in the same manner in every public institution, classroom, or office in Iraq during the Ba'ath era. The same exact practice is still followed today in Iraqi Kurdistan with the pictures of Kurdistan's President Masoud al-Barzani or his late father, Mullah Mustafa al-Barzani, and Jalal al-Talbani. The pictures of the first two figures are usually found in places controlled and dominated by the Kurdistan Democratic Party (KDP) in cities like the capital Erbil or Duhok; whereas the picture of the last figure is found in areas dominated by the Patriotic Union of Kurdistan (PUK) in cities like Kirkuk and Sulaimania.

While Kareem was sitting at his desk speaking on the phone, I looked at the three pictures of the Jordanian royal family members hanging above him, it made me think of how power is always over one's head, watching from above in many parts of the world. It occurred to me that this moment perhaps captures the complexity of the relationship between academics and the powers under which they live. I also thought how often these framed pictures hanging on the walls, right over the heads of Iraqi academics and professionals, have changed over the last few decades. With every change, these academics are forced to totally reinvent themselves, adopt a new "public transcript" (Scott 1990), and invent new survival tactics. The window in his office, rather than facing a nice sunny view, faced another big room, which was used as a space for Muslim prayers. It was one of the most unusual views from a department chair's office I had ever seen. I could clearly see many academics and students coming to the room and praying. Kareem, too, excused himself at every prayer time to go there and pray. Often when sitting in his office, I could hear the whispering lips of men praying. With the royal family pictures over his head and the prayer room right outside of his office window, I couldn't help thinking about an academic sandwiched between two eternally complex issues in any Middle Eastern university setting: politics and religion. Or, even more problematic, politicized religion in places ravaged by sectarianism like in Lebanon, Syria, and post-2003 Iraq.

Kareem said he had been chairing the department for the last two years. During our conversations, students often came into his office asking about grades, exams, and other academic and administrative matters. He seemed like a celebrity academic who was loved by most students, an observation that was further confirmed as I later attended some of his lectures in the classroom. I spent much time with him, observing how he lived his daily life. Kareem talked about his early days in Amman. He said that although he arrived in 2004, because of the occupation, he was unable to find a job until 2009. Between 2004 and 2009, he had to live on some savings and do some odd and menial jobs to survive. Even these odd jobs became harder to find over time because of the influx of refugees:

> Today, it is incredibly hard to find jobs in Jordan, especially if you are a working-class person. There is fierce competition, bitterness, and hatred between working-class Jordanians and Syrian refugees as we speak. These groups are competing for very limited resources. This creates animosity. The Iraqis, and the Libyans who arrived after, are usually not part of this competition because when they come here, they either have enough money to be allowed entry into Jordan or they are highly qualified and not competing for labor jobs. In the case of Libyans, many Jordanians despise them because some come with a lot of money and act with great self-entitlement. Of course, this does not apply to all. I have many wonderful Libyan students, who are brilliant and respectful.

I later discovered that at the time of my research, an Iraqi was only allowed residence in Jordan if they could deposit $50,000 in a Jordanian bank, or deposit $25,000 and own property. Some said that these conditions are subject to change annually. This is the government's way of ensuring that these people have enough funds to sustain themselves in Jordan. In a way, arguably, even some exiles are operating according to the corporate, capitalist business model. In 2009, through one of his prominent former professors in Baghdad (also now exiled in Jordan), Kareem was able to find his current academic job at this private university in Amman. "This university provided me with much-needed social prestige in Jordan. Being in exile, it is much better to say that you teach at a university than being jobless."

However, the most difficult thing for Kareem, like for many others, is the fact that they are almost exclusively hired by private universities and public universities in Jordan (and in Kurdistan) are seen as "more prestigious" and usually come with more job stability. As a result, public universities tend to prefer hiring "locals," which means Jordanians in Jordan and Kurds in Kurdistan, with few exceptions. Private universities, on the other hand, are for-profit and operate on annual contracts that may or may not be renewed. These tend to hire more qualified Iraqi and other Arab academics from countries like Egypt, Lebanon, and Syria. Since the Syrian war, there has been an influx of Syrian academics coming to Jordan seeking jobs and safety. There were already two exiled Syrian academics in Kareem's department at the time of my research. Kareem said: "The pay is good, but the job security is absolutely frightening."

Based on what Kareem and others shared, existence under such contracts is a double-edged sword: it can help you survive under expensive and unforgiving exile conditions. It can save your life after escaping war, threats, and violence, as most Iraqi academics experienced after 2003. However, when contracts are not renewed, which happens often and unexpectedly, academics are immediately disposed of with no income to live on, and with no place to go to if they don't get another contract with another university as quickly as possible. This, in turn, automatically terminates their residency status in Jordan as it does with Arab academics in Iraqi Kurdistan. Their salaries, their homes, and living standards in an expensive country like Jordan are relatively comfortable, but only so long as that contract gets renewed at the end of the year. Furthermore, the conditions that determine which contracts are renewed and which are not are dependent on many factors, as Kareem noted:

> These factors are governed by market forces. Some disciplines are more marketable and in high demand at private universities than others. The market's demands change from one year to another, which also changes who is hired, and whose contracts are renewed or terminated. It also depends on political factors such as the exiled academics' politics, sect, and how much they are liked or disliked by the department. If they do not like your politics, sect, or way of thinking, they can terminate you using the market demand as an excuse. There is also another factor which combines politics and economics. In difficult economic times, they can easily terminate Iraqi academics to replace them with Jordanians.

This comment reveals the complex ties between the economic and political aspects of these contracts, but more disturbingly, it reveals the extent to which privatized and corporatized universities deal with knowledge as a commodity to be bought and sold or even removed from the market altogether. One academic I met had a PhD in Arabic and Islamic studies. After her contract was not renewed, she was jobless and simply relying on her husband's work, also on a contract in Amman: "If his contract doesn't get renewed next year, we are done," she told me.

* * *

The issue of temporary contracts is just the tip of the iceberg. On July 6, 2014, I was on my way to meet with Sura M., an architectural engineer and a department chair at one of Jordan's best private universities in the field of engineering. Sura, introduced in Chapter 2, identified as a Shi'a who is married to a Sunni. She arrived in Jordan in 2006, after receiving a death threat in 2005 in Baghdad. When I arrived in her office, it looked much like Kareem's office in that it was tidy and decorated with nice furniture. At this time, I had already started to see a pattern of so many sad stories hiding behind fancy office furniture. I spent the entire day with Sura to see how she lived and interacted with students and staff. She said:

> exiled Iraqi academics turned out to be a blessing for Jordan and many Arab countries, because they now make the core of some of the best private universities in the Arab world. In fact, they have built from scratch many universities in places like the UAE and even here in Jordan. When I first arrived here, this department was at the bottom of the list in terms of competitiveness in architectural engineering. Now it is at the top of the list. It is second only to the Jordanian University, which is the best public university in the country.

While in her office, I observed Sura as a hardworking woman who showed exceptional skills in adapting to different life situations. She was firm and assertive when she spoke to staff and students who came by to ask for instruction. She seemed uncompromising when students came asking for favors. When one student came by asking whether she would mark her down on a paper for not having addressed part of a question, Sura told her that sadly there was nothing she could do to help her. When the student left, I asked Sura: "Do you fail students?" She said with emphasis:

> I do not fail students. Students fail if they do not work hard. They fail if they do not take their work seriously. I have always resisted this impulse at private universities to treat them as customers. This is one of the hardest

things for Iraqi academics to deal with in these for-profit universities in Jordan.

It also caught my attention that she was speaking in a Jordanian dialect: "You get extra respect when you speak in their dialect," she told me. As we discussed stages of her past academic life in Iraq, she tried to steer away from the sad memories there.

> Despite the dangerous situation in Iraq, I always made sure to go swimming. Nothing stopped me from practicing my hobbies in Baghdad. I learned how to be firm from my father, who was an Iraqi diplomat in France. He taught me never to compromise no matter how tough life gets. I miss my father so much. He left a big gap in my life. He died in Baghdad while I was here. The sectarian violence was at its climax then. I could not attend his funeral. I will never recover from this wound.

When we started chatting about the Jordanian chapter of her life, she said: "Exile gave me even more independence and added strength to my personality as a woman." She went on,

> but the real feeling of exile comes from the fact that our lives are tied to contracts here. Once these contracts are terminated, everything is over … My husband and I never wanted to leave Iraq, until his sister was shot in the head by a militia group and after I received a death threat. When we left Iraq, instead of supporting me, my university in Baghdad considered me as having resigned without any rights or benefits. I was not even granted pension after many years of service.

Sura discussed at length the problem of the many academics who were threatened and forced out of their former academic posts in Iraq and had lost many years of service. As we saw earlier, in some cases, subsequent post-occupation Iraqi governments have enabled academics to simply apply for early retirement and get their pension while living in exile or internal displacement.

I met many interlocutors who, despite not having reached retirement age, were simply "allowed" to retire and are now living on their pension in exile or internal displacement. Sura noted that it is critical to take notice of how the post-2003 Iraqi sectarian governments got rid of many academics from the previous era by simply doing everything they could to force them to retire early. This, some noted, is a form of "premature academic death" for those no longer wanted by the new political powers in place. From the multiple accounts shared by interviewees in this regard, this could be considered as yet another form of academic cleansing, that is, forcing those "unwanted" under the new sectarian governments to retire early, which is often tied to forcing them out of the country.

Still, many were not fortunate enough to have their retirement applications and paperwork approved in Iraq. It all depended on the time-frame, and how well connected they were. Others said they had to pay bribes to officials in Baghdad to have their applications approved and/or processed faster. There is a huge irony in that academics must bribe officials to get a pension in return for their "premature academic death." In a way, this reminds me of how the Iraqi government under Saddam Hussein executed certain dissidents and charged their families the cost of the bullets they used for their execution. The most affected academics were those who had a record of academic service of 30 years or more, then received death threats in Iraq, and had to leave empty-handed without a pension. In exile, most private universities that usually hire them do not count their years of service in Iraq. They must start from scratch. This, I discovered, amplifies the feelings of exile and alienation for many. Academics felt so much pain for having lost 30 years or more of their academic service for nothing in return.

In Jordan, the situation is slightly better than it is for those academics who are internally displaced in Iraqi Kurdistan. Both Kareem and Sura confirmed that the social security law in Jordan can include non-Jordanian citizens in specific cases and upon meeting certain strict conditions. First, the academic must be hired at a place that specifically notes that their position is covered by social security by the time they reach the retirement age. For Iraqis in Jordan, they can retire at the age of 60 and receive pension, provided they have 15 years or more of service in Jordan before the age of 60 but not after. Most academics are unable to meet this strict condition for one reason or another; mainly because most never have their contracts renewed for 15 years in a row, or reach the age of 60 after having worked for 15 full years in Jordan. In some cases, Sura said, if the academic has 13 or 14 years of service and reaches the age of 60, they can pay the difference to the social security office and still be eligible for receiving pension. But, again, few people can meet these strict requirements.

It is precisely these uncertainties and insecurities that make Sura unable to celebrate all the gains she had made in exile, especially her achievements at the department that she now chairs.

When you live by contract as an academic, your entire life and future are up in the air ... I also cannot help mourning everything we lost in Iraq. I feel I gave all my life to Iraq for nothing in return. I feel a great pain *for* Iraq and *from* Iraq. All the years of hard work in preparing generations of students are now history ... I worry that even my children may not see Iraq as more than a job opportunity in the future.

* * *

Sameera S., a professor of chemistry in Amman, also introduced previously, echoed what Sura said about living under contracts but also added that these precarious and uncertain conditions "make exiled academics feel that even their contributions are displaced" because, in these for-profit universities, academics are seen as contracted laborers providing a service to customers (students), and often this relationship ends once the transaction is over:

Being here is hard. It has destroyed my academic and scientific life ... I am not in my country. I do not feel as privileged and satisfied with my contributions here as I did in Iraq. It is not the same to teach Jordanian students as teaching Iraqi students who would never forget me, who would remember me and honor me beyond their education years. Here, I do not have that. It is not the same as working hard in your country, in your own place, leaving a fingerprint. Here everything will end once the contract ends ... In Al-Mustansiriya University in Baghdad I walked around my campus proudly, with my head high and with dignity. Here I am just a number in a contract. And even so, many local academics may hate me and see me as a rival stealing the bread from their mouths.

What is particularly significant in Sameera's description of lives tied to contracts is not only this strong sense of mourning but also what she calls a "displaced contribution," which is precisely the result of living and existing under precarious contracts and uncertain conditions. Academics do not feel that their contributions matter. Many told me that such conditions discourage them from even wanting to make any contributions in the form of producing knowledge for such an unfair and greedy for-profit academic system. The idea of a "displaced contribution" was expressed by multiple academics I met. More so by those in Iraqi Kurdistan than in Jordan, which, once again, blurs the line between internal displacement and exile.

I was shocked one year later to hear several internally displaced academics in Kurdistan use the exact same words of "displaced contribution." It made me realize that those in Jordan and Kurdistan have many more experiences in common than I had initially thought. It also shows that academics can feel as alienated in internal displacement as they do in a foreign country. Interestingly, this feeling of "displaced contribution" is not simply a product of being in exile; it is a product of working at exploitative, for-profit, private universities that is strongly felt even inside post-occupation Iraq. In this way, it is a clear example of academics alienated from their academic labor and from students, as universities are becoming increasingly corporatized and commercialized.

* * *

The issue of living under contract becomes even thornier for academics from the medical field in Jordan. On June 9, 2014, I went to visit a prominent Iraqi medical doctor and professor in the field of immunotherapy. Reem T. was one of the top doctors in Iraq for many years. She left Iraq several times for different reasons. She said that she was critical of Saddam Hussein's regime, although she is a Sunni from the former strongman's hometown of Tikrit. She first left in 1997 to protest the sanctions because "as a doctor I saw so many people dying in hospitals, not only from lack of medicine, but sometimes for absurd reasons like power outages that killed patients on ventilators." Reem was living in a nice house in Jordan. When I arrived, an Asian maid opened the door. Everything in the house reflected an upper-class taste. Although Reem was dressed in a business-like way, her face looked sad, as though in a permanent state of mourning. She had to leave Iraq because of sectarian violence and came to Jordan through Scholar Rescue Fund (SRF). When I met her, she had recently finished a research project with the SRF and had been living on her life savings and her pension from Iraq.

Reem holds a BSc from the Medical College in Cairo University obtained in the late 1960s and a PhD in immuno-allergy from Paris obtained at the end of the 1970s. She taught at medical colleges in Mosul and Baghdad from 1974 until 1997, when she left for Jordan because of the sanctions. She then returned to Iraq in 2001 and worked there at multiple university hospitals from 2001 until 2011. In 2011, she had to leave again because of sectarian violence. She feels "at home" in Jordan. She made it clear that she is grateful for Jordan and the Jordanian people for being hospitable to Iraqis during these difficult times. Yet, "there are many problems," she added. When I brought up the issue of living under contract, she said that for those in the medical field it is even more complicated:

We, Iraqi doctors and medical professors, suffer from many things. Iraqi doctors cannot practice here, unless under the name of a Jordanian doctor. Physicians here suffer more than other academics because most universities have enough staff, and it is extremely hard for us to get academic posts.

Reem said that there are many things she appreciated about being in Jordan, especially its proximity to Iraq and the fact that many Jordanians appreciate and sympathize with what happened to Iraq, yet:

exile is exile at the end of the day. This is not our country. Even if you work for a Jordanian doctor, you only get a small percentage [of the money], when in reality you pretty much do all the work. There is no doubt that local doctors here do take advantage of junior Iraqi doctors. They often make them work for free.

For Reem, this issue was way beyond contracts being renewed or not. When I asked her how she felt about losing everything she had in Iraq, I received one of the most emotional responses in this research. I saw tears welling in her eyes as she said:

I have no hope in life. At this point, I am only thinking about death. The war killed all my ambitions. I think I have a serious depression. I try to overcome it with my strong personality. On top of that, since I came to Jordan, I have been fighting breast cancer.

A long silence filled the room. There was a strong feeling of sadness and deep emotions for her and me. I could not utter a single word after that statement, so I decided to "be with her" in my silence rather than in my words. She shed some tears. I then tried to brighten the atmosphere by talking more about her past and present research interests and hobbies. She told me that she had authored many research papers in the past on asthma management, bronchitis, and iron deficiency. She had also done research on the side effects of TB vaccines.

Reem herself realized how sad the atmosphere had become, so she started asking me questions about my own life, family, and journey. For about twenty minutes or so, as often happens in fieldwork, we switched roles: I became her interviewee and she the interviewer. As I shared more with her, she said, "I am fluent in Russian, French, and English. I also love reading literature. I love how Somerset Maugham captures human emotions. And today more than ever I connect with the works of Albert Camus." I left Reem's house, but her face and story have been dwelling in my head ever since. Her sad and mourning dark eyes captured everything I wanted this work to articulate. Reem's life was one of a lost past, a present she rejected, and a future that is up in the air, like a plane traveling between continents.

* * *

Beyond the precarious contracts for exiled academics, many testimonies captured the daily reality of the corporate private universities in Jordan. Sometimes, the most compelling insights come from the least expected places or individuals. In June 2014, in Jordan, I had a chance to spend a few days observing and participating in the life of Jasim S., an exiled Iraqi academic specialized in the field of economics and finance. Jasim holds a BA from the College of Commerce, University of Baghdad, obtained in 1969 and a PhD from the Berlin School of Economics obtained in the mid-1970s, where he focused on studying economic relations and international finance. He has a long academic experience in Iraq where he taught and researched from 1980 until 2001. In 2001, he left for Oman seeking better economic opportunities. In 2005, his contract in Oman was not renewed, so he returned to Iraq, despite his opposition to the occupation. As expected, he told me, "I couldn't cope with what was happening. I soon found myself forced to run for my life because of sectarian violence."

Jasim came to Jordan for a teaching opportunity. When I met him, he was the chair of the department of accounting and finance at a private university located on the outskirts of Amman. He picked me up once or twice a week for a few weeks and we drove together to his campus. What struck me in his daily life, while attending some of his lectures on finance and public versus private sectors, was that he was careful to remind students that the "market doesn't always have the right answers for society's problems." He went into detail about the market's failures. I never expected to hear these insights in a finance class at a private university by an exiled Iraqi professor working under a precarious contract. When he left his lectures, while walking from different classrooms to his office, I often saw students chasing him asking questions about their grades or asking for signatures for this or that type of paperwork.

On one occasion, I shared this observation with him. I asked how come I did not see any students simply asking him questions about something he taught or said in class. I asked whether they only come after him for administrative matters. I also expressed my admiration for comments he made in class about how the market functions. I wanted him to comment further on what he thought about the private sector in his own situation, as an exiled, contracted professor who teaches at a private, for-profit university. Jasim said that from his experience in Iraq and other Middle Eastern counties where he has lived and taught, private universities are never as good as public universities in standards because "students in these universities pay for their classes, and so they expect to pass and get good grades in return." He then gave me a concrete example to demonstrate some problematic aspects of private education from his experience in Jordan:

We had an MA student from Kuwait in this department—a lovely, but a very lazy student. This guy insisted that we should pass him and award him the MA degree. I refused to do so. However, I kept getting phone calls from many high-profile people to influence our department to grant him a degree that he did not deserve. Because of his strong connections, we eventually got calls from the Cultural Attaché at the Kuwaiti Embassy followed by a call from the Iraqi Embassy. The latter was trying to influence me and some other exiled Iraqi faculty who teach here. Eventually, under much pressure, we had to pass him and get him out of here. The point is, you see, these things were not common in Iraqi public education and so they are really hard for many of us to deal with here. In Iraq, the student was not a customer. The state not the students paid our salaries. The professors were strict and able to stick to their values and high standards. Private education as we know it here and now, challenges and undermines all of this.

Jasim's story reflects one of the most challenging issues academics in Jordan and Kurdistan must deal with in these spaces. They used to have more say on how to teach and on whether to pass students. Now they are disempowered by contracts and are expected to compromise much of their ethics and standards. In this case, the contract and the for-profit university are not simply economic matters. They are political. They impose the rule of the market, which if they refuse to submit to, they will be forced to deal with a series of other economic and political consequences as demonstrated in Chapter 4. Few interlocutors spoke favorably about this shift from public to private in their lives. Few academics did not complain about how this new reality has seriously affected their lives, teaching style, and academic standards.

One week later, these challenges were put into action in front of my eyes. I was sitting in Jasim's office as he was chatting with two other faculty members—both exiled Iraqi academics. They were talking about another mutual academic colleague who had recently died. They said that his last wish was for his body to be buried in Iraq, but because of the dangerous circumstances, it was not possible to fulfill his last wish. One of the academics, consoling everyone in the room, said:

It's OK. Jordan is like our second home. Many Iraqis have died and have been buried here in the last few years. What can we do if the security situation in Iraq does not allow us to live there? It does not even allow us to die and be buried there.

I learned from them that some Iraqi academics who have died in Jordan have been buried in a cemetery in the city of Irbid.

After this chat, Jasim's colleagues left. In a few minutes, a Jordanian MA student came into the office and they started talking about his MA thesis

proposal. Based on the conversation, it seemed
was far from ready to start writing. Jasim told h
readings he needed to do, some ideas he needed to de
consider his proposal ready. The student seemed enrag
having to do further work. Within a few minutes, the tone o
tion changed. The student started speaking rudely to Jasim insis
is ready to write his MA because he wants to be done, "I have a jo
for me and I am not going to waste my time on this. I am not payin
to keep me stuck here forever," he said loudly and stormed out of the offi
I did not comment, though I noticed that Jasim was embarrassed that this
had happened in front of me. I waited for him to make the first comment.
He said:

> You see what I mean when I talk about this difficulty of moving from
> public to private sector in higher education. I am a specialist in these
> matters. I am trained to understand the value of the market. The market
> may succeed in certain contexts, certain businesses, or certain insti-
> tutions, but higher education is just not one of them. The principles of
> for-profit privatized institutions are in disharmony with higher education
> values and knowledge attainment. Education is not about profit. It cannot
> be. I am aware that in the West they have great private institutions, but
> we cannot compare their circumstances, cultures, and history to the way
> things are done here. Our continuous political upheavals in the region
> have prevented us from building healthy private universities not afflicted
> with corruption and power abuses.

Here we see again the strong connection between higher education and political circumstances in the region. When I asked Jasim, and other interlocutors
later, to explain why and how they thought that private universities in the
West differ from those in Iraq and Jordan, some thought that the difference
was mainly that private universities in the West do not solely rely on tuition
paid by enrolled students. They also receive funding from diverse sources
and endowments, which allows them more freedom for relatively better and
freer academic environments. In Iraq and Jordan, one interlocutor noted,

> We rely on students' money to operate, so they have a significant influ-
> ence on standards. They kind of make or break us, if you think about it.

...nic rigor are undoubtedly com-
...cause of this fact.

...e office of Hala N., a biologist
...rmacy department at one of
...ogy at Mosul University in the
...rch in the field of biology at
...aught in Iraq for many years

...looked organized, with many
...y, biology, and pharmacology. There were also handmade
items, some with "thank you" cards attached to them. I expressed admiration for the displayed items. She said: "these are all gifts from my students
here to show their gratitude for helping them with teaching, research, and
other types of academic support." She then started crying and reached out
to a tissue to dry her tears:

> I had many handmade gifts from my students in Iraq, but I left them
> all behind. I lost many things after the war. We had to leave the country
> on very short notice after my husband and I received a death threat. We
> took our four children overnight and came to Jordan. I wish I could have
> brought all my students' handmade gifts and cards with me to show them
> to my children and grandchildren one day.

Throughout a few visits I paid to her office on different days, I noticed how
meticulous and helpful Hala was with all the students who came to her office
asking questions related to papers, exams, and specific topics in pharmacology. On one occasion, I asked her about how exiled academics were forced
into different academic settings, namely, public to private and for-profit universities. I told her that many interlocutors felt uneasy about this shift, so I
wanted to understand how she felt about it.

Hala said that to understand how exiled academics feel about this,

> one has to understand the context from which we come. We come from
> Iraqi public education that was strict with high standards, but we also

lived and studied under wars and sanctions. So, now we must deal with for-profit institutions that have very different values. We are in a different time, teaching very different types of students. This is not a matter of us being an arrogant older generation looking down on today's students in these universities. It is a matter of different ways of studying, thinking, and academic rigor.

I asked Hala to elaborate further, she said, "I have to tell you how I studied, under what circumstances before I tell you how I teach now for this to make sense." She gave me an example of how she did her MSc research in biology during the UN sanctions on Iraq when she had to do research under difficult circumstances, lacking academic resources. At that time, she was pregnant and had to take care of all household chores as a mother and a wife:

During those days, I researched animals in cages, so imagine me pregnant, drawing blood from animals, going back home preparing bread and cooking meals, and so on. The harsh sanctions forced all women to prepare everything at home from scratch. We even made things like cheese, yogurt, and jam from scratch because most such products in the market were of poor quality. Also, imagine, one time, I spent six months researching some animals I was watching daily on a farm as part of an experiment. Before the end of my experiment, an American air raid nearby destroyed the farm and all my animals escaped from their cages and were stolen. I lost all the hard work I had been doing for months. I studied under such circumstances. Still, our Iraqi professors were strict and expected high quality work.

Likewise, Hala said, her PhD, was right after the occupation in 2003, under even more difficult circumstances:

During my PhD research, Iraq was invaded. Universities had to close for a few months. This hindered my research, because I was researching animals and had to watch them for six full months at a time, but the interruption due to bombing made that impossible. In fact, during one raid, school stopped and when I came back, I saw that the cages in which I had kept my research animals, which were Japanese quails, were stolen. We were near a neighborhood that had many farms and poor people, so they would break into the university and steal animals and equipment with any raid or bombing.

Just around the time Hala started writing her dissertation, she was threatened and had to leave the country for Jordan. She had to write her dissertation in Amman with minimum supervision: "I couldn't meet with my committee members or adviser. In fact, I had to change many committee members and I had to change my topic several times because most committee members were either killed or had left the country."

Hala managed to finish her dissertation from Jordan and went for one last time to Baghdad in 2005 to defend it, when sectarianism was at its peak: "My committee members, I remember, said 'let's do this as quickly as possible and leave before 1pm!'" She told me that her adviser supported her greatly to go through this difficult time: "My adviser recently died of cancer. It is one of the saddest events in my life. He was a wonderful human being." Hala cried once again when speaking about her late adviser: "you see this is where we come from to this private setting. This is why we have strong feelings against these money-making machines."

At that point, Hala made sure to clarify that she loves Jordan very much and that she truly feels "at home" there.

This country has kept me safe. It has kept my dignity intact, after what happened to Iraq. I am forever indebted to Jordan. It has opened many doors for me. But, still, when we talk about private education, we have to be honest in evaluating its pros and cons.

Hala said that she could not even compare her previous Iraqi students with her current Jordanian students, "because we are talking not only about two different countries, but also different times and different places, so the comparison is neither possible nor fair." However, she believed that this does not mean that one cannot evaluate private education in Jordan on its own terms:

What I see now and here is shocking compared to how I was educated and how I taught in Iraq. Students here want to get information as fast as possible. Many do not want to work hard. They expect to get high grades, to travel, to have it all, but they also want to do very little work ... The respect in the student–professor relationship is also different ... Students nowadays are afraid of books. Imagine, I must teach them to accept and love this thing called "a book." They only want lecture notes, like summaries of things rather than in-depth information. They are afraid of writing essays, so I must do everything possible to make them love writing essays, as opposed to just multiple-choice questions. I do this by bringing essays into every quiz or exam and allotting few points from the total grade on that, so they break the ice and learn how to do it and love it without losing much of the overall grade. There is no way they could graduate from here and not know how to write acceptable essays.

Hala expressed serious concerns about students in private universities who expect "easy passing." She said that of all places, a department like theirs should not allow this. She admitted that adjusting to these kinds of students has been hard for her and for many other exiled Iraqi academics she knows.

I personally never passed any student without truly believing deep down that they deserved it. I am especially careful with topics that are a matter of life or death, like drugs, because then people's lives will be in the hands of these students when they work at pharmacies.

Hala was one of multiple interviewees in Jordan who emphasized that the way Iraqi academics have dealt with this dilemma in Jordan is "rather than lowering our standards to the mediocre requirements and expectations of for-profit universities, we brought these universities up to our own standards," she told me. I found this comment, which I heard a version of from multiple academics in Jordan and Kurdistan, revealing. It reflects a form of resistance by these academics to cope with and even to try to change their new reality, despite the risks entailed. Yet, this is certainly no easy task for academics under such fragile and precarious conditions.

During my time in Jordan, I was able to meet some Jordanian academics who have worked side by side with exiled Iraqi academics. Some of them provided even more chilling accounts of how some Iraqis are treated at Jordanian universities. They shared details that Iraqi academics were either too hesitant to share, or they simply shared in subtle ways. In July 2014, I met with Waleed C. for lunch. Waleed is a Jordanian biologist educated in two top US universities and currently teaches at a university in Amman. Waleed discussed many challenges to "academic freedom" at Jordanian universities, including difficulties in his case where there are many faculty members who even oppose the teaching of Darwin's "evolution theory" based on religious grounds. He complained about corruption at the administrative level in many Jordanian universities where he had studied and taught. He noted this to highlight how hard it must be for exiled Iraqi academics to exist under contracts. For example, at his current university, "presumably one of the best in the country," the hiring and firing processes are highly dependent on tribal connections. At the university where he did his BSc before going to the USA to pursue his higher education, "it was pretty much a place with tribal connections, where a certain tribe ruled, and it was either impossible to hire someone from another tribe, or, if they did, the pressure on that person would be immense." The fact that things are tied to tribal connections produces many other consequences that undermine higher education. This includes, but is not limited to, who gets funding to do research, promotion standards, publications, and so on:

> Many faculty members are basically buddies from the same tribe hanging out in this or that department. All they need is to publish in some mediocre journals to get their next promotion. They evaluate publications with a point system that consists of three levels: level three—the lowest—in which you have to publish at places equivalent to a daily newspaper. The second level is simply publishing in some local scientific or academic magazines and journals. The first level—the highest with more points—is when you publish in international peer-reviewed journals. However, the latter would be the worst peer-reviewed journals in the West. In brief, the system is designed to enable corrupt, mediocre, and unqualified professors hired through connections, bribes, and side-deals to get their awful-quality works published. They have created criteria that are just good enough for their poor academic performance.

Waleed also talked about higher-level, more established Jordanian academics like deans. Many of these high-level academics "pretty much do nothing other than public relations to promote their self-image." In the department where he was teaching at the time, for example,

> the dean and his wife pay local newspapers to turn their trivial events, like attending a party to support high school students, into big news. They are

constantly on Facebook or other social media sites promoting their activities. As soon as they post something stupid, they get hundreds of likes and flattering comments from like-minded people.

Waleed emphasized that he shared all these challenges that he, as a Jordanian professor, struggles with to help me put into perspective what exiled Iraqis living under contracts have to struggle with in their own lives in Jordan:

Iraqi professors are in very precarious positions even if they end up holding the position of dean. No matter what their qualifications or performance, they are always under contract. They have to succumb to such triviality. Some, of course, like it this way. Iraqi professors also have to constantly trash the Shi'a in order to be accepted in Jordan. The first thing they have to prove is that they are "like" Jordanians, which means: they are Sunnis, they find Shi'a disgusting, and so on.

There are many important points in Waleed's narrative above. First, I was certainly able to observe some of the challenges he articulated during my time in Jordan in general, especially those related to sectarianism. Second, several Iraqi interviewees have insinuated the existence of these challenges, though in subtle ways for understandable reasons. It is clearly unsafe for them to articulate them in the same way that a local Jordanian professor would be able to. This already reflects a serious lack of social, political, and academic freedom for these academics. Third, the interlocutors' concerns about the move from the public to the private, for-profit sphere of education in exile can help us deduce the existence of these challenges. Fourth, while many Iraqi academics in Jordan were hesitant to outright complain about the academic atmosphere they live under in these private universities, those in Kurdistan were in many ways more direct about articulating these challenges. One could think that Waleed's narrative above is somewhat an exaggerated case of "venting," yet my time in Jordan and Kurdistan proved that it does in fact capture many of the challenges the exiled and the displaced academics must endure to survive in these spaces. What Waleed described about hiring and firing, publication standards, promotions, and the way connections work strongly resonate with my observations in Jordan and later in Kurdistan.

LIVES UNDER CONTRACT:
THE CORPORATE UNIVERSITY IN IRAQI KURDISTAN

Hatim S., an academic in the field of computer science, is fortunate to be among the few displaced academics who have a job at a public not a private university. Most internally displaced academics, especially in recent years since the spread of ISIS, work under precarious contracts at one of Kurdistan's 18 private universities. I first met Hatim in September 2015 in Duhok and we continued to meet regularly throughout most of my time in Iraq.

Hatim holds a BSc and an MSc in computer Science from Mosul University obtained between 1997 and 2000. He then earned his PhD in the same field from Malaysia's Science University (MSU) in 2010. Throughout his academic journey, he has taught and researched in Jordan, Germany, Malaysia, and then returned to Iraqi Kurdistan, where he has been teaching since 2012. In total, he told me, he had experienced four different academic systems. I learned from him that, like in Jordan, most internally displaced academics in Kurdistan are hired by private rather than public universities because the latter are important spaces in the semi-independent Kurdish region that prefer its public institutions to be concentrated in the hands of the Kurds. "It is part and parcel of Kurdistan's ethno-nationalist objectives to hire mostly Kurds in their public institutions, including public universities," he told me. Even the University of Duhok, a public university that was established in 1992, shortly after Kurdistan's semi-independence from Iraq, has been moving in that direction. The university used to hire more Arab academics in the past due to shortages in its Kurdish faculty, but over the years, more educated Kurds from the West and other parts of Iraq have been returning to Kurdistan, which has made more "local" expertise available.

With ISIS invading Mosul and other parts of Iraq, the region and the university have recently tightened their hiring practices by seeking to give preference to hiring "locals." Given the geographical proximity between Duhok and Mosul (about 45 minutes by car), the two cities—one predominantly Kurdish and the other predominantly Arab—have always had strong ties. Some of my Kurdish friends from Duhok told me that they often went to Mosul for doctors' appointments and returned on the same day. Others talked about how so many Kurdish students studied in Mosul, which has some of Iraq's best universities.

However, after Mosul's takeover by ISIS, relations between the two cities deteriorated, and Arabs from the Mosul region became suspect and strongly discriminated against. Many Kurds equated Mosul and its Arab residents with ISIS at the time of the research. Other minorities from Mosul like Yazidis, Assyrians, and Kurds were embraced as ISIS victims. This situation was strongly reflected in academia, with universities in Kurdistan becoming hesitant to hire displaced Arab academics from Mosul. Hatim felt this in his daily life. Being at a public university, he is a permanent hire—in theory. When we talked about his life in Kurdistan, however, he asked rhetorically, "Is anything permanent these days?"

Before coming to Duhok and before ISIS, Hatim was doing a postdoc in Germany.

I could have stayed there, but I came here because I was promised this full-time, permanent position. Yet, because the academic atmosphere in Iraq is so tied to the political one, it turns out that being here a full-time is not guaranteed whatsoever ... Alas, even if the academic job is permanent, the political stability is always temporary here. This gives me many sleepless nights. The political situation determines my academic situation.

Hatim lives in Duhok with his wife and two children. He is a devoted father and husband, even though he always feels that he is not doing enough for his family because academia drains most of his time. When he and I went shopping for simple groceries for his family, he sometimes received calls from his wife to check on him. Before picking up his cell phone, he would jokingly look at me and say: "Excuse me, I have to take this call from the Ministry of Interior." Before ISIS occupied Mosul, they used to go back every few weeks to visit his family and in-laws now trapped there. After ISIS, this became impossible. Their families have been cut off from each other and neither side can visit the other. "We only communicate through the internet," he said. "If I go back to Mosul, I'll be killed by ISIS. If I am asked to leave Kurdistan tomorrow, my wife and I have no place to go to." He paused for a bit and added:

Now I consider myself a failed academic because I am trapped here. This is yet another form of academic embargo for us. We thought the UN sanctions were awful, but this is much harder. I am also a failed parent because I cannot give my children enough time and attention. I must work so hard here for fear of being dismissed from my position that I do not have much time for my wife and children. Can you imagine that my children, both not ten years of age yet, now know everything about ISIS? I had to tell them. I had to explain to them why we are trapped here; why they cannot see their grandparents, aunts, and uncles left behind in Mosul anymore.

Despite these difficulties, Hatim emphasized to me that his problem is not with the idea of living in exile per se; it is in living in a certain type of exile that absolutely "hates you and can push you out at any minute." He added, "The freedom exile provides varies from one place to another. It depends on the red lines set in place in each exile." For Hatim, given the history and the difficult relations between Arabs and Kurds in Iraq, "which was mostly not our fault, but the fault of the former Iraqi regime," the displaced Arab academic who has no other place to go to but Kurdistan and under contract, this is the most difficult place one can inhabit now. During one of our meetings, he said,

> In Germany, exile felt more bearable. At least you can go out and see nice streets and shops and forget your pain. Here you go out for a walk and you remember your pain even more intensely. Everything reminds me of how bad the situation is for me. Everything reminds me of where I am from, and my difficult position in this small city.

* * *

The last few months of my research were spent mainly working with a small group of internally displaced academics at a modest private university in Kurdistan's capital, Erbil. During these months, I spent a great deal of time with academics displaced mostly from Mosul and Baghdad. In Erbil, the issue of living under contract at a private university was even more intense and strongly felt than in Duhok's public university.

Aboud R., the chair of the English department at the university in question, also introduced previously, holds MA and PhD degrees in Linguistics from Mosul University. Like many in his department, he came from

Mosul to work in Erbil before ISIS. However, as soon as ISIS invaded, he found himself trapped. Aboud is one of the few academics in this research who had a favorable take on for-profit, private universities employing faculty under such precarious contracts, though this was not without some contradictions that emerged as I kept meeting with him regularly in his office as well as attending his classes between January and April 2016.

When I sat in his office for the first time (in early January 2016), one of the first things that caught my attention was the personnel files of his department's faculty members, many of whom are internally displaced and with whom I got to work throughout my time in Erbil. Most files had the name of the employee and their academic rank written in Arabic. All the folders, except Aboud's, had the rank of "Assistant Lecturer," which is the lowest rank to have at the department. Aboud was at the rank of a "lecturer." No folder had any rank above that. I asked him about why an entire department did not have at least one or two faculty members with higher academic ranks. His explanation was that it is because the Iraqi system of academic promotions is "backward and extremely bureaucratic." It is so bureaucratic that it discourages most faculty members from attempting to advance. Furthermore, to get promoted, faculty need to submit peer-reviewed research. What often happens is that:

the process of evaluation is filled with malice. Peers either know each other and so they practice "you scratch my back and I'll scratch yours," or they know each other but hate each other, so they can dismiss very good research to prevent promotions. This turns many academics into each other's enemies rather than "peers." What often happens is that much good research gets shot down and lots of mediocre works gets published.

After some time, I saw Aboud looking at my recorder anxiously. I asked if he would rather I turn it off. He said: "I would appreciate that." As soon as I turned it off, he opened up even more and said:

Also, this is a private university that only cares about money. The owner of this university is a businessman. This is important. He has lots of investments and tons of money. He has nothing to do with academia or knowledge. One day he simply decided that he should open a university to increase his profits. So, here we are. Now, what this means is that the administration here would rather have contracted faculty at the lowest academic ranks possible, so they do not have to pay them a lot of money.

I then asked him how money works in this context. He said that an assistant lecturer in his department gets the equivalent of US$1,200 per month, and a lecturer gets about US$1,600. He then provided some figures and numbers evaluated in Iraqi dinars (IQDs) that explain why the university would rather not have higher ranks among its contracted faculty members:

> If you have a department where you need 15 faculty members to cover your hours: the salary of a full professor with a PhD is about 5 million IQDs. An assistant professor gets about 4.25 IQDs, the lecturer gets about 3.5 million IQDs. The MA holders, which are the real laborers for the university, get the smallest salaries. They make about 1.5 million IQDs. We have about 3.5 million IQDs difference between the salary of a full professor with a PhD and that of the assistant lecturer with an MA degree. So, having more MA holders—like assistant lecturers—saves this university a great deal of money. It is often the case that you could hire three MA holders for each PhD holder who applies for the rank of a full professor. There is also a huge difference in the amount of labor you would get from an assistant lecturer versus a full professor. MA holders work about 15 hours per week just on teaching, whereas full professors teach for about 6 hours. The three MA holders I would hire will cover 42 hours of work per week for much cheaper than the PhD holder at the rank of a full professor. This is precisely why you have mostly assistant lecturers at any given Iraqi university rather than full professors.

The figures provided by Aboud help to explain why internally displaced academics are living under such precarious conditions. Aboud's comments resonated with those of another interlocutor, who said that,

> this turmoil in Iraq has provided the greedy private sector with a huge reserve army of displaced academics who are willing to do anything for any price to save their lives. This is also the case in Arab countries like Jordan.

When I asked him about contracts, Aboud said,

> by the way, many faculty members at this university are academics who
> were in Jordan, whose contracts were terminated, so they had to return
> to Iraq. And because the areas where they come from are dangerous like
> Mosul, Anbar, and other places, they had no choice but to come to Kurd-
> istan and work for this university.

I found this comment revealing. It shows how these academics are caught
in vicious cycles between exile and internal displacement. They are thrown
from one place to another, and every place wants to give them short-term
safety in the form of a contract for as low a price as possible. One of the
significant results of these short-term contracts, as I found from attending
many lectures in Jordan and Kurdistan, is a lack of political, intellectual, and
academic freedom. The contract is a constant reminder than one is temporary and could be dismissed any moment, and therefore that they had better
keep their mouths—and brains—shut.

When I asked Aboud about what it meant to have one's life bound by a
contract, he said that people tend to seek settlement and security in life, and:

> whereas there are many positive sides to that, there are also negatives.
> When you are settled, you can create with safety. But in other ways,
> settling can produce a routine that kills creativity … This routine will
> start to curb your creativity. Yet we have examples that contest both sides
> of this argument, that is, people with stable lives who are creative and vice
> versa. Under the pressure of a contract, however, you must create, you
> must act, and you must compete … In my view, to be insecure and living
> under contract is better for creativity.

Aboud told me that his vision comes from direct experience of having
worked in the more secure, but stagnant and stifling public sector in Mosul
before.

Based on everything he shared, I asked how his vision would apply to
the internally displaced or exiled academics for whom living under contract
goes way beyond issues of creativity and competition. It is a situation in
which a contract and a residency card are literally a matter of life or death.
He agreed that the psychological pressures in this situation are much greater

than those experienced in places that are not torn by war and violence as Iraq is. Still, Aboud insisted, contracts and market-driven education were "better for all parties involved." He added, "for example, if we open a sociology department in this university, you will hardly have any students willing to pay to enroll in it." When I asked what it means if knowledge itself is subject to the rules of the market, Aboud said:

> the more you are connected to the market, the higher your creativity becomes, because your creativity, like capital, will constantly have to be increased. You must remain relevant to succeed. If sociology does not attract paying students, then it is not worth having it in our university. One of my professors from Mosul once taught me a memorable point. He said, "Why do you think that academics of linguistics write all these wordy books. They spend an entire book stating ideas that can be stated in a simpler way and in a few pages. It is because that is how they make a living. You write so that the editor can edit, so the publisher can publish, and individuals can purchase the book. All these actors profit from this long and wordy book."

There was one big irony that Aboud left unsaid. As I spoke with more faculty members in his department over time, one of them who knows him very well and who was the one who introduced me to him in the first place, casually told me later that Aboud was extremely afraid of losing his own contract. I learned that Aboud had been frantically applying for jobs in case his contract was not renewed. Based on multiple comments from faculty in Aboud's department, it is fair to state that Aboud's praise of "living under contract" is itself a result of his fear of losing his contract.

* * *

Sadiq T., who was also an assistant lecturer at the same university and department in Erbil, had a different take on what it means to have their academic, political, and social existence tied to contracts. Sadiq teaches poetry and fiction. He holds a BA and an MA in English literature from Baghdad, and an MA in Middle Eastern Studies from the UK. He moved to Erbil with his wife and two sons from Baghdad in 2013 because of sectarianism and marginalization. Having talked to his department chair, Aboud, about contracts and productivity, I wanted to have Sadiq's take on the same issue.

> The claim that living under contracts increases productivity is rubbish ... If you don't have any loyalty to your employer from the start; if the new-comers are not incentivized; if you put faculty under huge pressures, the first outcome for us is a feeling of futility. You feel like this place is a waste-land. I cannot grow in a wasteland.

Sadiq emphasized:

> If I am brought here under a contract with the assumption that I am always transitory, if my contract is terminated or not renewed, then I won't be serious about things at all. Instead, one becomes a diluted and less serious version of who they are. With the increasing hostility against Arab faculty here, I feel that my replacement is already considered by default, because of who I am, because of my sect, my language, and where I come from.

Sadiq noted that these contracts make most internally displaced academ-ics feel that they are living in a "pathetic academic situation" because all they care about is to "kiss ass" for fear that their contracts are terminated. The most interesting point in all of this was yet to be discovered. At a dif-ferent meeting with Sadiq, I said: "We have talked a lot over the last couple of months about living under contracts. Can I actually see a copy of your contract? I would like to see it to analyze it." He said, with a loud sarcastic laugh:

> We are never given a copy of the contract. It does not exist as a hard copy. Nobody has it. You can ask all the other faculty and you will see that nobody actually has a copy. It is a verbal contract that the administration can revoke at will. So, perhaps, when you write about this aspect of our lives, make sure to call it "lives under contracts that don't even exist in a hard copy."

After checking with multiple interlocutors, they all confirmed that they are never given a copy of their contracts. Sadiq said that not having a copy of a contract that makes or breaks their lives is the "ultimate form of denying access to one's livelihood and existence." The fact that this is practically a one-sided contract—from the administration's side—shows that these academics cannot negotiate, contest, or hold power accountable for any breaches or transgressions committed against them. This shows a frightening new face of how the commercialization and corporatization of higher education in war-torn countries is working.

As I kept talking to other faculty members in Sadiq's department, I found that internally displaced Arab academics are not even allowed to own a house under their names. Some bought houses but they had no right to register their new houses under their names. This is exactly the policy that the former Ba'ath regime applied in cities like Kirkuk. Many Kurds and other minorities like Turkmen and Assyrians during that time had to either register their houses under the name of an Arab sponsor or were forced to change their "ethnicity" on their national IDs to "Arab" in order to be able to register property under their names. This was part of the "Arabization" process at that time, though people found many ways to get around it in order to keep their houses. The exact same practice in Kurdistan today struck me as a perfect case of "an eye for an eye and a tooth for a tooth," a philosophy, as Gandhi said, "makes the whole world blind."

All of this was brought into stark relief as I sat in an office shared by multiple internally displaced faculty members and a lecturer came in with a frightened look on his pale face and shouted: "Did you hear the horrible news about Bassam?" Bassam was a faculty member teaching there with an MA. He had requested a leave of absence from the university to pursue his PhD in Malaysia and had been granted the leave. However, after he had already left for Malaysia, he received another email from the administration stating that if he did not return to his post within three months, it could be terminated. Since his family was living in Erbil, he decided to abandon his PhD and return because, otherwise, his family would be left without any support. He returned from Malaysia and rented a new apartment in Erbil. As soon as he resumed work at the university in spring 2016, he was notified on his first day back that his contract had been terminated. So, he lost both options. There was nothing he could do about it, especially, as noted before, he did not even have a copy of his contract. Bassam, from ISIS-occupied Mosul, had no place to go to. The faculty in the room were discussing how to provide support to deal with his crisis that could become their crisis at any minute. One of the touching moments was when two other Kurdish faculty members came in and expressed their dismay at what happened. They, too, offered to do everything they could to support their colleague.

* * *

In Iraqi Kurdistan, the issue of shifting from public to private university was even more intense because the quality of private institutions in Jordan, according to many interviewees, is much better than in Iraq. Private universities in Iraq are relatively new compared to their counterparts in Jordan. Moreover, Jordan has not witnessed the violence and instability that Iraq has. During the Ba'ath era, there were few private institutions, heavily regulated by the Iraqi Ministry of Higher Education "to ensure that they don't give students easy passes or turn into money-making machines," Aboud, a lecturer of Linguistics at one of Erbil's private universities told me. I remember, growing up in Iraq, most people looked down on students who went to private universities and institutes. They were usually students who did not get high GPAs on their last year of high school, so their only way to get accepted at a relatively good school was to pay for it. Public universities were more competitive than private ones. They also reserved their tuition-free seats for students who worked hard to receive higher grades. In that sense, Iraqi public universities during the Ba'ath era were designed to allow for social mobility for all Iraqis.

Aboud still saw many problems with the private university in post-2003 Iraq, including the one where he now teaches in Erbil. He told me that he found the private university in Mosul, where he worked for many years before 2003, was still "much better" than what they have today because, "the laws under the Iraqi state before 2003 required a private university to be part of a syndicate or an established board of trustees, or a council of at least nine academics." What this meant in practice is that the state did not allow private universities to operate for the sake of making profits only. Aboud provided a useful comparison from first-hand experience between how private universities operated before 2003 and how they operate today:

> The private university where I taught in Mosul before 2003 was established by the syndicate of Iraqi accountants and editors in Mosul. The syndicate received 1 per cent of total profits every year. The rest of our income was allocated for salaries and university spending. This is not

the case in Kurdistan today because we have a single individual owner of the university who seeks to get as much profit as possible. Every saved or earned dinar matters for him. The owner here, who is a business-man, wants the income to cover salaries, university spending, and, more importantly, to make a good profit for himself. This is usually done at the expense of academic standards, to be fully honest. This literally means that the biggest loser in the process is the academic and the research standards of the university. We did not have this problem under the Ba'ath model of private universities. In those days, if a student were absent for a week, we would get rid of him without looking back. We were obliged to dismiss students who would be absent for a certain number of days. We would do that without thinking twice about university profits. We had part of the surplus every year—no matter how much profit we made—that would go to the university's bank account, to be used when needed. Here, the surplus goes to the pocket of the individual owner who would never mind having as much profit as possible.

Aboud's narrative explains why many displaced academics struggle with the current model of the private university, where most of them are hired in Kurdistan. In fact, the university where he works in Erbil is not only one of the biggest employers of displaced academics in Kurdistan but it also has several branches in the region.

To put all this into a real-life scenario, Aboud said, "let me ask you a question: if you have a first-year student who is in a bad academic standing, would you let him pass or not, as an academic?" I said that I would fail such students. He responded:

Well, that is what we did in private universities during the Ba'ath era. Here and now, we have to do everything possible to pass him on the first year to ensure he will pay us for the next four years. To ensure we will profit from his enrolment. If we really have to fail him, it can't be in the first year because the chances of him dropping out altogether are higher in the first year, whereas chances of him dropping out after failing at a more advanced year are lower, because the student would have already invested too much time and money into his education to drop out. This is why we almost have a 100 percent passing rate in the first year to retain students. If they fail in the second year, they will still come back. Now, remember, at private universities here, we already admit students of the lowest grades to begin with—those whose grades were not good enough to get accepted into public universities. As one of my colleagues puts it, "we get the bottom of the basket!" The student here is already incompetent and then you have to pass them on the first year. It is definitely an undeserved pass.

Aboud noted that despite these challenges, he still worked hard with students to better prepare them. He believed that a good professor "should have a 100 percent passing rate in his classes." This comment contradicted his narrative above. It can be analyzed in two ways: first, it could be that Aboud does work hard to help every student succeed. I attended multiple lectures of the "Phonetics" course he was teaching that semester. He seemed well prepared for each lecture and I saw that he tried hard to keep students focused and engaged. However, a second way to analyze his comment is in relation to the pressure of the contracts under which displaced academics live. This pressure certainly forces many displaced academics to compromise their teaching standards. Aboud once proudly noted: "In many of my courses the passing rate is 100 percent. The president of the university says that all my students must be geniuses!"

Over time, I learned from multiple faculty members, that the president of the university in fact micro-manages all details of academic life on campus, especially things related to student enrollment and retention. He also has absolute power over every single contract of every faculty member. This made it clear to me that student enrollment/retention is a key priority for the internally displaced academics, so they do not risk their contracts being terminated or not renewed at the end of the year. In fact, multiple interviewees told me that the president of the university is not only a businessman concerned primarily with profits but he also is an "authoritarian dictator who speaks to faculty in the most humiliating ways." In March 2016, one faculty member with whom I worked for months and had become a close friend, invited me to "get a taste of how horrible our university president is." As I was getting ready to attend a class with another faculty member in his department on that morning, the former told me,

Forget the class. Come to my office in half an hour so we can go together to this big meeting with the university president. I want you to hear how

he speaks. I want you to see him with your own eyes, so you know what I
have been talking about all this time.

In half an hour, we were both in an auditorium with about 300 faculty
members present.

The president opened the meeting speaking in English: "We are here for
one and one reason only. We are here because students are not attending
classes. This means that there is a serious problem and laziness with those
managing their attendance—the faculty." His tone was angry and he spoke
in an authoritarian and threatening voice. He then said that students were
not skipping classes because they are "lazy," but because they are not being
adequately engaged in the classrooms. He spoke for about 30 minutes in
ways that reflected a clear form of power abuse, promising severe punishments, if faculty failed to adhere to his orders:

You need to catch your class. If you do not catch your class, the administration will not catch you. We have too many holidays. You are too relaxed.
Students are even more relaxed. From now to the end of the semester, I
want you to have a quiz in every single session in every single class. You
have to be present. If I wanted an online university, I would have had one;
I would not need you all here. If we remain like this, our ship will sink.
We cannot afford empty classrooms. We cannot afford more and more
lecturers sitting in one room sipping one cup of tea after another, while
hundreds and thousands of students are just walking around campus
taking pictures, enjoying a sunny spring day, and having fun. What is happening is an alarm for the university, faculty, and staff, and we have to do
something about it as soon as possible. If students do not come to class,
you must go out and search for them … You all must take responsibility, or you will be replaced with someone who can do so. From now on, I
want every faculty member to contact any student who is missing classes
by email or even through Facebook. I want you to try to talk them into
attending classes. You must let them know that if they do not attend, they
will be dismissed. We do not want their money … Tomorrow I want to see
all this implemented. I may not come personally to each classroom but I
will send lots of watching eyes to see how it is being implemented. I have
eyes watching all of you from people among you and from outside!

Some remarks in this speech deserve attention. The first one, which I discussed with several interlocutors after the meeting, relates to the president's point when he noted that students who do not attend classes should be dismissed, "we do not want their money." I was told that this is just rhetoric that the president uses in such big meetings; if faculty actually dismiss students because of absence, the faculty may risk having their contracts terminated. A few faculty members told me some had their contracts terminated because they took such actions, "the administration only cares about money. They will punish us if we dismiss students for absence. Students know this fact, which is why they feel emboldened not to attend classes in the first place," one instructor in the English department told me. Another faculty member said that:

if the administration was honest about dismissing students who do not attend classes, they would have dismissed half of their 5,000 currently enrolled students. Just consider this, in the month of March, usually students attend 5–7 days of classes out of the entire month. They skip the rest of the month for this holiday or that. The main one being the Kurdish New Year, Nowruz.

Second, I asked a few faculty members how they would explain students paying so much money for education, yet not attending classes. Don't these students, I wondered, feel like they are burning up their money in doing so? One faculty member said that it is because:

this behavior is part and parcel of the overall society that is littered with this mentality of wanting all kinds of privileges without working hard to get them. They basically do not want knowledge; they only want that piece of paper called a "degree" and whatever privileges that are associated with it.

Aboud, the chair of the English department, said that these students' behavior is like "someone who enters a supermarket, pays tons of money, and leaves empty-handed." I still found these explanations inadequate. Having spent one year in Kurdistan, I interacted with many students who graduated with bachelor's degrees but were unable to get any type of jobs, whether at the public or the private sectors, because of the deteriorating economy.

I saw many bachelor's degree holders from different disciplines who were working as taxi drivers, guards, and other jobs either menial or totally unrelated to their education. Therefore, there is also an element of despair and hopelessness when students become so detached and indifferent about their education because they know that it will not pay off after graduation. The issue from the students' perspective is critical and it perhaps should be a subject for a separate research.

One chemistry lecturer in Duhok, who had taught in Basra and Baghdad before 2003, said that the Iraqi state used to have guaranteed jobs waiting for students after graduation.

> We had many industries that were thirsty to take any graduates from such departments as biology, physics, chemistry, and others. Today, all Iraqi industries are destroyed. Our students in Kurdistan graduate knowing that there is no place to take them. We, faculty members, also know that it is unlikely for most of our graduates to get good jobs. I know many of my students who now work as taxi drivers. To be honest, we feel embarrassed to pressure our students to work harder when we know that they won't even get a job after graduation.

This comment provides a more plausible explanation as to why even students paying for their education seem to be so hopeless and in despair when it comes to their prospects.

* * *

Given all the challenges with private education in Iraq, private universities, unsurprisingly, have problems with accreditation. One interviewee, a department chair at a private university in Duhok, told me that Baghdad and Kurdistan each have their own ministries of education and higher education, and Baghdad does not recognize degrees from private universities in Kurdistan, "we have 18 private universities in the region. None of them is recognized by Baghdad. The political divide between them has not made things better. Politics is always in the way of education in Iraq."

Most interlocutors also complained about the introduction of "quality assurance" into private and public universities after 2003. This is like the "student course evaluations" practice done at Western universities. For displaced faculty, their contracts are seriously affected if they do not get "good" evaluations. Being in extremely fragile situations, many displaced academics who have no place to go to expressed deep concerns about these evaluations. One academic in Duhok said, "Quality assurance makes education a joke. I see so many academics passing undeserving students to get good evaluations and to secure the renewal of their contracts. It is a vicious cycle." Others mentioned that even more concerning is the fact that, like their contracts, copies of these "evaluations" are never shared with faculty to know how they are doing. They are simply sent to the administration and the latter takes actions accordingly. Many are surprised to suddenly hear that they have been terminated based on evaluations they had never seen. One interlocutor said:

> These evaluations are not even designed with a space for students to write meaningful feedback. They simply have some absurd questions that students must answer with "strongly agree" or "strongly disagree" kind of feedback. They are useless, yet they do seriously affect our lives.

During my graduate studies in the USA, I have seen many academics who trivialize teaching and award students grades they do not deserve to ensure getting a good evaluation, especially part-time adjuncts teaching under precarious contracts and junior faculty on the tenure track who want to ensure that their teaching evaluations are stellar by the time they are up for tenure. As such, there are significant connections between the situation of exiled and displaced Iraqi academics and Western academics operating under the neoliberal corporate university in Western countries. After all, the infection of neoliberalism is coming from the West to the rest of the world.

THE CAMPUS AS "CONCENTRATION CAMP"

The more time I spent at private universities in Kurdistan, the more I was shocked by the reality of the lives of displaced academics in these spaces. In mid-January 2016, I was introduced to Mohsen Z., a displaced academic at a private university in Erbil. Mohsen was a young junior academic specializing in Teaching English as a Second Language (TESL). He obtained his education from Mosul University and then went to the USA as a Fulbright Scholar, where he pursued his MA in TESL. He could have stayed in the

USA, he told me, but "staying there is not a solution. Our country is bleeding and if we do not help, nobody will help us. Time has proven repeatedly that if you don't help yourself, nobody will help you." As soon as he started his contract at the private university in Erbil, ISIS invaded Mosul. He was, at the time of research, trapped alone in Erbil while his family was trapped in Mosul. Mohsen loved the English language. He spoke in English with me most of the time. He only spoke Arabic when he cracked jokes that would not have been as funny if translated into English, or when he shared his love poems written in Arabic. He shared his small office with three other displaced faculty members and he was known as "the poet of the room." Every time I went to visit the office in between lectures, he made tea for everyone and read his latest love poem to me and his other colleagues. I once joked with him about a recurring theme in many of his poems about "a woman who betrays her lover after he had sacrificed everything for her." He said:

That is what happened to me, man. I loved a woman in Mosul. I sacrificed everything for her. Her family rejected me because I was "just an English teacher." She did not even try to fight for our love. She simply married a rich man chosen by her parents. I do not think I will ever trust any woman in this world.

One of his colleagues in the room joked: "Oh, don't believe him, he is dying to have a girlfriend but there are no takers."

Mohsen often described the campus as a "concentration camp." I heard this from multiple other interlocutors on his small campus, so I asked him to explain exactly what he meant by it. He said that on top of being displaced, existing under a contract, and having no place to go to if terminated, this campus is like a "concentration camp" because it operates on a punch-in–punch-out system. The university used a fingerprinting machine to track faculty members' hours and attendance. Most interlocutors found this deeply insulting and dehumanizing. I asked Mohsen how he felt about it, he said:

You are fingerprinted when you get into work and when you leave. Faculty here are just prisoners. If you have any urgent chore to take care of, you are forbidden from leaving campus. You could be terminated if you leave campus without permission. They are trying to suffocate faculty as much as possible. This is so humiliating. For example, on a given day, if you finish your lectures say at 11am, you still have to wait on campus until the end of the day at 2.30pm, which is when you are allowed to leave campus. You cannot leave campus to take care of a chore, even if it is within walking distance. If you try to leave, the guards at the door are instructed to let you know that you cannot leave. These security guards know each one of us and they are clear about not letting us leave campus to take care of any urgent business. For example, especially in our case, we often must go to do paperwork, renew residency cards, and so on, but they do not let us do this during workdays. They ask us to postpone it to the weekend. Never mind that they do not apply these rules fairly and equally to everyone. Displaced Arabs are scrutinized much more than everyone else.

I went to campus regularly and left at the end of the day with faculty members whom I had become friends with over time. I noticed how they had to punch in and out at the same time every day. They had to enter no later than 8.15am and leave no earlier than 2.30pm. I was told that if they arrived a few minutes late, they would receive a warning from the administration. Likewise, they were not supposed to stay beyond 2.30pm every day—none of them had a desire to stay anyway. The small size of the campus also contributed to amplifying this feeling of being at a "camp" or a "prison" as many referred to it.

The feeling of being in a "concentration camp," I discovered, is not only limited to their lives on campus. Many academics told me that, especially after ISIS, Arabs increasingly suffer from discrimination in the streets of Kurdistan. Cars with number plates of cities like Mosul, Anbar, or other predominantly Arab, especially Sunni cities in Iraq, get vandalized or outright destroyed in some cases. Some interlocutors shared that they are often profiled in the streets or at checkpoints simply because of their looks, the fact that they do not speak Kurdish, or when they are heard speaking Arabic. To avoid such situations, one interlocutor said,

I shop at the same grocery store owned by a friendly Kurd. At this point, he knows who I am. He knows my story. He does not discriminate against me. I try to shop at the same places where I am known by the sellers.

Another said: "Many of us hang out in certain cafés where a number of displaced Arab men go to smoke shisha and visit with friends. That's our only breathing space." One day I went out to a café with a faculty member. On the way, there was a "surprise checkpoint" set up in the street. Surprise checkpoints are very common in Kurdistan (and Iraq in general) for security reasons. Yet, many of them are not just there to catch the "bad guys" but also to interrogate or harass anyone who is not a local or who does not have a local ID, or has expired residency papers. I noticed how the faculty member looked distressed and anxious. When we arrived at the checkpoint, I greeted the officer in Kurdish and he immediately let us pass. "You're so lucky to speak the language. It can save you so much pain," he told me. When I asked how their families deal with these conditions, some told me that their wives or other family members try to socialize with each other. For those whose family members are trapped in Mosul or other dangerous zones in Iraq, they simply stay in touch via social media. Many single displaced faculty members who live alone in Erbil or Duhok simply avoid going out as much as possible.

A few interlocutors said that when they go out in Erbil, they prefer to go to malls or to majority Christian neighborhoods like Ankawa district. Such places are more "tolerant and sympathetic" to displaced Arabs. One interlocutor had both of his children placed at a Christian daycare. "Even though I am a Sunni Muslim and I pray five times a day, I feel safe leaving my children here. These people accept everyone. If we Muslims were peaceful and loved each other like Iraqi Christians, Iraq would not have been destroyed as it is now," he said to me one morning after he dropped his children at the daycare on his way to the university.

I went on long walks in the evenings in Ankawa frequently. It was clear that many Arabs went there to shop, eat at restaurants, or simply to walk in the streets. In addition to the many displaced Christians from the Mosul area, the presence of displaced Arab families, including many from Syria, was clear. Many felt safe to walk around, to speak in Arabic without being profiled or discriminated against. I paid a few visits to several Christian convents in Ankawa and spoke with a few nuns who shared with me that they welcome any refugees and displaced people. They try their best to help them. One of the nuns, speaking in neo-Aramaic, said:

We do not have enough resources to help everyone, but, as you see, we have turned much of the property of these convents and cathedrals into temporary shelters to help these people in their distress and hardship. I am sure God is happy to share his home with refugees. We also try to help them by teaching them manual skills like making handmade items to sell in the shops or simply have their own kiosks set outside our property to make a living. We teach many displaced young girls knitting, broidery, or to make women's accessories to sell to other shops. We have dealt with a few cases of raped women who escaped violence. We helped them by providing them with a peaceful space for recovery at the convent. As you see, the district is filled with displaced people from many parts of Iraq and Syria.

One of my close Kurdish friends, who works as a consultant for different NGOs dealing with refugees, said that Kurdistan has received thousands upon thousands of Iraqi and Syrian refugees. "Up until the Syrian war, Iraq was a place from which refugees escaped. We didn't expect to suddenly become a place to which people would come seeking refuge."

The issue of feeling like one is living in a "concentration camp" on and off campus for these academics was felt even in terms of accommodation. Most interlocutors in Erbil and Duhok lived in neighborhoods that were gated and guarded, and were almost exclusively inhabited by displaced people from other parts of Iraq. This fact created a segregated environment between "locals" and "displaced locals." This segregation is determined by and divided according to ethnicity, language, and the residency status. These conditions are at once like "concentration camps" as well as "internment camps." It is a situation that strongly reminds us of Hannah Arendt's words in her well-known essay, "We Refugees," where she writes: "Apparently nobody wants to know that contemporary history has created a new kind of human beings—the kind that are put in concentration camps by their foes and in internment camps by their friends" (Arendt 1994: 111). In this case, the boundary between concentration and internment camps is blurry as is the boundary between friends and foes.

Equally pertinent to the Iraqi case of internal displacement, especially in connection to the internally displaced academics who likened their lives to being in a "concentration camp," is how Giorgio Agamben theorized the "camp" and the existence of people in a "state of exception," but in a place in which different laws are applied differently to different people. In "What is a Camp?" Agamben examines the concentration camps in Nazi Germany by asking how such events could have taken place in these camps (Agamben 2000 [1996]: 36). To answer this question, he argues that rather than considering the camp as a historical fact, we must see it as "the hidden matrix and nomos of the political space in which we still live" (Agamben 2000 [1996]: 36). Agamben argues that the camps were not born out of ordinary laws, but rather, they were born out of "the state of exception and martial law" (Agamben 2000 [1996]: 37).

The consequences of the 2003 occupation of Iraq (sectarianism, violence, terrorism, and ISIS) have turned the country into divided zones of life and death; camps where the displaced live with no options to go elsewhere, yet where also different sets of laws are applied to different people. Iraqi Kurdistan, despite its serious efforts to help the internally displaced, is an example of such a space for the internally displaced. Agamben writes:

The camp is the space that opens up when the state of exception starts to become the rule. In it, the state of exception, which was essentially a temporal suspension of the state of law, acquires a permanent arrangement that, as such, remains constantly outside the normal state of law.

(Agamben 2000 [1996]: 38, original emphasis)

Agamben asserts that the camp is not simply an "external space." Indeed, "what is being excluded in the camp is *captured outside*, that is, it is included by virtue of its very exclusion" (Agamben 2000 [1996]: 39, original emphasis). Thus, it is precisely because of the camp's existence in a "state of exception" that everything is possible in them. And because inhabitants existing in such spaces:

have been stripped of every political status and reduced completely to naked life, the camp is also the most absolute biopolitical space that has ever been realized—a space in which power confronts nothing other than pure biological life without any mediation.

(Agamben 2000 [1996]: 40)

Agamben emphasizes that rather than asking how such inhumane acts were committed against other human beings in these camps, we must ask how could human beings be so deprived of their rights "to the point that committing any act toward them would no longer appear as a crime" (Agamben 2000 [1996]: 40). More importantly, Agamben shows that these camps not only represent a political space of modernity but also how power constantly changes its tactics and methods of how to create such spaces of exception, which have now become the rule. As such, it is critical, he argues, that we learn to recognize the camp "in all of its metamorphoses. The camp is the fourth and inseparable element that has been added to and has broken up the old trinity of nation (birth), state, and territory" (Agamben 2000 [1996]: 43). Much of what Agamben states applies to the case of displaced Iraqis, as we saw in how academics struggled through sectarian violence, as well as in their new spaces in exile and internal displacement.

A case that perfectly illustrates the existence of displaced academics in a "state of exception" was that of Abdullah M., an assistant lecturer of law and legal English at a private university in Erbil. Abdullah lived in Mosul, moved to Erbil for a job and, like many of his colleagues, was trapped in Erbil after ISIS invaded Mosul. Also, like them, he lived under a contract and his existence in Erbil was bound by a residency card. However, his case was more complicated than others because he was born in the district of Makhmur, about 65 kilometers from Kurdistan's capital, Erbil. Makhmur is a small agricultural city populated by Arabs and Kurds. During Saddam Hussein's rule, as part of the Arabization process, the district was made part of Ninawa governorate (Mosul) in 1996, even though the district is about 115 kilometers from Ninawa and only 65 kilometers from Erbil. After 2003, the district was brought back administratively under Erbil. This made the Kurd residents of the district de facto locals of Kurdistan, and therefore, they do not need residency cards to live in other parts of the region. That rule, Abdullah told me, is not applicable to Arabs from Makhmur. In theory, like the Kurd residents of Makhmur, Abdullah should not need a residency card to be in Erbil, but because he is an Arab, this law does not apply to him. He is in a "state of exception" or exclusion. On one occasion, Abdullah expressed his deep humiliation at being excluded while others from the same district are not. "I cannot wait for Mosul to be rid of ISIS to go back and have my dignity back and live with my family. If Mosul gets liberated tomorrow, you can count me as the first one to return," he said. Another faculty member in Abdullah's department said:

The need for residency cards in your own country confirms the notion that we do not belong here, that we are not wanted here. This practice is designed to kick us out of here when no longer needed. It always gives you a feeling that you are transient, and if you do come here because you have no other options, it makes it hard for you to be serious about your contributions to this place because these contributions will never pay off.

Upon close examination of these precarious conditions of different citizenship and residency rules and multiple exclusions, and the feeling of being in "concentration camps," it becomes clear that this is no coincidence in a world increasingly governed by neoliberal capitalist modes of existence.

The Iraqi case, in many ways, resembles what the anthropologist Aiwa Ong examines in her work *Flexible Citizenship* (Ong 1999). Ong shows how different types of unequal and, for many, cruel forms of citizenship and belonging that we see worldwide are both conditions and products of late capitalism. She coins the term "graduated sovereignty" to challenge the assumption that "states" are destroyed by late capitalism and the market, and to show how the state subjects "different sectors of the population to different regimes of evaluation and control." In doing so, states create different "zones" of law from within (Ong 1999: 217). For example, in Malaysia, with its three main ethnicities (Malays, Chinese, and Indians), the state created six different zones of "graduated sovereignty." These zones include "the low-wage manufacturing sector, the illegal labor market, the aboriginal periphery, the refugee camp, the cyber corridor, and the growth triangle" (Ong 1999: 218). In each of these zones, Ong argues, the state has different laws and forms of discipline to keep each population under control. In this way, as in the case of the conditions under which exiled and displaced Iraqi academics live, Ong shows that rather than assuming that the power of the state has ended, we must seriously consider that states have refashioned and reinvented themselves to accommodate the rules of the market. For Ong, this is one of the most distinct characteristics of the modern transnational state, and therefore that of the "flexible citizenship" that determines who is included in certain zones and who is excluded. Ong's concept of "graduated sovereignty" captures the complex ways in which the modern form of the state contributes to transnational capitalism. If we consider that Iraq was invaded and divided into different zones to control its resources and people by capitalist neoliberal powers, then Ong's analysis is relevant and applicable in this case.

*   *   *

Sadiq T., the English literature assistant lecturer also in the same university in Erbil, shared more nuanced details about how displaced academics live their daily lives in Kurdistan. He said that an Iraqi academic suffers from multiple exclusions inside and outside of Iraq. From experiencing sectarian violence in Baghdad, studying in the UK, and now teaching in Kurdistan, Sadiq said that being an Iraqi academic, "you suffer from imposition. You are already a suspect wherever you go." While he loves traveling around the world, participating, and learning from different peoples and cultures, Sadiq rejects "hybridity" as promoted by the Euro-American scholars because being the "hybrid" or:

> so-called citizen of the world, as many Westerners like to repeat uncritically, all depends on your place in the power structure of that world. If you are colonized, occupied, and marginalized, this model is not ideal for you. You will never truly be considered "a citizen of the world." This model only works for the privileged.

Furthermore, while acknowledging that there is no such thing as "pure cultures," Sadiq finds that "hybridity" is Eurocentric, and therefore it alienates and marginalizes many people, especially from war-torn countries who do not have the privilege of traveling or existing freely wherever they want. "I am not the other. I am not the periphery. I am the center of my own universe." Yet Sadiq does feel he is on the "periphery" in Kurdistan, before even traveling beyond the Iraqi borders:

> As a Sunni Arab, you feel this is not your time and place at all. I happen to be part of a segment against whom all kinds of stereotypes are created. When the students attend your lecture, when you meet with the president of the university, anything and everything you say is usually politicized and taken out of context. If you talk about why a Nowruz break should take one full month, practically sabotaging much of the spring semester

167

of the academic year, they will tell you that it is a political symbol, you must hate freedom, Kurds, and the Peshmerga.

For Sadiq, to exist in such an environment where people like him are excluded, and where they are treated exclusively in political terms, is the ultimate form of exclusion. As we were chatting one day about his struggles, he raised the question:

You may wonder why they bring us here, if they have all this animosity toward us. Well, we are considered cheap labor for them. It is an economic issue. It is convenience. It is similar to what Jordan does to Iraqi academics. If we had a decent state that would guarantee our rights and dignity, I would automatically choose to be in Baghdad. I would choose to teach in Baghdad, not just because I am from Baghdad, but because I would not want to waste my time justifying my existence and innocence as I do here. Imagine, here, even on an official holiday, Arab faculty are still expected to show up. Think about this, we come to an empty campus on certain official holidays. The campus is empty but we still have to come. The point, for me, is simple: they are giving us hell while they can for as long as they can.

Like other academics in his department, Sadiq said that the rule used to be that if a lecturer came to an empty classroom, they were supposed to wait for 15 minutes and then leave. As part of "retaining students," he showed me a new official order from the university administration written in Kurdish stating that now faculty are expected to wait for 50 minutes in an empty classroom: "Do you see the amount of humiliation here? We are expected to wait for almost one hour in an empty classroom. The administration actually sends people to ensure the enforcement of this absurd rule," he said.

During my research time in the Kurdistan region, I discovered that the line between the economic and the political issues for displaced academics is hazy and blurry. Since the economic crisis in Kurdistan, there have been enormous pressures on private universities to stop hiring displaced Arab faculty and to replace the existing ones with Kurdish staff. At the end of December 2015, while visiting Sadiq in his office, he said:

Last week four Arab heads of departments were kicked out. Legally, they cannot just kick them out, so the official way of putting it is "they stepped out." Each one of them was called by phone and told that they must submit their resignation/stepping-out letter and send it to the presidency of the university. What happened is they stepped out of their administrative positions, though they were still working as regular contracted faculty. They were replaced with Kurds. The chairs of departments here are unqualified with mediocre education and skills. The professor you just met here in my office is an Iranian Kurd. He has a fake PhD degree. He was initially hired with an MA from Tehran University, which was real, but then he forged a PhD just to get a raise in his salary. He claimed a forged degree from a university that does not exist. It does not even have a website. This is a real scandal. The evidence is graphic ... his title was changed to a Lecturer. It is supposed to be from [university name omitted]. You can check it out. It does not exist. It is a virtual university. They only have a Facebook page with a couple hundred likes. Even though most faculty in our department know about it now, nobody does anything about it. This is what they want—mediocrity. Make-believe qualifications. In brief, the Arab academic for them is just a transitory actor who can be replaced with the first Kurd who has the slightest qualifications. Once they find your replacement, you are immediately pushed out of the door.

According to Sadiq, many displaced or exiled academics can survive these inhumane conditions through developing and adhering to "bad habits" that help them forget the misery of their existence:

> Our life can easily produce much cynicism and bitterness, this is why many shield themselves with bad habits, as Jean-Paul Sartre says. I often feel that I must either adapt to these awful habits of this existence; migrate, which is not an option for me; or simply become extinct. As a result, you hear many displaced academics speaking about absurd things after classes like women's breasts, receiving love letters from female students, the dollar exchange rate, invitations to dinners with powerful people, and so on. This is their way of coping, it seems to me. You never hear intellectual conversations. You never hear suggestions to have a conference or a lecture about what it means to be a displaced academic in this place.

They are too afraid to discuss what really matters. Today's academics are turned into people who can discuss everything except what matters. Their primary job is to simply beat around the bush. That is it!

Sadiq's words above resonated in many ways. First, during my time doing this research, I did observe many of the issues he articulates here. I heard (and overheard) many faculty conversations similar to the ones he describes. At another level, I noticed several faculty members who avoid talking about issues deemed too "controversial," or that might endanger their positions or status in any way. This is understandable for the exiled and the displaced who are in extremely fragile and sensitive positions. Yet, in the long run, avoiding serious actions can also have serious effects on their lives. Silence rarely, if ever, changes the status quo. I met one female academic in Sadiq's department who literally shared with me one of the most shocking "coping mechanisms" for the internally displaced faculty. This academic is a female displaced from Anbar, who had lived in Jordan for many years. When I asked her how she coped with living in internal displacement and under precarious conditions, she responded: "I intentionally try to stay superficial and shallow. I avoid any deep conversations with people here. It's my way of coping with and forgetting my reality." This comment, among others, emphasizes Sadiq's earlier remarks, citing Jean-Paul Sartre, on how displaced faculty find such "bad habits" therapeutic. Sadiq added that these "bad habits" are the only means of survival left to them:

> This means no matter how bad habits are, with all the negative connotations attached to them, and rightly so, they do provide you with a safe resort. In fact, assuming the role of a displaced person in Kurdistan becomes a habit after some time—a bad one.

Sadiq's comments on the "bad habits" as a means of survival show how what starts as a "temporary state of displacement" can go on for much longer than expected, and therefore, the only way to adapt to this prolongation is through adopting these "bad habits," if the displaced or the exiled person is to survive all these pressures. Sadiq used the notion of "bad habit" referring to the philosophical concept of "bad faith" (*mauvaise foi*) used by Jean-Paul Sartre and Simone de Beauvoir, who show how human beings "under pressure from social forces adopt false values and disown their innate freedom hence acting inauthentically" (Childers and Hentzi 1995: 103). Sartre and de Beauvoir argue that because we are "condemned" to be free, free choice is inescapable. Yet, social pressures, while they do not make us forget that we are "free to choose," they can in fact make us consciously and intentionally choose to deny ourselves that freedom. Sartre provided multiple examples of how this may work. Two notable examples are of a café waiter and a woman who go on a first date (Sartre 1993 [1965]: 160–69). Both individuals in Sartre's examples choose to deny their freedom of choice by using that very freedom. They do so, he argues, not because they do not know that they are free but because they choose not to "acknowledge" their freedom because it is too painful to deal with at the moment they choose to act in "bad faith." Moreover, Sartre and de Beauvoir show that humans usually deny themselves the freedom to choose by internalizing that their actions are governed by external powers beyond their ability, which becomes their way of saving themselves from the pain and anguish that result from having acted in "bad faith," rather than in practicing their "free choice," regardless of the consequences. That is, the external moral system becomes "a tool to moralize otherwise immoral acts, leading to negation of the self" (Sartre 1993 [1965]: 160–69).

Another variation of this idea was articulated in literature before Sartre by George Bernard Shaw. In his play, *Caesar and Cleopatra*, Shaw challenges how we think about "duty" in society. One of the characters, Apollodorus, states bluntly: "when a stupid man is doing something he is ashamed of, he always declares that it is his duty" (Shaw 1913: 60). For Sadiq, many displaced academics are forced to act in "bad faith" to survive, to cope with the fact that:

we should revolt, we should take serious actions against the humiliating and dehumanizing choices we are forced to make at this place. The longer I live here, the more I understand what an Iraqi poet meant when he stated, "existence is a closed door."

Sadiq, like many interlocutors I spoke with, noted how the situation of internally displaced academics is such that they are denied the right to speak their first language, Arabic, in many settings. Over time, many of his colleagues were forced to lecture strictly in the English language to avoid any discrimination from students. He asked whether the fact that some displaced people choose to "bury their language" is not in itself another manifestation of acting in "bad faith" because they choose to do so consciously to avoid the painful reality they have to face if they choose to openly speak in Arabic, whether on campus or in the street. Yet Sadiq acknowledged that the issue of the language is much more complex for academics. It is not just about the language, it is about who is speaking it. It is not just a language, it is all the political connotations that come with the language, particularly with the speakers of that language.

6
Language as a Metonym for Politics

Between my time in Jordan and Iraqi Kurdistan, I found the Kurdish language to be one of the most difficult issues interlocutors dealt with daily. Language is so critical that, to many, Arab countries like Jordan feel less "foreign" and "alienating" than northern Iraq. Language challenged and blurred the boundaries between "home" and "exile"; "belonging" and "not belonging"; "existence" and "erasure" of the human, academic, and political lives for this population. In Jordan, multiple interlocutors shared that they had had an opportunity to either go to Iraqi Kurdistan or to come to Jordan. They chose the latter because they felt more alienated in Kurdistan than in an Arab country. This sense of alienation was attributed to Kurdistan's ambitions for independence, implemented through strong ethno-nationalist practices and policies. Many found the Kurdish language as a metonym symbolizing much more than just a language. It is a political, economic, and a social tool. As a result, Arabic speakers can be subject to multiple forms of discrimination and exclusions both on and off campus in Kurdistan.

Many academics do not necessarily have the choice to move from their violence-ridden areas to an Arab country because, with the worsening economic conditions in the region, it is increasingly hard to find academic posts anywhere. Many of those who worked in Arab countries and whose contracts were not renewed had no choice but to return to Iraqi Kurdistan as the last refuge available to them. These academics go through cycles of internal displacement and exile, based on their contracts and limited options.

It must be noted that not every Arabic speaker suffers in Kurdistan. Many displaced minorities from other parts of Iraq who do not speak Kurdish as well as many Syrians, Lebanese, and other Arab nationals who live in the region do not experience language oppression to the same extent that Iraqi Arabs, particularly Sunnis, do. Kurds are primarily Sunni Muslims with diverse ethnic backgrounds but, nonetheless, they share the same religion as

Sunni Arabs. The explanation as to why Sunni Arabs suffer the most from speaking Arabic (or from not speaking Kurdish) is because of their positionality and history. It is not about speaking Arabic, it is about who is speaking Arabic. It is about the speaker more than the spoken language. It is about the history of the Kurds and the Sunni Arabs in Iraq. The latter are seen as the embodiment of the transgressions committed against some Kurds during the Ba'ath era, particularly during Saddam Hussein's rule. Yet, as we saw in previous chapters, to connote Sunnis with the ruling party and former governments of Iraq before 2003 is an oversimplification. It is a convenient construct that has contributed to sectarian violence with the Shi'a as well as other ethnic tensions, as in the case of the Kurds versus the Arabs. Many interlocutors acknowledged that many Kurds suffered during Saddam Hussein's rule. Yet, as one academic put it: "They should not punish us for what happened in the past. We are not the ones who caused this suffering. They are punishing the wrong people." Others emphasized that many Iraqis had suffered equally from different forms of oppressions and exclusions before 2003, and so "today we need a culture of reconciliation rather than revenge," one interlocutor said. As such, to understand the lives of the internally displaced in Iraq, it is critical to understand how language shapes the daily academic, political, and social lives of displaced academics in Kurdistan.

THE POLITICS OF LANGUAGE ON CAMPUS

Hatim S., introduced previously, is a computer science professor. He is from Mosul and is currently living and working in Kurdistan. During one of our conversations, he told me about the challenges he faced with languages in exile. He noted that his suffering in these terms is not just restricted to Kurdish,

> the Germans also refused to speak English in many cases when I was there doing my postdoc. They did not care whether you lived there permanently, or you were there just as a tourist for a few days. I suffer greatly from not speaking Kurdish here.

These experiences led him to believe that "language is the real exile," and the more unforgiving the exile is in terms of whether one speaks its language or not, the more intense that feeling of not belonging becomes. I found this statement powerful, particularly if we consider how the entire pan-Arabist project started by making language the key element to creating an Arab "home" and "self," after long periods of colonial domination. Now it seems as if things are back to square one.

To gain a deeper understanding of how language works in the lives of displaced academics, I attended many lectures to see how things played out on campus and in classrooms. In mid-October 2015, after classes for the new academic year had started, I attended multiple lectures with Hatim. All his lectures were taught in English. In one lecture, he delivered part of a course he taught titled "Graphic Designs" in two parts on the same day: part one on theory followed by part two in the lab. In the theory part of the lecture, I found Hatim to be an exceptionally meticulous, professional, and friendly professor. I observed how one Kurdish student asked him a question in Kurdish even though it was known that the professor only speaks English and Arabic. Hatim did not understand the question. Another Kurdish student interpreted for him. When the student asked the question in Kurdish, there was a clear sign of discomfort and unease on Hatim's face. It seemed hard for him not to be able to understand his students. I noticed that Hatim consciously avoided using Arabic to further explain certain concepts for students.

At one point in the lecture, Hatim was explaining a difficult concept in English. It was clear from the student's expressions that they could not grasp it. Hatim, then slipped and explained one term in Arabic, but he soon caught himself as if committing a crime. He immediately switched back to English. At another point in the lecture, one student raised his hand and asked: "what does the word 'overlap' mean?" Hatim paraphrased the meaning of the word in English. He then quickly and under his breath said the word in Arabic and carried on.

He was then interrupted by another student who asked another question in Kurdish and added provocatively: "do you speak Kurdish?" Hatim responded, "No. I don't. Please try to ask your question in English?" After a few minutes, Hatim was interrupted once again by another student who asked in Kurdish, "How do we differentiate between the RGB colors?" Hatim, not understanding the question, responded, "Maybe if you ask in English, I could understand your question and know how to help you." The student responded in Kurdish with a disrespectful tone: "Maybe if you spoke

Kurdish, you could understand my question and help me." Hatim ignored the comment and kept lecturing.

In the second part of the lecture in the lab, Hatim was present, but most of the instruction was done by two female assistant lecturers. One of them was a Kurd and the other an Assyrian Christian. There, I noticed two things: the Kurdish lab assistant spoke in Kurdish and students responded positively to her instructions and directions. The Christian woman did not speak Kurdish because she, like Hatim, was displaced from the Mosul area. She switched between Arabic and English, but everyone seemed to understand and responded positively to her. Nobody objected to the fact that she was using Arabic. Nobody gave her a hard time as was done in Hatim's theory lecture earlier on the same day by the same class. It was then when I started thinking that *it wasn't simply about speaking Arabic, it was about who is speaking Arabic.* Hatim's positionality, a Sunni Arab from Mosul, highly influenced how Kurds reacted to him speaking in Arabic. This observation was further confirmed over time when I attended other lectures with other interlocutors in different departments and universities in Duhok and later in Erbil.

In one instance, I observed a Shi'i professor of business management lecturing exclusively in Arabic with no problems. However, as a pattern, most Arab interlocutors, whether Shi'a or Sunni, were extra careful and tried to lecture exclusively in English to avoid any confrontations or uncomfortable situations related to language. Other minorities who were not fluent in Kurdish seemed relatively relaxed about language in general, though not fully comfortable either. In some cases, it was sad to see that some academics' English was not good enough to lecture exclusively in English, but it was the safest option for them given the time and the place. English, as the colonial language of the old British colonizers and the present American occupiers, ironically, becomes a "shield" and a "lifesaver" for the displaced academics. Yet, as one interlocutor said when asked how he feels about "shielding" himself by lecturing in English:

The English language, as the language of the colonizers, is no longer the property of the English people alone. It is no longer even English. The English language has become a language of the marginalized, the oppressed, and the colonized.

After the lab lecture ended, I had a conversation with the Christian lab assistant working with Hatim. She spoke neo-Aramaic as a mother language, so we spoke in Aramaic together. I asked her about the language issue. She confirmed that it is particularly a problem for displaced Arab academics. She said that this issue has further intensified for Sunnis after ISIS, especially those from Mosul. She also confirmed that she does not experience any problems when she lectures back and forth in Arabic and English. She then confided in me that Hatim had a big problem in his first year at the department when he tried lecturing in Arabic. At that time, many students walked out of his class. Later, some complained to the department insisting that he never uses Arabic again.

I heard he was traumatized by that experience. He is a good, hardworking, and smart professor. It's a shame that such a good professor is treated like this by students ... They give him a hard time because of who he is and where he comes from.

Hatim was "told" by the department to use English in his instruction. However, since many students' English skills are poor, especially Kurds from Iran, Turkey, and Syria, the issue of language is far from resolved when instructing in English only. Some Iraqi Kurdish students asked him to switch back and forth between Arabic and English once again, but at that point, Hatim refused. He decided to stick to an "English only policy."

Throughout my research, I heard from several interlocutors how students acted out against them just because of who they are. Some said that students and administrators "gang up" against them taking advantage of their precarious and weak position as displaced people to get what they want. In some cases, some interlocutors shared, they are too afraid to even catch students cheating in exams because students could create a scene, scream at them, threaten to kick them out of the university or the region altogether. Indeed, language in this context is like a "battlefield" between students and displaced academics. The former often use it as a weapon to provoke, blackmail, or unfairly attack displaced academics. The system in place seems to be content using students and displaced academics as a "battlefield" to its own benefit. Power, in a sense, is pitting the two parties against each other and watching indifferently. In the end, it seems that both students and displaced academics lose the battle, while politicians in place win by keeping the status quo.

One interlocutor in Erbil told me that in some cases "students will try to know who you are, where you come from, and then provoke you, blackmail you, or gang up against you accordingly."

Later, I shared some of my observations related to language with Hatim when we were together in his office. He confirmed that they are accurate. He added, however, that for many, especially in the scientific fields, academics are simply accustomed to using English terms. Many would still choose to lecture in English or at least switch back and forth between Arabic and English even if they were in Baghdad, Mosul, or other parts of Iraq. This is especially the case for certain disciplines like computer science, chemistry, physics, biology, and others. Hatim said, in his field, he cannot imagine lecturing about many concepts without using English. "I may not mind reading poetry in Arabic, but certainly I cannot imagine reading computer science in any language other than English." On the other hand, he acknowledged the existence of the language problem beyond this matter. First, he said that language issues in Kurdistan today are a reaction to the former regime's Arabization policies. At the same time, they are also "an indication that things have not changed, but rather the oppressors and the oppressed have changed places." One week later, Hatim and I carried on talking about language. On that day, when I arrived in his office, Hatim looked delighted. He said:

> Today was a good day because I finally went to the *Asayish* [the official security organization in Kurdistan], and after some digging, they found that they had a digital record of my residency information. This means that the processing of my residency card will be faster. I feel a great relief because I can finally travel now. I have been locked up in this little city for the last two years of my life. I need to go out to breathe. I also want to exist officially in the system. They know me here at the department. I exist only through my university employee ID. In the street, I feel like I do not exist. I often walk and wonder who am I really?

Hatim's joy to have his residency renewed or processed is hardly an individual reaction. Many interlocutors told me that they feel "locked up," "imprisoned," "living under an intellectual and physical embargo," and other statements expressing a strong feeling of confinement. When I asked Hatim why he feels locked up in the city and cannot even go to Erbil, for example, he said that at checkpoints he must present a "green card" to pass because he is an Arab and not a local of Kurdistan. Non-Arabs, he added, can simply present their Iraqi IDs and go through.

Each person needs a different form of ID to pass, depending on who they are, where in Iraq they come from, their ethnicity, and so on. This absurdity, in my view, is the baggage of the former regime. The current system in place is a continuation of what the former one had established. Could they have changed things? Perhaps. But changing the head of the regime does not mean changing the system and institutions it had put in place. It could simply mean using the same old oppressive institutions for the benefit of the new winners.

For a moment, while sitting in his office, I thought with sadness how simple things like renewing a residency card can fill the day of displaced people with joy and relief. I know these feelings. Going through the asylum process in the USA, I have had many such moments from the time I applied for asylum, going to interviews, fingerprints, more interviews, more paper work, until one really "counts"—until one's human existence is acknowledged. It is somewhat understandable to go through this process in a foreign country, but it is extremely painful to have to go through it in what is supposedly one's own country. Still, even when one gets that "residency" renewed in their own country, or when they finally get that foreign passport that is supposed to make us "count" more than we did before, one discovers that one never really counts in the same way as everyone else. The processes of determining "who counts" (Nelson 2015) are much more complex than being acknowledged through an ID, becoming a number in the system, or through obtaining a foreign passport in exile. One will always be an American from Iraq, an Algerian in France, a "legal" Arab resident in Kurdistan, and so on. As a result, laws and regulations get applied to people in these spaces in ways that never forget—or forgive—their "origin," their past, their positionality, and their place on the ladder of power relations. What happens is at best like how the Austrian novelist, Robert Musil, describes: "All citizens were equal before the law, but not everyone was a citizen" (Musil 1995 [1930–1943]: 29). After a short pause, Hatim said:

To answer your question from our last meeting: yes, lecturing in English is definitely like a shield for me ... this is a historical problem. We have baggage that dates back to the times when Kurds were not allowed to use their language freely. What we are living now is a legacy, an inheritance, and a consequence of the policies of the former regime. The problem is that today things have changed, but some people still mistreat the Arabs who do not speak Kurdish because they think we refuse to learn the language. They think we look down on them by not speaking their language rather than considering that learning a new language is not easy. It does not happen overnight. It is even harder with age. I'm in my mid-40s now and it is not easy for me to learn a new language just like that ... We, internally displaced academics, have been thrown into this context against our will and we have to just deal with it ... The language factor does make a difference when it comes to how alienated one feels in a place. I now have two Kurdish neighbors: one of them speaks Arabic and the other does not, and so my relationship is naturally much stronger with the former than it is with the latter. This is not for racial or ethnic reasons, but simply because communication is smoother and more possible, and so the human connection becomes stronger too. Language is a passport that allows you into people's hearts and lives.

When I shared with Hatim some of my observations from his lectures about how the Kurdish students reacted to him not speaking Kurdish or to the fact that they could not understand English well enough to communicate with him, he said:

When I first came here, I asked the chair of the department "in which language should I teach," he responded, "listen, whichever language you use, some students will object!" However, there's a big irony here: the problems I face with lecturing in Arabic, even if few students do not understand it are much bigger than those I face when I lecture in English, even if more students won't understand it ... In Jordan I was not as careful as I am here. There, I had more freedom and a sense of adventure with experimenting with teaching styles and methods ... Language was not an issue, let alone an oppressive tool that could make or break my life as it does here. Losing my job here means leaving the region with absolutely no place to go to. It means losing everything without any alternative. This sadly means more and more compromises for me as an academic. When put under such circumstances, you start to compromise more and more. You compromise on things you never thought you would in your life.

The advice from the chair of Hatim's department is far from a sarcastic remark. During my time in Kurdistan, I heard many interlocutors uttering a version of this remark. When I asked one Kurdish academic specializing in chemistry, who used to live in Mosul but then was displaced to Kurdistan after ISIS, which language of instruction is best for students in Kurdistan, she responded: "We have to lecture in all languages and all dialects for our students to understand." Hatim was genuine when he stated in our early interactions that he truly loves lecturing in English, but it is equally true that he is deprived of speaking, lecturing, or publicly using Arabic. One does not necessarily negate the other. On our last meeting, he captured what had then become the crux of the matter on this chapter: "The problem is not with Arabic itself. It is with who is speaking it."

Some interlocutors made another important point to this effect by noting that not speaking Kurdish is not an issue in and of itself. It is, they believed, an excuse to mistreat and discriminate against them. One said:

Many British, American, and other European expats in Kurdistan neither speak Kurdish nor do they even bother to learn. Yet they are treated with the utmost respect, paid handsomely, and live comfortably. This shows that language is used as a tool to oppress certain people because of who they are.

The more I attended lectures with different interlocutors, the more I saw the intense effects of language on their academic lives. One interlocutor who specialized in economics told me that he does not speak Kurdish and his English is also poor. He then added that in his discipline,

We, fortunately, follow less of a descriptive style in lecturing. We follow more of a quantitative style of research, which eases the language problem for me. Furthermore, most of the economic vocabulary have no Kurdish translations, so most students prefer Arabic anyway. Well, they should prefer English but, they too, have poor English skills like I do. My students and I are even on this one.

Another interlocutor, Ghazi, an academic specializing in chemistry in Duhok, provided an interesting comparative lens between Arabizing higher education during the Baʿath era and the Kurdishization in Kurdistan today. He said that in the 1970s the Baʿath party started "Arabizing the curriculum" at Iraqi universities as part of "decolonizing education from Western influence." This had negative effects on certain fields in which English is the primary language of the literature available in these fields, or in which academics were trained, like in chemistry. Before imposing Arabic or Kurdish on the curriculum, "we have to remember that some of our best academics are trained in foreign countries. They are trained there in English not in Arabic or Kurdish." He recalled how Arabizing certain parts of the curriculum was done during the Baʿath era.

> At that time in 1970s, we had heated discussions about whether we should Arabize the curriculum. Some people were in favor of it to preserve the Arabic language. They argued that it is what they do in Germany and France, and in other places, and so we should do it too.

Ghazi lamented that the same problems the politics of "Arabization" produced in the past are now being reproduced by the "Kurdishization" in all walks of life, including in higher education. Ghazi believes that insisting on instruction in the Kurdish language is counterproductive in his field of chemistry. He finds that:

> some students use language issues as an excuse to cover their poor performance and their lack of hard work. There are also cases in which students say they do not understand English. For example, we use words like "hybridization" and "polarization" in chemistry. If you go to the UK, people will know the standard meaning of these words, but even native English speakers may not know how we use them in chemistry. Likewise, understanding these words in your language—Kurdish—is not enough. You need to know how they are used in chemistry, and this requires knowing chemistry well, regardless of the language of instruction.

Jenny, an Assyrian Christian assistant lecturer of chemistry said that the language problem is "like everything else in Iraqi academia, a political issue."

It is so serious that they often exclude many extremely qualified academics because of linguistic and ethnic factors.

Many qualified academics from other parts of Iraq are either Arabs or other non-Kurds. They do not hire them, despite shortages in faculty because of linguistic and ethnic reasons ... Let's be honest about this, the tribal mentality still rules education, hiring and firing, and how academia is run here, though it is done under the cover of modernity.

Jenny added that, as a result, displaced faculty who do not speak Kurdish are forced to instruct in English only. Yet, this makes things worse because most students have "awful English skills."

Jenny lamented that students and faculty are turned into a political, ethnic, linguistic, nationalist battlefield between multiple powers.

It is a catastrophe for a professor to stand up in the classroom and lecture in English when she knows that most students don't get it. We graduate 70–80 bachelor's students every year, but in reality, only 20–30 of them deserve their degrees.

On top of these problems, Jenny said that the Ministry of Higher Education in Kurdistan expects as many students as possible to graduate.

As many as possible should go through the pipeline. This is the unwritten rule in this region. To whose benefit? I do not know who such students can benefit. Obviously even the system in place is doing itself a disservice by graduating many unqualified students. There is politics in everything now. This is tribal education, tribal style of academics, dressed in modern clothing.

I asked Jenny to further explain what "politics" has to do with graduating many unqualified students in this context, she said:

Most of our students do not even get jobs. When I reprimand them for not doing their homework, they tell me that when they finish, they will most likely become taxi drivers ... We do not have companies and factories as we did before 2003 where chemistry students can work and be employed to apply their education. We are a consumer society par excellence today. We do not produce. We only consume. Now most graduates are becoming a burden on the region because they cannot find work—except those who have connections ... We are a university that graduates students only as a political gesture. It is only a public political display to show that the region is doing well after its separation from the central government in Baghdad.

Jenny's words matched my observations off campus in Kurdistan. When traveling between different places, I chatted with many young Kurdish taxi drivers who told me that they have bachelor's degrees in fields like chemistry, physics, economics, and others, but who, due to the economy and the job market, had no choice but to work as taxi drivers to support their families. Jenny, like some others, seemed angry at the system and the way the universities are constantly exploited for political purposes and by the political parties.

Jenny's office was simply a desk in a big shared room where other female academics from diverse backgrounds like Kurds, Arabs, Yazidis, among others, shared the space. I often hung out with them in the room to chat and observe their daily lives. These female academics spent their in-between lecture times in the office chatting, eating, laughing, and sharing stories. They seemed close and bonded, despite their different ethnic, religious, and linguistic backgrounds. Most of these women were master's degree holders at the rank of a "lecturer" or "assistant lecturer." They were assigned most of the teaching load in the chemistry department. The few PhD holders had their separate individual offices and, from what these women told me, "they did little to support our research or job advancement. They simply used us as cheap labor to teach tons of classes and labs," one Kurdish female academic, who was originally from Sulaimania, told me.

One day, while I was with them in the room, the chair of the department came and asked them to stop bringing food and tea to the room because "you're spending too much time eating, drinking, and making noise." One of the Kurdish lecturers was outraged by his "ungrateful attitude for all the work we do." As soon as he left, she put a sign on the door stating "Welcome to the Paradise Café" as a joke. On my last visit to their big office, Jenny, once again, expressed her outrage about how politics is preventing academics from realizing their full potential. She said, even if you choose to remain politically independent, as I have always been, they will keep nagging you to join this or that political party for such and such benefits. They often knock on the door here and ask me to pay the monthly party dues to one of the major Kurdish parties. They know I am independent but they act dumb. Basically, implied in this act is that they expect me to join and they remind me about it every month.

I said to her that what she said reminded me of how the Ba'ath attempted to recruit people. She responded with an old Iraqi phrase, "This cub is from that lion."

THE SOCIAL IMPLICATIONS

Many interlocutors shared that their families suffer a great deal because of language in internal displacement. One interlocutor, Iftikhar, introduced previously, a physicist who currently teaches in Kurdistan, said that the effects of displacement and exile are even harder for the children of academics because their children are usually younger and less able to cope with such circumstances:

Nobody ever talks about our children, their future, and their well-being. I worry so much about the destiny of my children. I will retire soon, but they are at the beginning of their lives. They are unable to get jobs here in Kurdistan because they do not have residency; and they do not have residency because they do not have a job or a sponsor in their own country, ironically. On top of that, they suffer many different types of discrimination and isolation for being Arabs. They miss their lives, their friends, and Baghdad, but are unable to go back. The psychological pressure on academics' children also affects how we think, act, produce, and teach ... Their future is incredibly vague and unknown currently. I feel so sad for them. Perhaps the only solution is for them to go abroad once and for all.

Iftikhar's point about the children of displaced academics was articulated several times during my research, including by some academics in Jordan whose children are unemployed, unable to get jobs, or unable to practice in fields like medicine and pharmacology, as discussed by some in the medical field previously.

Other aspects of the social implications of language emerged when one interlocutor in Erbil said:

> If I am in the street and someone picks a fight with me, I will not be able to respond or fight back because I am a loser in the fight in advance. If I spoke the language, the story would be totally different. I could at least seek justice.

This is not an imaginary scenario. On a different occasion, one interlocutor told me that her husband was "beaten bloody" in the street in front of her because he was heard speaking Arabic on the phone. Gülşen A., a Turkmen lecturer of computer science from a small village in the outskirts of Mosul, spoke at length about the social implications of language. I will never forget the joy in her eyes when I met her for the first time and greeted her in her mother language, Turkmen.

Gülşen came to Kurdistan to teach before ISIS invaded her small village. Overnight, her family became homeless and had to go through multiple displacements from Kurdistan, to southern Iraq, then back to Kurdistan. Since she started her job, she has been living in a small room at a student dorm on campus. "I cannot afford to live alone. Furthermore, I am not married and the society here is unforgiving about a young unmarried woman living on her own. I do not want to get married." Gülşen, like some others, has been trying to learn Kurdish to avoid the challenges that arise from language. In fact, recently, taking courses in Kurdish language has been made a requirement for the internally displaced academics, especially those working as "permanent" staff at public universities. Gülşen echoed what many said in that the problem is much beyond whether a displaced academic speaks the language or not. She remembered the early days when she first came to Kurdistan in 2006 and said:

> At first, we did not have the language dilemma that we are facing these days. I came to a very diverse place filled with minority people like myself. I felt for the first time in my life that this university was the right place to be. I met many Yazidis, Kurds, Christians, among others. It was a place that embraced minorities. In fact, many of my previous professors from Mosul had come here to teach.

Gülşen shared several first-hand stories that illustrate the social implications of language on the displaced and their families:

> When I go to the bazaar and ask how much the price of an item is, the man responds, "it is 2,000 dinars, but if you ask me in Kurdish, I will sell it for 1,000." Similar issues arise when you go to a government office to do any paperwork ... The other day I took my mom to the bazaar. She asked the store seller about the price of an item in Arabic. I had warned her not to speak Arabic, but she insisted it was all okay and that we used to come here and speak Arabic all the time and it was all fine. I told her that things have changed and gotten worse, but she did not pay attention to my warning. So, anyhow, she asked the seller "how much is this?" he said with an unfriendly look on his face, "5,000 dinars." I asked the same question in Kurdish, he responded, "my dear sister, this costs 4,000 dinars!" His facial expressions immediately changed. He became much friendlier when I asked. I have never encountered such a rise in racism and nationalism here before. Not with this intensity. Another example, my brother's car plate is from "Mosul" and if he parks anywhere where people are allowed to park, the traffic police immediately show up out of nowhere and ask him to move. If he says, "but others are parked in the same area," they tell him that he just cannot park there and that other plate numbers are local, so they are okay.

Gülşen emphasized that things have deteriorated much beyond Arabs or displaced people. She said that the rise of ethno-nationalism is also about who will eventually seize power, which is why it is an intra-Kurdish problem before it is a Kurd versus non-Kurd problem. In this regard, she shared some experiences from her classroom:

> There is a growing animosity even among the Kurds themselves—within the various Kurdish tribes. Even when I divide students into groups to do group projects, which is common in computer science, a Kurmanji speaker of Kurdish will say they will not work with student X, because he/she is a Sorani speaker of Kurdish. I often try to be understanding and excuse such behaviors since these students come right from high school, with that mentality, if you know what I mean. But I still cannot quite

accept it. It seems to me that the current structure has already been put in place and there is no return or undoing it.

What is significant in Gülşen's narrative is how the intra-Kurdish conflict is equally affected and shaped by language in terms of how the different speakers of the two main Kurdish dialects, Kurmanji and Sorani, treat each other. In this way, people are not only classified through languages but also through dialects. There is the Arabic versus Kurdish language as a metonym for domination on the one hand; and there are the Kurdish dialects as a metonym for politics in this struggle over power on the other hand. It is a case in which there are multiple layers of localism, and therefore different languages and dialects, competing. This challenges the usual narrative about the world becoming increasingly globalized or just one "small village." It is a case in which globalization is capitalizing on and feeding off localization. For certain places, to be dominated by globalization, they must be made as local and excluding of other nearby localities as possible. In the case of Iraqi Kurdistan, this can be traced to the two major Kurdish political parties that have been struggling over power since the 1990s.

Gülşen said that over the last couple of years she had been trying to improve her language skills to "fit in" as much as possible and to avoid being discriminated against, though she feels that there are no guarantees, given the rise of hatred and racism against the non-Kurds:

I have worked hard to become better in Kurdish ... I have attended multiple courses to improve my language skills. Yet people will always know, from my looks or my accent, that I am not one of them. I am an outsider. Once they detect that, they will insist on who I am, where I am from, and such questions ... To be a displaced person immediately puts a question mark around your identity, your humanity, and your existence. You become a strong target for classification. For example, my family rents an apartment at a building owned by one person. I have noticed that he treats them differently than other tenants simply because they are not Kurds and they are displaced. He makes it clear that they must pay their rent right on time without any delays, because he worries that displaced people are poor and may not have enough funds to pay at any given month. He does not scrutinize other tenants in the same way he does with my family ... He speaks Arabic, but whenever my brother speaks with him, he responds in Kurdish only. The language is basically imposed on you whether you like it or not.

When it comes to the two Kurdish dialects, I have observed that for Kurmanji speakers, the Sorani dialect, which is the standardized Kurdish, represents the bourgeoisie class trying to have full control of Kurdistan. Therefore, its speakers can easily come across as "snobs" and political rivals. There is a general impression that the Kurds of Sulaimania see themselves as the most "progressive," "sophisticated," and "civilized." There is also a stereotype that they look down on others, especially the Kurmanji dialect speakers.

To gain a more nuanced understanding of the complexity of the intra-Kurdish struggle reflected in the two different dialects, I had multiple conversations with one of my Kurd friends, a Kurmanji speaker who lives in Erbil. She was exceptionally well positioned to speak about this issue. While not an academic, Tara K., is experienced in doing academic research, working with NGOs, as well as working with multiple government institutions in the Kurdistan region. Given her long and diverse work experience, Tara had extensive knowledge about the complexity of the region. She, too, has suffered greatly (socially and professionally) as a Kurmanji dialect speaker in Erbil, where most people speak the Sorani dialect of Kurdish. Tara said that the Sorani speakers "claim to be the real, pure Kurds because their Kurdish dialect is purer or stronger than ours."

Having lived in Erbil for many years now, and having had many professional and academic achievements, she said:

I was going to get a job at the Kurdistan parliament, but was not granted it because my standard Kurdish was not "pure" enough. That is, it was not Sorani enough. They actually cited that as a reason. They said that my Sorani was not strong enough, even though I was the strongest candidate for the position. The Sorani dialect has been imposed as the language of the new ruling bourgeoisie class here. They control most institutions and offices in Kurdistan.

Tara said that some people have gone as far as making absurd claims like "Tara doesn't even speak Kurdish!" This remark reflects how by speaking the "less" acceptable or standardized dialect of the same language, one is accused of not speaking the language altogether. It also considers a speaker of the "less desired" dialect to be "less pure." Tara's narrative shows how languages and dialects become tools that impose and perpetuate certain notions of who is "pure," who is "impure," and therefore, who poses a "danger" to the status quo. We also see that, whereas the language issue in the case of Arabs versus Kurds is a metonym for politics, in the case of the two Kurdish dialects, it is a metonym for power and class struggle. It must be acknowledged that many Sorani Kurds believe that power in the Kurdistan region is in fact concentrated in the hands of Kurmanji Kurds, especially when it comes to the most sensitive positions in the government. The topic of the two Kurdish dialects in Iraqi Kurdistan is beyond the scope of this book, and it deserves a separate research.

Yet, Tara does work for the public sector in Kurdistan's government. So I asked how she deals with her daily work as a manager who does not speak, write, or communicate in "pure" Sorani. She said,

> If we want to correspond in Kurdish, which I need to do from time to time, I can write, but it will not be "standard." I usually ask for help from someone who is good in Sorani. They write it and I sign it as a manager.

According to Tara, the Kurds in Sulaimania, who speak Sorani dialect that has been standardized in the rest of the region, see themselves as the most "authentic" and "pure" Kurds of all. They see, for example, Kurds in Duhok as "backward" and "tribal." Tara also emphasized that the language issue is even worse for Arabic speakers who live in the region:

> Just as Saddam's government had all kinds of unwritten laws against Kurds and other minorities, we have similar unwritten laws against the Arabs today. History is repeating itself. However, you might have already noticed in the street, one thing that's surely changing in Kurdistan is that the average Kurd has concluded that neither the Americans nor the Europeans are genuine allies ... The Sykes–Picot Agreement has expired and now they are re-bordering, re-drawing boundaries for the entire region. So, this time it will be based on an ethnic, sectarian, and nationalist basis. They are just using us as a political card in Iraq and the Middle East in general. Most Kurds cannot believe that all these international powers are unable to defeat ISIS. The rise of ISIS has created much awareness about what is really going on ... The Western powers have made the situation so

bad in the region that the Palestinian cause has been totally erased from public memory.

Tara found the overall situation for all Iraqis discouraging. She acknowledged that she is not a "typical Kurd" in that her life experience, education, and work have opened her eyes to many issues more than what would otherwise be allowed for the average people in the street.

There are many important issues that emerge from Tara's narrative as well as what previous interlocutors have shared so far. Most of these narratives make it clear that the issue of language is primarily an issue of power, class, and domination. Language is used to establish new forms of power, governance, and produce new elites. This issue is hardly new or unique to the Iraqi/Kurdish context. Yet, its importance and prominence has re-emerged more intensely than ever in many war-torn parts of the world.

The issue of the standardization of language was central in Antonio Gramsci's thought. In fact, recent scholarship has shown how language is the main "entrance point into Gramsci's political and cultural thought" (Ives 2004: 1). Gramsci initially became familiar with the concept of "hegemony" by closely examining how it was first used in linguistics (Ives 2004: 43). Moreover, much of Gramsci's important and understudied contributions to language emerged from the linguistic debates in Italy in his time—the attempts to standardize the Italian language across Italy by imposing the Florentine dialect. It is during these times when Gramsci found "language as a political issue ... to government policy around language, educational language, curricula and everyday language practices. He combines this with the rich metaphorical power of linguistic concepts as tools to help analyse political circumstances" (Ives 2004: 5). For Gramsci, *la questione della lingua* (the language question) was key to state formation. Indeed, Gramsci's focus on language "helps address how our subjectivity is constituted by forces external to us, and yet, at the same time, we as subjects make choices that collectively determine our lives" (Ives 2004: 7).

The significance of the case of language, whether as a metonym for power between Arabs and Kurds or as a power tool in the intra-Kurdish struggle, has been perfectly captured by Miriam Cooke's study on Arabs in the Israeli society (Cooke 2015: 141). Cooke argues that "Israel is an asylum. In the first instance, it was an asylum for European Jews (Ashkenazis) until they turned the asylum into their state." In a section titled "Language and the

Asylum," Cooke shows that classifying people in Israel was not only through Arabs versus Jews, but also Ashkenazi Jews versus Mizrahi Jews: "the integration of Oriental Jews into Israeli society can be attained 'only through Ashkenazisation'" (Cooke 2015: 152). Likewise, in the case of Arabic versus Hebrew, Cooke writes, citing an interview with Shimon Ballas: "The two languages could not co-exist; one had to replace the other ... Language in this context is not merely a skill, it is an essential part of identity that must be broken to change" (Cooke 2015: 152). Cooke concludes that, in the case of Israeli Arabs, exile is in the "*barzakh* between the forbidden Arab past and the unattainable Israeli present. Jewish Arabs are simultaneously in both and neither" (Cooke 2015: 145). For Mizrahi Jews, Cooke shows that the gap with the Western Ashkenazi Jews has increased rather than decreased over the decades (Cooke 2015: 155).

In another important case that captures racial hierarchies in Black America, James Lorand Matory's ethnographic work at Howard University shows through what he calls "ethnological schadenfreude," how in attempting to distinguish themselves from the stigma associated with and imposed on Black African Americans, "many black ethnics refashion themselves through 'anti-African American' identities" (Matory 2015: 3). Matory, drawing on works of thinkers like Pierre Bourdieu, shows that this refashioning of identity is ultimately an expression of "class hierarchy." Matory's findings match the Iraqi context in two important ways: first, in the way that the demonization of "Arabs" through the Western discourse of "terrorism" has made the Kurds often refashion themselves by overemphasizing that they are neither Iraqis nor Arabs. They do so not only as part of their ambition to have an independent state but also as part of distancing themselves from any negative stereotypes associated with Arabs. The Kurdish language plays an essential role in this process. Second, in the intra-Kurdish case, the Kurmanji versus the Sorani speakers of the Kurdish dialects distinguish themselves from each other as part of the struggle over power and social status.

DO SAD STORIES EVER END?

Ultimately, the combination of the conditions experienced by exiled and internally displaced academics create what I call a "plan B mode of existence." Many academics I knew in all my research sites spoke in one way or another about how these difficult, precarious, and unpredictable academic, social, and political realities make them always already in the mode of thinking, preparing, and plotting for a "Plan B." For example, many assistant lecturers or lecturers with MA degrees told me that they apply for PhD programs in places like Malaysia, India, Turkey, Cypress, or any other countries that can offer them admission even before they decide to pursue a degree as a "Plan B," in case their contracts get terminated.

On my last week in Erbil, I went to the campus of the private university where Sadiq, the assistant lecturer of English literature was teaching. He invited me for a cup of coffee at the cafeteria and said we could hang out at the library. As we were at the cafeteria waiting in line to get our coffee, he looked around and said,

> Every day in this place makes me more and more convinced that my role as a lecturer is basically sitting on the fence watching a pathetic show taking place. The show is between two parties: the administration, which consists of predator businessmen; and the paying students, the customers. My job description is to simply fulfill their needs while keeping my mouth shut. How can we think and teach? How can we produce meaningful knowledge at a place that is the opposite of what thinking and teaching are about?

After we picked up our coffees, we went for a short walk around the small campus. It was a beautiful spring day with carpets of green grass and wildflowers covering the campus and the surrounding areas. I thought about how much I would miss Sadiq when I leave Iraq, as he had become a dear friend. I saw him put his coffee cup on a bench, kneeled and started petting a street cat that approached him fearlessly meowing and begging for her morsel for the day. He then stood up and said, "Let's head to the library, my friend." We did.

Sadiq, on that day, confided in me that he goes to the library for a simple reason:

> To be away from all these faces that I do not want to see anymore. I want to leave this place. I am now looking for a job outside of academia, despite my love for teaching and thinking. I cannot do this anymore. I must also be honest with you, your presence in my life over the last few months

and the questions you have asked me have made me more determined to make a serious move about my life.

I was speechless. Sadiq then said that I should not feel bad about it, "it is not like it's your fault. You just asked me questions that, amid my hectic and crazy life, I never had time to think about, let alone honestly confront." As we sat in the library, he opened his laptop and told me that lately he had been spending so much time at the library looking for jobs outside of these exploitative private universities. After a short pause, he said: "Do you know how I imagine the end of a university like this owned and ran by a businessman?" I said I did not and I wanted to know how he imagined it. He continued:

I imagine that this university will not end as a university. It will end being in the hands of another investor, another businessman who will show up one day on campus; look at its structure, its buildings, and gardens, and suddenly decide that this space would be more profitable if it were turned into, say, a luxury apartment complex. That is it. It is the end of the story. You see, investors and businessmen have become the creators—and the destroyers—of our lives.

In the library, which was at the basement of a big building that houses other administrative offices in its upper floors, Sadiq asked: "Do you notice the precise location and setting of this library?" I asked what he meant by that. He said:

Well, look at all these nice buildings and places on this small campus, but of all places, the library is practically just at the basement of this building. The basement is important here because it speaks volumes about the priority of the library on the agenda of those running the place. It is, like its location, at the bottom of their priorities. This indicates the place of knowledge as far as they are concerned. This speaks volumes about how, to them, knowledge and research are inferior, and so is the place of the academic who deals with and produces this stuff.

While still in the library, around 1.30pm, the president and the owner of the university came in surrounded by a few high-ranking administrators. They all headed to the circulation desk where a Kurdish worker was sitting. I had seen the employee at the circulation desk many times during my time on campus. I had a few short conversations with him. He is a simple villager who is not trained as a librarian, but who somehow managed to become better at the job. We suddenly heard the president screaming at this guy in Kurdish. Sadiq begged me to pay attention to what is going on because he does not understand Kurdish. I listened to the president harshly reprimanding the simple villager for not displaying some faculty books properly at the entrance of the library to make the entrance "more attractive and inviting." The face of the circulation desk employee turned red in total embarrassment. The president screamed in front of everyone telling the administrator standing next to him: "Make sure to cut one week's worth of his salary for negligence." The administrator responded, "Yes, sir!" As soon as the president and his aides left the building, Sadiq looked at me and said in English: "You now know what I mean when I tell you this place is for knowledge reduction not for knowledge production!" By the time I started writing this book, Sadiq had already left the private university and found, in his words, "a more tolerable place" working with a European "humanitarian" organization.

7
Final Reflections
Home, Exile, and the Future

The journey of this book started as a project to tell the story of exiled and displaced Iraqi academics in post-occupation Iraq. As I finished writing it, I found that, in telling their stories, these academics ended up telling a very important story about Iraq itself. With their first-hand, intelligent, and analytical voices, I find the testimonies captured in this book indispensable for understanding the effects of the US occupation on Iraq. Moreover, these testimonies speak volumes about why what was done to Iraq should never happen again in another country.

The first part of the work examined life during the Ba'ath era in nuanced and holistic ways to explore these academics' struggles as they worked tirelessly to build their country. The second part examined these academics' post-US occupation stories both inside Iraq (right after the occupation) and in exile. I showed how the reconfiguration of the Iraqi state—the shift from a secular, unified, one-party system, into a divided country ruled by the occupying forces and their appointed sectarian and ethno-nationalist leaders and militia groups, produced the Iraq we have today. The stories reveal that the occupation and the subsequent Iraqi governments used death threats and assassinations, sectarianism, and "de-Ba'athification" as methods of governance to restructure Iraqi society, institutions, and culture.

I then explored how academics' relatively stable jobs in pre-occupation Iraq have now been turned into what I call "lives under contract" in exile. Such lives entail living under precarious and temporary contracts, being tied to residency cards subject to annual renewal or termination at the mercy of greedy, for-profit private universities operating according to the neoliberal ethics of education and knowledge production. Iraq's exiled academics now live in constant fear and in what can be called a "plan B mode of existence" under the most fragile conditions. They are constantly fearing the next day and thinking about alternative options (Plan Bs) to survive. While an extreme and violent case, *Bullets in Envelopes* shows that the conditions of Iraqi academics in exile are part and parcel of global trends marked by the commercialization and corporatization of higher education adversely affecting academic, social, and political freedoms of writing, thinking, and speaking truth to power. As such, countries and societies are being totally reshaped (and destroyed) in alarming ways. *Bullets in Envelopes* is about academics, but it is not written for academics only. The stories in the book prove that the Iraq War is far from over. Instead, it has been happening over and over in other countries too.

* * *

During my last few days in Iraq, I went on a short road trip around the north. I wanted to embrace for one more time its hills and mountains, fields, waterfalls, springs, lakes, flowers, streets, buildings, and skies. On my last day in Erbil, I paid one last visit to the convent that supports the internally displaced in the Christian district of Ankawa, followed by a visit to Saint George's Church, where I was baptized as a child. I took a short walk in its small and magical rose garden. I smelt every rose my nose could reach. The scent of the roses filled me with life and hope. Next to the convent, there was a shrine under renovation. Most of the workers doing the renovation were displaced Christians from the Mosul area. As I entered the site, they all surrounded me and greeted me warmly. "Are you here to light candles and make a wish?" one displaced old man asked me. "Yes, I am." He immediately ran to Virgin Mary's statue right on the opposite end of where I was standing, picked some candles, and came running to hand them to me. He then said, "Let me get the priest's permission to open the door and let you inside the shrine." He did.

As I was lighting the candles, I started humming one of my favorite hymns, "My Home is your Home," by the Lebanese diva, Fairuz. I always loved this hymn because, in it, Fairuz speaks directly and honestly with God. She allows her sorrow to flow like a river as she tells God:

My home is your home, I have nobody
I called your name so much
until the horizon has expanded
I waited for you at my door

and at every other door
I wrote you my pain on the setting sun...
Do not neglect me, do not forget me
I have no one but you
Do not forget me...
My country has turned into an exile
My path has been covered with thorns and weeds
Send me someone tonight to check on me...
...
I waited for you at my door
and at every other door
I wrote you my pain on the setting sun...

While humming these words, a few things crossed my mind. First, it occurred to me that, despite being one of the most meaningful and powerful hymns for many Lebanese people during Lebanon's long civil war, the hymn was first sung in 1972, three years before that war had erupted. It was as though Fairuz knew beforehand what was coming as she says, "my home has turned into an exile." I thought how artists, writers, and thinkers who are genuinely and strongly connected to their time, place, and peoples always sense disasters before they befall. They are not magicians with crystal balls. They simply use their other well-trained senses, beyond the five senses, to feel the upcoming earthquake, to sense the eruption of the upcoming volcanoes, the approaching hurricanes. They signal what they sense in their works, while many people do not take their warnings seriously.

Second, it occurred to me that Fairuz, in her hymn, is speaking to God about exile. It occurred to me that there are some striking similarities between God and exiled people. Like these people, God has often been a political and a politicized figure in history. Like exiled people, God's power lies in his existence everywhere and nowhere. That is how many exiled people feel. They have a multiple existence but multiple existence can also be akin to non-existence. God, therefore, is the ultimate expression of exile. God—if God exists—should understand the meaning of exile more than anyone else.

As I finished lighting the candles in the shrine, I remembered that I had asked most exiled academics at the end of every encounter to share some final words about how, after all their experiences, they would define "home" and "exile" today. I also asked most of them to share some final reflections on their hopes, pains, dreams, and wishes. It is to their final words and wishes, as I share some of them below, I lit these candles in the shrine.

Deema

I feel lonely in London. I want to write many books, but given everything I have been through, I lack confidence. Writing is an extreme act of self-confidence ... I am not married because I do not believe in marriage. I still do not have an academic job or any job for that matter. The image people had of me as a strong, intelligent woman at the university in Iraq cannot be fathomed by people here. All they can see is a jobseeker, or just a failure, I am sad to say. This is especially hard for me because in the Middle East—and probably in most parts of the world—women are defined by one of the two roles: either as a wife and a mother, or as a proud working woman. I currently have neither...

Farah

You know how overwhelmingly rejuvenating the scent of Iraqi roses is? I have never smelt any roses like Iraqi roses. Ever. I always missed them here in London. When my sister died, I went to Iraq in 2003 to attend her funeral. I took a quick visit to my late mother's old house now occupied by other family members. I saw lots of roses in her garden. I decided to cut a few branches to bring them and plant them here in London to remind me of home. I hid them well and managed to get them past security points in the airports. I planted them in my garden here. When they bloomed, to my disappointment, they still did not have that strong scent. They smelt like any British-grown roses. This is "home," my dear Louis... "Home" for me is just a container for our ancestors, our loved one's bones. It is a place where memories once lived and thrived. Today it is just those distant memories. Nothing else.

Shereen

Living in exile is hard. I do not take a lunch break at my current university in London because I feel some inferiority complex in dealing with Westerners due to what I have been through. There are huge cultural differences. Adapting has been extremely hard. I am not like other young refugees who can do a better job adapting. Here, faculty come by sometimes and knock on the door announcing lunchtime. They like to hang out at this time every day. I always find excuses not to go. When I do hang out with them for lunch, I feel that their talk, their style, their interests, their daily activities are so alienating and disconnected from my life experience. I try not to talk, but then I also try not to make them feel that I am distant. I try to smile, but I find it hard to find a mutual topic of interest. I feel we are from two different worlds. My previous position in Baghdad was very different. I was so close to everyone. People knew how I felt without me saying a single word ... I try to get accustomed to life in exile. I try to be involved even in areas that do not interest me as a female scientist, like women's rights! I try to be involved even when I am not really interested. This is my way of adapting ... Here everything is about grants. You have to have projects/research ideas and get grants to work on projects. We did not have any of this in Iraq, so it is really hard to get accustomed to this system of constantly having to market yourself. I am struggling in every way you could imagine. I find it hard to ask people questions because they may think I am stupid, or that Iraqis are not qualified enough ... In return, as a woman, I feel freer. I can do anything I want by myself, and nobody would bother me...

Israa

The role of the academic and the intellectual amid all this is to give hope. There is hope ... My role is not to be an impediment in anyone's way, even in the way of those who hurt me and hate me ... I am ready to intellectually support and advise any students through the University of Baghdad from my place here in Amman ... Some of my former students and colleagues in Baghdad make me feel guilty for not being there with them in this struggle, but I always remind them that I did not leave at will. I left by force when my husband was kidnapped. I never wrote a diary in my life, except for those days when my husband was kidnapped because they were the most difficult days emotionally and psychologically ever. They were truly hard times...

Issa

There is a difference between being a "native" and a "resident" of a place. So, for me, I do have a native place, it is Iraq. At the same time, I honor the exile in Jordan that has helped me and given me a shelter, so it is also my new home ... One way to overcome exile is to make sure we do not get alienated from each other as humans ... We should do everything possible to avoid getting alienated from ourselves. That is the only real battle. The only battle worth fighting...

Jasim

I refused many offers to go the West. I had several opportunities, including resettling in the USA through the International Organization for Migration (IOM), but I refused. I want to be here in Jordan, despite all the difficulties. The culture here suits me more. And, more importantly, I want to keep an eye on Iraq...

Kareem

I fear dying here in Amman. I want to go back to my friends and tell them about what happened to me in exile. My mother's passing here in November 2013 was a loss as big as losing Iraq. It was the hardest thing. Mother is belonging. You belong to your mother. Your country, symbolically, is like your mother—it gives you lots of things that your mother gives you. They are both wells of love and kindness.

Hiba

There is too much violence around the world. It is so harsh out there that it feels impossible for us to be able to change society, affect policies, increase awareness, fight ignorance, and still make a living in exile. As a result, most Iraqi academics and intellectuals choose solitude and exile. I wanted Jordan to be a temporary station in my life of exile, but now I am more frightened than ever that exile is my permanent destiny...

Hazim

For the new generations, "home" is connected to self-interest; it must be a profitable place. It is a pragmatic place. This is precisely how those who chose to settle in places like Europe and the USA think of the concept of home. For me, "home" is the place where my people are being tortured as we speak now. It is a place where I grew up and where my dreams grew up with me. It is a place where I learned how to serve people. I am not the first one to say this, as many poets and philosophers have said it before me: a human being finds himself in what he gives to others. To realize yourself, you have to serve others and to give to them tirelessly. Home is not to establish yourself in the European sense of the word—to look for what only benefits you as an individual. Here in Jordan, I do serve people, but this service is at a humanist level. At home, my service takes a different dimension, it becomes a national duty. Right now, I feel that I have not given Iraq the care and work it deserves, but I do not have a choice in that. This is precisely why I have been trying to resort to online education, so that I can help Arab, Iraqi, and international students whom otherwise I would not have a chance to reach out to. Exile took so much from me at the psychological level. Exile is suffering, sleepless nights, and anxiety; but exile also gave me priceless opportunities to learn more about other experiences, other countries, and other people. I have authored five academic books since I settled in Amman, all of which are taught in several universities in the Arab world.

Hanadi

My hope for the future is that we get rid of this ideological, political, and religious game. There is hope that Iraqis will gradually wake up and start to believe in home and citizenship rather than ethnic, religious, and sectarian divides. It will take time, but it will happen. I know it will happen.

Zainab

I am unhappy and uncomfortable overall. This situation, the hardships, the wars, being exiled to Amman, and more importantly, my husband's illness really broke my back. I married this man because I loved him, despite the age difference and our different ethnic backgrounds ... I used to be known among people for my smile. I do not smile anymore. My intellectual life is not what it used to be. I have authored 18 books, many of them are taught as textbooks in Arab countries like Bahrain and Sudan. However, the last two years in exile have been so hard on me. My daughter left for the USA. My son got diabetes. My ill husband may not live long. I shoulder all the responsibilities around the house. I feel so tired and do not know how long I will manage to do all these duties. I always wanted a husband with my father's attributes and my husband had perfectly fulfilled that. He has always been loving, kind, helpful, and supportive and always there for me, but his illness changed things. I used to be pampered by him all the time. You can call it an Oedipus complex. I loved my father so much. More than my mother, God rest her soul ... My husband reminded me of my father. I did not look tired, overweight, and neglected like this. It is true that I am not beautiful by the highest standards, but I looked decent before I was hit by all these hardships…

Hala

War and exile have taught me to love myself, to reconcile with myself and with others. They taught me to forgive, to return offenses with goodness. Exile gave me many things, but war and exile robbed me of the opportunity to go see my favorite man in the world—my father—for one last time before he died in Baghdad. I will never recover from this wound. My father was a just man. He loved his sons and daughters in the exact same way. He gave us all the freedom we wanted to be whoever we wanted. When I was an undergrad studying biology, his favorite thing in the world was to have lunch with me and listen to my college stories and adventures … I am sorry to be very pessimistic, but I think that Iraq will only get worse. Many people have died. It is impossible to forget those who have died. There is so much hatred and feelings of revenge between people. It takes a great degree of awareness to learn how to have a dialogue that allows people to eventually mend the wounds and forgive each other…

Sameera

As much as we love the homeland, when the homeland rejects me, when it cannot allow me to exist, then the meaning of home must also change. When I go to Baghdad now, I feel alienated because people have changed, or those I knew have left altogether. In fact, even my own family changed. People, even within the same family, have changed in different ways as a result of these circumstances. I still feel pain and cry every time I walk in Baghdad's streets, but I also like my dignity and I want a better life. If a foreign place is going to offer me dignity and a comfortable life, I accept that. What happened has changed me in so many ways. Now I care and love myself more than ever. I used to compromise who I was as a woman and an academic. Now I put myself and my well-being first. After all my sacrifices, I came out empty-handed, so this taught me how to reconsider my love for myself. Exile is offering more than what my country has or is able to offer me. Jordan has offered me security and dignity. The USA might offer the same. It may offer me new opportunities. Alienation is something inside of you. You can treat it by reconsidering your life, making new friends, looking for new ways of life, interests, and healthy relationships. Iraq is unable to offer any of that at this time...

Abbas

Iraq is not home. It is foreignness. I do not feel it is my homeland because a human has no value in Baghdad. I feel more respected in Kurdistan than in Baghdad, given what I have experienced ... Nothing makes me sadder than the fact that my country was totally destroyed. We used to live, love, and enjoy every bit of Baghdad, which was the most beautiful city I have ever known. We used to walk its streets and alleys every day of the year. It never ever occurred to us that it would be destroyed like this. It never occurred to us that such ugly reality would befall Iraq. I have not been to Baghdad since I left it 12 years ago. I cannot go back. I do not want to go back because I do not want to see what has happened to it. I will not be strong enough to bear all this destruction, to see it before my eyes ... [Abbas breaks down crying].

Hatim

Iraq as a homeland attracts us as a magnet but, at the same time, it repels us and pushes us away. It is the most difficult home to be part of. At this point, the worst thing that could happen to you is to be an Iraqi living in Iraq. If you are an Iraqi living abroad, you are better off. If you are foreigner living inside Iraq, you are fine. But if you are an Iraqi living in Iraq, that is the worst position to be in! In brief, being an Iraqi, defies all the laws and theories of physics and chemistry!

Gülşen

The most difficult question you could ask me is to define "home." I cannot express what it is. I miss my village a lot. If you travel the whole world, you will always miss the land where you were born, the soil where your body was conceived. Waking up every morning, looking at the fields, smelling all kinds of fresh natural scents, the smell of hot bread baked with wood fire in mud ovens, the women on their way to the fields, including me and my sisters. We used to get up at 4am and go together to the field. We mostly grew cucumbers and potatoes because they were in high demand, but they also required much harder work than other produce. Even during the UN sanctions, growing these two crops was better for us to make living. But we worked from the early hours of the morning till late evening ... For me, my late father was everything. He was home! Even when I miss the village today and want to see it again, it is simply because he loved it, he was in it once. I miss every place his feet had stepped on. Home is the place that enables you to discover yourself and my father was the one who helped me discover who I am. He is a man who happened to live in and love that small Turkmen village where I was born and raised. After my father's death, places ceased to have any big impact on me. I can survive anywhere. No place is my home anymore. I do not feel places anymore. The village will always be home because of what it meant to my father.

Latifa

My dream is very simple: I want to be safe. As an academic, I wish that the next generation will be as faithful as academics as we were to our students. As dedicated as we were during the UN sanctions on Iraq, even though we made next to nothing for a living and we lived in poverty. For me, my part is almost over, I hope the next generation will be more dedicated.

Aboud

My feeling in Kurdistan is like a delayed feeling of exile, a delayed feeling of alienation. It did not happen at first, it showed up later with changing circumstances and discourse. You know in linguistics, particularly in pragmatics, we use the terms "explicit" and "implicit." Implicitly, you are displaced, but sometimes you look at everything around you and that can have a soothing effect that makes you forget or simply turn a blind eye to the fact that you are actually displaced. Yet, sometimes, with a single remark or situation, it all comes back to you and confirms the fact that you explicitly do not belong here. A very simple example, my son comes back from school looking very sad. When I ask what is wrong with him, he says that the Kurdish kids at school call him "Da'esh! You are ISIS!" This hurts you so much, so you know that these children who call your child these things are hearing them from their families and the grown-ups surrounding them. An eight-year-old child will not just call his classmate "Da'esh" without hearing it a lot at home or on TV. The encounter of my child at school becomes like a mirror of the milieu in which we are existing. Of course, this does not mean that all people think this way. My neighbors are Kurds and they are so kind and respectful, but politics and the propaganda machine and the media are making a huge negative impact on people. Furthermore, no matter what paperwork you must deal with here, the first question asked is "where is your residency card?" An Iraqi should not be asked for a residency card in his own country. When you need proof of residency in your own country, this is the ultimate expression of exile. You are exiled in your own country. If an Arab is caught at any checkpoint without this card, it would be a big deal. You will be treated like someone who crossed borders into a foreign country without a passport. [Aboud starts tearing up and choking back his tears.]

Omer

The definition of "home" for me has become quite cynical and bitter. It is this: I have two houses that I wanted to be my homes but I cannot live in either. I have one house in Baghdad and one in Anbar, but I live displaced in a rented place here in Erbil. I have two homes, but I am homeless because of sectarianism and violence. Oh, and there is one more huge irony in my story that you must mention: since all my IDs are originally from Baghdad because I was a resident of that city for most of my life, and since I escaped it under threat of sectarianism, Baghdad has refused to grant me a single dinar from the money they allocate for displaced people. The reason they cite for denying me is that I am from Baghdad and so I do not qualify for the displaced people's support...

Sadiq

Home is a lost dream that I will never be able to retrieve. Exile is what is left after that loss. It is like being boxed in an elevator for the rest of your life with people you may or may not like, but you have no choice until that elevator stops and you are set free—which is when you die ... Furthermore, I am more certain than ever at this point that "home" is definitely not a flag for which we have to fight and die. The flag—any flag—is appointed by the hunter. I find that all flags do not represent a nation. What represents any nation is the untold stories, the silenced stories of its people. The louder we become about flags and such rhetoric, the weaker and less secure we are in our supposed homes. The truth is very simple, and it is this: a mother on the last minute of her life, on her deathbed, tells her son: "be careful, son, when you sleep cover yourself and protect yourself from cold," this is the ultimate truth of what home is. The homeland is the time when you truly feel that you do not have to talk about a lot of things because they are already granted to you as a human being—it is all those things that go without saying...

*   *   *

It was a beautiful spring day in April 2016. The previous night's rain had washed the streets of Erbil and had given the green grass and wildflowers in the fields and along the sides of the streets, and in between the houses, yet another lease on life. It would not be long before summer's unforgiving heat would arrive and dry everything to a crisp until the first rainfall that usually comes sometime between October and November. As a child, I still remember the smell of the first rainfall after summer's dry months. That encounter between Iraq's dry lands and the first rainfall in autumn remains my most favorite fragrance in the world. I could not believe I was in the car on my way to the airport. I was leaving Iraq already. My sister and brother-in-law were driving me to the airport.

The radio was on, playing a contemporary version of the Kurdish folklore song "Ha Gulê" sung by the Iraqi Kurdish singer, Zakaria. As he sang "*Diwerin gula biçînin*" ("come, let's plant flowers"), it occurred to me that most folkloric songs in Arabic, Kurdish, Aramaic, Turkmen, Persian, and Turkish have flowers as a recurring theme. If it is accurate to say that our folklore reflects our long history and rich culture, then it follows that these languages and cultures have often cared about planting and sharing flowers. I remembered hearing that version of Zakaria's song for the first time when I was an undergraduate at the University of Baghdad. I danced to it for the first time at an Assyrian Christian wedding I was invited to by a dear friend in Baghdad in May 2002. That night, my friend and I danced like crazy. I have always loved dancing to this song. Its melancholy yet upbeat melody always convinces me to move my body. Even if I listen to it after having the worst day possible, this song would simply turn me into a dancing Zorba the Greek. At that moment, Zakaria's words seemed at once ironic and painful, "come, let's plant flowers"? I wished that everyone would take these words seriously. We need to plant fields of flowers not mines for each other. Yes, this was my only and final wish to add to the list of my interlocutors as I was leaving Iraq. I wish I could convince all Iraqis from all their different backgrounds to plant flowers.

Here I was again on an airplane. Here I was again up in the air, landing just for short periods of time in transits to connect from one flight to another, to fly from one continent to another. Here I had just left Iraq, the home that I am no longer sure is a home anymore. Here I was once again heading to my exile. And just as returning to Iraq after ten years in exile made me feel as though I was back inside my mother's womb, leaving it felt like a rebirth of some sort into this harsh world. I was excited about how much I had learned, changed, and grown throughout this research at human, scholarly, and spiritual levels. Yet, I was horrified about what was ahead. I was horrified that I had to turn all these stories, experiences, images, and moments into one book that would do justice to all interlocutors. I was horrified about how to ever put the first line on the paper to tell this story, let alone finish telling it. I confess that I hate finishing stories. Stories should never end.

The book is over, but the battle for a decent life and a more tolerable world is not. The book is over, but I hope that the stories of my interlocutors will start a new dialogue, a new language, and a new way of looking at things. I hope this work will make many other works possible. So, now that this work is finished, I hope that its life shall begin.

Notes

INTRODUCTION

1. For works that have made arguments along these lines, see Naomi Klein, *The Shock Doctrine* (2007); Raymond W. Baker, Shereen T. Ismael, and Tareq Y. Ismael (Eds.), *Cultural Cleansing in Iraq* (2010).

CHAPTER 1   A NUANCED UNDERSTANDING OF IRAQ DURING THE BAʿATH ERA

1. See list the history of UNESCO's International Literacy Prizes, UNESCO 2016, available at: www.unesco.org/new/en/education/themes/education-building-blocks/literacy/literacy-prizes/history/.
2. For a good source that provides detailed information and analyses of the structure of the Iraqi educational system, see James Frey (1988).

CHAPTER 2   THE BAʿATH ERA: IRAQI ACADEMICS LOOKING BACK

1. This point also applies to Turkmen, Assyrians, and other minority ethnic groups within Iraq.
2. Also cited earlier by scholar Eric Davis, *Memories of State* (2005), 221.
3. For examples of scholars who made such arguments, see Suad Joseph, "Elite Strategies for State Building: Women, Family, Religion and the State in Iraq and Lebanon" (1991); Amal Rassam, "Political Ideology and Women in Iraq: Legislation and Cultural Constraints" (1992).
4. Hizb al-Daʿawa (Islamic Daʿwa Party), also known as the Islamic Dawa Party is a Shiʿi political party in Iraq, which was established in 1957 by Mohammed Sadiq al-Qamousee and Mohammad Baqir al-Sadr in the Iraqi city of Najaf. The party was established in Iraq with the support of the Iranian governments following the Iranian Islamic Revolution. The main aim of the party within Iraq was to promote Islamic ethics and to counter secularism. As a result, the Baʿath regime was a foe to the party. After the First Gulf War, the party's agenda became more aligned with that of the USA—both acting as strong opponents to Saddam Hussein's regime. Most of the party's leaders were persecuted by the Baʿath regime and were forced into exile as a result. However, after 2003, many returned to Iraq and assumed different political positions, especially after some of its members moved

to the Islamic Supreme Council of Iraq (SCIRI). It must be noted that, unlike other Islamic Shi'i oppositional parties, al-Dawa was opposed to the invasion of Iraq. For a recent scholarly work that provides detailed analyses of the history of the party, see Bernhardt (2012).
5. For further reading on the genealogy of the term "terrorism" in Western discourse, see Lisa Stampnitzky (2013).
6. For example, books like the four-volume seminal work *Asha'ir al-'Iraq* (*Iraqi Tribes*) authored by 'Abbas al-'Azzawi was banned in Iraq among others. For further analysis on this, see Davis (2005: 238–39).

CHAPTER 3   THE UN SANCTIONS: CONSENTING TO OCCUPATION THROUGH STARVATION

1. For examples of such studies, see UNICEF results of the 1999 Iraq Child and Maternal Morality Surveys, available at https://fas.org/news/iraq/1999/08/990812-unicef.htm; and Sarah Zaidi (1997).
2. Denis Halliday interview in *Salon Magazine* is cited in Ramon Das (2003: 26).
3. Al-Mutanabbi Street, named after the famous Iraqi poet Abu al-Tayyib Ahmad al-Mutanabbi (915–965), located in Baghdad's historic downtown, was for generations a bookselling and exchange center. The street was traditionally lined with many cafés where Iraqi writers and intellectuals gathered. On March 5, 2007, a car bomb exploded on al-Mutanabbi Street killing and wounding more than 130 people and causing significant damage to the historic street and its businesses. An anthology, reflecting on the historical and symbolic importance of this street published in 2013, featured responses to the bombing by Iraqi and international intellectuals, poets, and writers. For more details, see Beausoleil and Shehabi (2013).

CHAPTER 4   THE OCCUPATION: PAVING THE ROAD TO EXILE AND DISPLACEMENT

1. The cleansing methods were used by the sectarian and ethnonationalist political actors, who were enabled and appointed by the occupying forces.
2. Ashura falls on the 10th of Muharram in the Islamic lunar calendar. It is considered a major religious day of mourning for Shi'i Muslims worldwide that commemorates the martyrdom of Imam Hussein which took place in the year AD 680 in Karbala in modern-day Iraq.
3. Traditionally, Iraqis (especially women) wear black when a family member or a loved one dies. Some wear it for the first 40 days, others wear black for one year as a sign of mourning.
4. See the original CPA document titled "Coalition Provisional Authority Order Number 1: De-Ba'athification of Iraqi Society", available at: www.iraqcoalition.

org/regulations/20030516_CPAORD_1_De-Ba_athification_of_Iraqi_Society_.
pdf, accessed October 7, 2016.

5. For a full list of all regulations, orders, memoranda, and public notices issued by the Coalition Provisional Authority in Iraq from May 2003 until June 2004, see CPA Official Documents, available at: www.iraqcoalition.org/regulations/, accessed October 8, 2016.

6. See the original CPA document titled "Coalition Provisional Authority Order Number 2: Dissolution of Entities," available at: www.iraqcoalition.org/regulations/20030823_CPAORD_2_Dissolution_of_Entities_with_Annex_A.pdf,, accessed October 8, 2016.

7. See the original CPA document titled "Transition of Laws, Regulations, Orders, and Directives Issued by the Coalition Provisional Authority," available at: www.iraqcoalition.org/regulations/20040628_CPAORD_100_Transition_of_Laws_Regulations_Orders_and_Directives.pdf, accessed October 8, 2016.

Bibliography

Abdul Majid, Saman (2003) *Les Années Saddam: Révélations Exclusives* [*Saddam's Years: Exclusive Revelations*] Paris: Fayard.

Abdullah, Thabit (2003) *A Short History of Iraq*. London: Pearson-Longman.

Abdullah, Thabit (2006) *Dictatorship, Imperialism and Chaos: Iraq since 1989*. London: Zed Books.

Abu Zeed, Adnan (2016) "Decline of Higher Education in Iraq Continues." *Al-Monitor*, September 22, www.al-monitor.com/pulse/originals/2016/09/iraq-university-education-academic-accreditation.html.

Abu-Lughod, Lila (1989) "Zones of Theory in the Anthropology of the Arab World." *Annual Review of Anthropology* 18: 267–306.

Aburish, Said K. (1997) *A Brutal Friendship: The West and the Arab Elite*. London: Victor Gollancz.

'Aflaq, Michel (1963 [1959]) *Fī sabīl al-Ba'th* [*On the Way of Resurrection*]. Bayrūt: Dār al-Ṭalī'ah.

'Aflaq, Michel (1971) *Nuqṭat al-bidāyah: Aḥādīth ba'da al-khāmis Min Ḥazīrān* [*The Starting Point*], 2nd edn. Bayrūt: al-Mu'assasah al-'Arabīyah lil-Dirāsāt wa-al-Nashr.

Agamben, Giorgio (2000 [1996]) Means without End: Notes on Politics. Minneapolis, MN: University of Minnesota Press.

Agresto, John (2007) *Mugged by Reality: The Liberation of Iraq and the Failure of Good Intentions*. New York: Encounter Books.

Al-Ali, Nadje (2007) *Iraqi Women: Untold Stories from 1948 to the Present*. London: Zed Books.

Al-Istrabadi, Feisal (2008) "Seven Questions: The De-Bremerification of Iraq." *Foreign Policy*, January 16, http://foreignpolicy.com/2008/01/16/seven-questions-the-de-bremerification-of-iraq/.

Al-Solh, Minh (n.d.) "Al-'Ada'a Al-Amreeki Lilramz" ["American Animosity Toward the Symbol"]. *Alakhbar*. www.alakhbar-usa.com/AAguide/aflaq-Safir.html.

Al-Wardi, Ali (1995 [1954]) *Wu'ath al-Salatin* [*The Sultans' Preachers*], 2nd edn. London: Kufaan Publishing.

Arnove, Anthony (Ed.) (2000) *Iraq Under Siege: The Deadly Impact of Sanctions and War*. Cambridge, MA: South End Press.

Arendt, Hannah (1994) *Essays in Understanding, 1930–1954*. Edited by Jerome Kohn. New York: Shocken Books. Baker, Raymond W., Shereen T. Ismael, and Tareq Y. Ismael (Eds.) (2010) *Cultural Cleansing in Iraq: Why Museums Were Looted, Libraries Burned and Academics Murdered*. London: Pluto Press.

Bibliography

Beausoleil, Beau and Deema Shehabi (Eds.) (2013) *Al-Mutanabbi Street Starts Here: Poets and Writers Respond to the March 5th, 2007, Bombing of Baghdad's "Street of the Booksellers."* Oakland, CA: PM Press.

Bernhardt, Florian (2012) *Hizb ad-Da'wa al-Islamiya. Selbstverständnis, Strategien und Ziele Einer Irakisch–Islamistischen Partei Zwischen Kontinuität und Wandel (1957–2003).* Würzburg: Ergon Verlag.

CEOSI (Campaña Estatal contra la Ocupación y por la Soberanía de Iraq) (2013) "List of Iraqi Academics Assassinated in Iraq during the US-led Occupation." Iraq Solidaridad, Electronic document, www.iraqsolidaridad.org/wordpress/wp-content/uploads/2013/11/List-of-Iraqi-academics-assassinated-November-2013.pdf. Last Updated on November 7, 2013.

Chandrasekaran, Rajiv (2006) *Imperial Life in the Emerald City: Inside Iraq's Green Zone.* New York: Vintage Books.

Chatterjee, Piya and Sunaina Maira (Eds.) (2014) *The Imperial University: Academic Repression and Scholarly Dissent.* Minnesota, MN: University of Minnesota Press.

Chatty, Dawn and Bill Finlayson (Eds.) (2010) *Dispossession and Displacement: Forced Migration in the Middle East and North Africa.* Oxford: Oxford University Press.

Childers, Joseph W. and Gary Hentzi (Eds.) (1995) *The Columbia Dictionary of Modern Literary and Cultural Criticism.* New York: Columbia University Press.

Coalition Provisional Authority (n.d.) CPA Official Documents. Electronic document, www.iraqcoalition.org/regulations/, accessed October 7, 2016.

Cooke, Miriam (2015) "Jewish Arabs in the Israeli Asylum: A Literary Critique." In Roger Allen and Robin Ostle (Eds.), *Studying Modern Arabic Literature.* Edinburgh: Edinburgh University Press.

Das, Ramon (2003) "Human Rights and Economic Sanctions in Iraq." *Human Rights Research Journal:* 1–27.

Davis, Eric (2005) *Memories of State: Politics, History, and Collective Identity in Modern Iraq.* Berkeley, CA: University of California Press.

Doumani, Bishara (Ed.) (2006) *Academic Freedom After September 11.* Boston, MA: MIT Press.

Fanon, Frantz (2004[1961]) *The Wretched of the Earth.* New York: Grove Press.

Feith, Douglas (2008) *War and Decision: Inside the Pentagon at the Dawn of the War on Terrorism.* New York: HarperCollins.

Ferguson, Charles H. (Dir.) (2007) *No End in Sight: Iraq's Descent into Chaos.* Documentary film, www.youtube.com/watch?v=Ga5CcwMHKBI.

Foucault, Michel (1995 [1975]) *Discipline and Punish: The Birth of the Prison.* New York: Vintage.

Franzén, Johan (2011) *Red Star Over Iraq: Iraqi Communism before Saddam.* London: Hurst.

Frey, James (1988) *Iraq: A Study of the Educational System of Iraq and a Guide to the Academic Placement of Students in Educational Institutions of the United States.* International Education Activities Group Washington, DC: American Association of Collegiate Registrars and Admissions Officers.

Fuentes, Carlos (1990 [1981]) *Myself with Others: Selected Essays*. London: Collins Publishers.

Goethe, Johann Wolfgang von (2014) *The Maxims and Reflections of Goethe*. Translated by Thomas Bailey Saunders. Createspace Independent Publishing Platform.

Hegel, G.W. Friedrich (2006 [1910]) *The Phenomenology of Mind: Volume 1*. New York: Cosimo.

Ives, Peter (2004) *Language and Hegemony in Gramsci*. London: Pluto Press.

Joseph, Suad (1991) "Elite Strategies for State Building: Women, Family, Religion and the State in Iraq and Lebanon." In Deniz Kandiyoti (Ed.), *Women, Islam & the State*. Philadelphia, PA: Temple University State.

Khuḍayrī, Batūl (2004) *Ghāyib* [*Absent*]. Bayrūt: al-Mu'assasah al-'Arabīyah lil-Dirāsāt wa-al-Nashr.

Klein, Naomi (2007) *The Shock Doctrine: The Rise of Disaster Capitalism*. New York: Metropolitan Books.

Makdisi, Ussama (2000) *The Culture of Sectarianism: Community, History, and Violence in Nineteenth-Century Ottoman Lebanon*. Berkeley, CA: University of California Press.

Marx, Karl (2000) "Engels to Conrad Schmidt in Berlin." In *Marx–Engels Correspondence 1890*. Electronic document, www.marxists.org/archive/marx/works/1890/letters/90_08_05.htm.

Matory, James Lorand (2015) *Stigma and Culture: Last-Place Anxiety in Black America*. Chicago, IL: University of Chicago Press.

Mazawi, Andre E. and Ronald G. Sultana (Eds.) (2010) *World Yearbook of Education 2010: Education and the Arab "World": Political Projects, Struggles, and Geometries of Power*. New York: Routledge.

Mbembe, Achille (2003) "Necropolitics." *Public Culture* 15(1): 11–40.

Mignolo, Walter (2009) "Epistemic Disobedience, Independent Thought and Decolonial Freedom." *Theory, Culture & Society* 26(7–8): 159–81.

Musil, Robert (1995 [1930–1943]) *The Man without Qualities, Vol. 1*. Edited by Burton Pike. London: Vintage International.

Nelson, Diane (2015) *Who Counts: The Mathematics of Death and Life After Genocide*. Durham, NC: Duke University Press.

Ong, Aihwa (1999) *Flexible Citizenship: The Cultural Logics of Transnationality*. Durham, NC: Duke University Press.

Pilger, John (2004) "John Pilger on Why We Ignored Iraq in the 1990s—and Why the Media is Doing so Again." *NewStatesman*, October 4, www.newstatesman.com/node/192511.

Plett, Barbara (2000) "UN Sanctions Rebel Resigns." *BBC News*, February 14, http://news.bbc.co.uk/2/hi/middle_east/642189.stm.

Rabinow, Paul and Nikolas Rose (Eds.) (2003) *The Essential Foucault: Selections from Essential Works for Foucault, 1954–1984*. New York: The New Press.

Rassam, Amal (1992) "Political Ideology and Women in Iraq: Legislation and Cultural Constraints." In Joseph and Nancy Jabbra (Eds.), *Women and Development in the Middle East and North Africa*. Leiden: E.J. Brill.

Richards, Leila (1999) *Living Under Sanctions in Iraq: The-Oil-for-Food Program and the Intellectual Embargo*. Philadelphia, PA: AFSC.

Said, Edward (2000) *Reflections on Exile and Other Essays*. Cambridge, MA: Harvard University Press.

Said, Edward (1979 [1978]) *Orientalism*. New York: Vintage.

Sartre, Jean-Paul (1993 [1965]) *Essays in Existentialism*. New York: Citadel Press.

Sassoon, Joseph (2012) *Saddam Hussein's Ba'th Party: Inside an Authoritarian Regime*. Cambridge: Cambridge University Press.

Schiller, Nina, and Georges Fouron (2001) *Georges Woke Up Laughing: Long-Distance Nationalism and the Search for Home*. Durham, NC: Duke University Press.

Scott, James (1990) *Domination and the Arts of Resistance: Hidden Transcripts*. New Haven, CT: Yale University Press.

Seale, Patrick (1990 [1988]) *Asad: The Struggle for the Middle East*. Berkeley, CA: University of California Press.

Sharara, Hayat (2011) *Idha Al-Ayamu Aghsaqat [If the Days Turn to Dusk]*. Damascus: Al-Mada P.C.

Shaw, George Bernard (1913) *Cesar and Cleopatra*. New York: Brentano's.

Spagat, Michael September (2010) "Truth and Death in Iraq Under Sanctions." *Significance*: 116–20.

Spivak, Gayatri (1988) "Can the Subaltern Speak?" In Cary Nelson and Lawrence Grossberg (Eds.), *Marxism and the Interpretation of Culture*. Urbana, IL: University of Illinois Press.

Stampnitzky, Lisa (2013) *Disciplining Terror: How Experts Invented "Terror."* Cambridge: Cambridge University Press.

Tejel, Jordi, Peter Sluglett, Ricardo Bocco, and Hamit Bozarslan (Eds.) (2012) *Writing the Modern History of Iraq: Historiographical and Political Challenges*. London: World Scientific.

UNESCO (2016) "History of Prizes: International Literacy Prizes." Electronic document, www.unesco.org/new/en/education/themes/education-building-blocks/literacy/literacy-prizes/history/.

Van Dam, Nikolaos (2011 [1979]) *The Struggle for Power in Syria: Politics and Society Under Asad and the Ba'th Party*. New York: I.B. Tauris.

Yako, Louis (2015a) "Memories of the UN Iraq Embargo." *Counterpunch*, May 15, www.counterpunch.org/2015/05/15/memories-of-the-un-iraq-embargo/.

Yako, Louis (2015b) "From Iraq to Ireland: Heather Flowers and Mutual Human Experiences." *Counterpunch*, September 18, www.counterpunch.org/2015/09/18/from-iraq-to-ireland-heather-flowers-and-mutual-human-experiences/.

Zaidi, Sarah (1997) "Child Mortality in Iraq." *The Lancet* 350 (October 11): 1105.

Index

n refers to a note

Index

Christians xviii, 162–3, 197
citizenship 166–7
Coalition Provisional Authority (CPA)
74, 98, 99, 100, 109
Committee for Intellectual Soundness 26
communist academics 6, 22, 24–5, 26, 27, 30–1, 34
concentration camps 163–5
Cooke, Miriam "Language of Asylum" 191–2
Council for At-Risk Academics (CARA) 24, 77, 84
Covenant Society 16

Da'awa Party 49, 50, 209–10n4
Da'esh 145, 190–1
Das, Ramon 58
Davis, Eric 36, 53
  Memories of State 20–1
de-Ba'athification 75, 98, 99, 100–4, 107–8, 109–11
"developing countries" 14, 86
disaster capitalism 85
displaced academics 4, 6, 93, 113–4, 131–2, 148–9, 152, 154, 159–60, 167–70, 188

education x, 17–19, 23
Egypt, universities in 117
embargoes *see* sanctions
English language 176, 178, 182–3
ethno-nationalism 3, 187
exile 3, 119–20, 122, 129, 146, 198–9

Fairuz "My Home is Your Home" (song) 197–8
Faith Campaign 42
Fanon, Frantz xv, 14
Farag, Iman 117
Farah, Ilyas 21
Feith, Douglas J. 57, 99
Foucault, Michel 76

Franzén, Johan "Writing the History of Iraq: the Fallacy of Objective History" 34, 109–11
Friedman, Milton 85
Fuentes, Carlos 59

Garner, General Jay 99–100
Gide, André xiii
God 198
Goethe, Johann Wolfgang xii
graduated sovereignty 166–7
Gramsci, Antonio, and hegemony 191
Gulf War (1990-1) 13–14, 62

Halliday, Denis 57, 58
Hebrew language 192
Hegel, Georg Wilhelm Friedrich, and "slave-master dialectic" 14
history, re-writing of 109–11
Husayin, Fu'ad 110
Hussein, Saddam 31, 34, 39, 42, 52, 69, 121, 124–5

Iran-Iraq War 13, 22–3, 49
Iranian Revolution (1979) 32
Iraq
  occupation by Britain 16–17
  historical unity of 15
  invasion of Kuwait by 13–14, 40, 57, 63
  nationalisation of oil industry (1972) 18, 21
  Ottoman era 15–16
  US invasion of (2003) 73, 86, 164
  for other topics relating to Iraq
    see the topic, e.g. sectarianism, sanctions
Iraq Atomic Organization 32–3
Iraqi Communist Party 6, 18, 19, 21, 22, 24, 34, 35
Iraqi Cultural Centre, London 24, 27
Iraqi passports xiv–xv
Iraqi Petroleum Company 21

217